LEBANON

The Fractured Country

LEBANON
The Fractured Country

DAVID GILMOUR

St. Martin's Press, Inc.   New York

© David Gilmour 1983, 1984

All rights reserved. For information, write:
St. Martin's Press, Inc., 175 Fifth Avenue,
New York, NY 10010
Printed in Great Britain
First published in the United States of America in 1983

ISBN 0-312-47739-2

Library of Congress Cataloging in Publication Data

Gilmour, David (David Robert)
Lebanon, the fractured country.

Bibliography: p.
Includes index.
1. Lebanon—Politics and government. 2. Lebanon—
History—Civil War, 1975. I. Title
DS87.G54 1983   956.92'044   83-40525
ISBN 0-312-47739-2

To John Reddaway and Michael Adams
friends and mentors

Contents

Preface

I visited Lebanon for the first time in 1971 and stayed for a while in Beirut. It was my introduction to the Middle East. Beirut was the city where I made my first Arab friends and where I began to learn something of the politics and problems of the Arab world. Three years later, I returned and decided to live there.

I went not because I was involved or even particularly interested in Lebanese politics. Beirut was the intellectual capital of the Arab world and the natural home for anyone wishing to learn about the politics of the region. I had been in the city for only a brief period before fighting broke out in Sidon in February 1975, yet during the last weeks of peace I managed to travel through most of the country and to meet people from the different communities living in Lebanon. I had numerous letters of introduction and I rang people up and went to see them regardless of their political or confessional loyalties. In almost every household I visited — Christian or Muslim, Lebanese or Palestinian — I was treated with kindness and generosity. Some of the friends I made then will dislike and disagree with many of the things I have said in this book. Naturally I regret this but can only say to them that I have written about their country as I saw it.

Lebanon's civil war began more than eight years ago but in the West there is still much ignorance about its origins. The initial quarrels among the Lebanese have been largely forgotten and people now concentrate on the war's international aspects. The country has certainly suffered greatly from outside interference: some areas of it have been occupied in turn by Palestinian, Syrian and Israeli forces as well as by the Lebanese army and various Lebanese militias. There have been a few cases of foreign intervention, such as the sending of UN and multinational peacekeeping forces, which have been at least partially beneficial. But more frequently the behaviour of outside powers has been unscrupulous and hypocritical. The United States, for example, interfered in the war mainly in order to promote its own interests and those of its ally Israel.

In this book I have concentrated on trying to explain the Lebanese dimension to the conflict. It was, after all, a *civil* war even if in later years much of the fighting was done by foreign armies. Neighbouring, and not so neighbouring, countries exploited the conflict for their own ends, but only because there was a conflict for them to exploit. Propaganda sometimes asserts that the Lebanese were a peaceful people whose problems were all caused by others. It is not true and never has been. Throughout 1975, the first year of the war, the battles were fought very largely between rival Lebanese militias.

Lebanon was a young country with barely thirty years of independence when it erupted into a war that was at least as savage as the Spanish civil war forty years earlier. It was a young and also an artificial country carved out of Greater Syria by France, the mandatory power, in 1920. Throughout its short history Lebanon was troubled by disorders and in 1958 it suffered its first, comparatively mild, civil war. In the following pages I have tried to explain why political strife and instability were endemic to Lebanon, and why the Lebanese people were finally driven to settle their differences on the battlefield. If I have written at some length about the country's history, it is because I believe that the civil war cannot be explained except as the legacy of that history. The religious antagonisms, the cultural divide, the weakness of government had been apparent for decades. They made Lebanon what it was: a country with no unity, a country without a sense of nationhood, a country whose citizens were loyal not to the state but to their religious communities. It was thus a country without immunity to those more modern problems caused by rapid economic growth and social dislocation. The Lebanese were not able to agree on these issues just as they were unable to agree on what to do about the Palestinian Resistance Movement. By the 1970s it seemed that every new political development merely led to a deepening of those divisions that had bedevilled the country for so long.

I decided to write this book in the autumn of 1982 to try to counter what is in danger of becoming the 'official' version of the Lebanese tragedy. After General Franco's victory in 1939 Spanish history was entirely re-written to suit the victors and two generations of Spanish children were brought up on a thoroughly mendacious interpretation of their past. It seems to me that we are witnessing a similar attempt to re-write contemporary Lebanese history so as to mislead not only the people of Lebanon but the rest of the world as well. After the Israeli invasion of Lebanon in the summer of 1982, a number of self-proclaimed experts began writing to *The Times* and other papers with their version of recent events. These people, who were supporters of either the Israelis or the Lebanese Phalangists or both, claimed that the Lebanese civil war was not really a civil war at all but a war forced upon the Lebanese by the activities of the Palestine Liberation Organization. This interpretation, so its advocates believed, would go some way towards justifying Israel's devastation of Beirut and the Phalangist massacres of Palestinian refugees.

When you first hear a ludicrous propaganda claim you tend to dismiss it as ridiculous. But then you hear other people repeating it and before long it has become accepted as a part of history. It was for this reason that I decided to write a book with the aim of explaining to a Western audience the problems of Lebanon's short and troubled past.

None of my Lebanese or other Arab friends have been involved in this book or indeed knew that it was being written. But I would like to record my gratitude to some of them for what they have done over the last ten years to help me understand the problems of Lebanon: Nadim Dimechkie, Fuad and Salwa Es Said, Leila Baroody, Walid and Rasha Khalidi, Myrna Bustani, Walid Jumblatt, the late Samia Abul Jubain, Anwar Arida, Roseline Eddé, Ramez and Riad Dimechkie, Najib and Rima Shehadeh, Khalil Maccawi, Samia Costandi, Sami Alami and the late Henri Eid.

John Reddaway and my father, Ian Gilmour, read the manuscript with great care and made many valuable suggestions. So did Charles Glass, who knows Lebanon as well as anyone, and was thus able to save me from making a number of errors. I am grateful to all of them. I would also like to thank Derek and Pamela Cooper for information on the siege of Beirut, Hillary Metwally for typing out most of the manuscript, the librarian and staff of Chatham House for their help in providing books and journals, and Oliver Van Oss for suggesting that I should write the book.

D.G. April 1983

Chronology of Events

1920 San Remo Conference offers France the mandate for Syria and Lebanon. Proclamation of the State of Greater Lebanon.

1926 A Constitution is approved by the Lebanese Representative Council. Lebanon becomes the Lebanese Republic.

1936 Franco–Lebanese Treaty.

1940 Lebanon falls under the control of the Vichy French.

1941 British and Free French forces enter Lebanon and take control of the country.

1943 Lebanon declares independence. Bishara Khoury becomes president with Riad Solh as prime minister. The principles of government are contained in the unwritten National Pact.

1945 Lebanon joins the Arab League.

1947 United Nations General Assembly votes for the partition of Palestine.

1948 First Arab–Israeli war. Lebanese forces play a limited role. A majority of the Palestinian people are driven from their homes.

1952 Bishara Khoury is forced to resign from the presidency. Camille Chamoun succeeds him.

1956 Gamal Abdel Nasser nationalizes the Suez Canal. Egypt is invaded by Israel and later by Britain and France.

1957 Chamoun endorses the Eisenhower Doctrine. Controversial parliamentary elections result in a victory for Chamoun's supporters.

1958 Revolution in Iraq destroys the Hashemite monarchy. Civil war breaks out in Lebanon. The Lebanese army remains neutral but the United States sends marines to Beirut. Chamoun leaves office in September and is succeeded by the army commander, Fuad Chehab.

1964 Chehab steps down from the presidency and is succeeded
      by Charles Helou. The PLO is set up under the auspices of
      the Arab League.

1967 The third Arab—Israeli war results in the Israeli conquest
      of Sinai, the Golan Heights and the West Bank of the Jordan.

1968 Israel begins retaliatory raids against Palestinian refugee
      camps in Lebanon. Israeli commandos destroy 13 civilian
      aeroplanes at Beirut International Airport.

1969 The Lebanese army, backed by the Phalangist militia, goes
      into action against the PLO. In November the army and
      the PLO sign the Cairo Agreement regulating the guerrillas'
      activities in Lebanon.

1970 In the presidential elections Suleiman Frangieh defeats
      Elias Sarkis by a single vote.

1970 *September*: Civil war in Jordan. PLO transfers its head-
      quarters to Lebanon.

1973 *May*: Fighting between the PLO and the Lebanese army.
      October: Fourth Arab—Israeli war.

1975 *February 26*: Marouf Saad is mortally wounded in Sidon
      demonstration. Further demonstrations, for and against
      the army, follow in Beirut.
      April 13: Phalangist gunmen massacre Palestinians in Ain
      el-Roumaneh. Fighting erupts in several areas in Beirut.
      May 7: Ministers from the Phalangist and National Liberal
      parties resign from the government.
      May 15: Rashid Solh resigns as prime minister.
      May 18: Fighting begins again in Beirut.
      May 23: Formation of a military government under
      Nureddin Rifai.
      May 26: The military government resigns.
      May 29: Rashid Karami is asked to form a government.
      June 30: After further fighting, Karami forms a six-man
      cabinet with Chamoun as minister of the interior.
      August: Fighting breaks out in Zahle and Tripoli.
      September: Phalangists launch an attack in the centre of
      Beirut. Fighting continues in the capital for the rest of the
      year.
      December 6: Black Saturday massacre.

1976 *January*: Maronite forces begin blockade of Palestinian refugee camps. Mainstream PLO forces enter the war and retaliate by assisting troops of the National Movement in the siege of Damour.

January 14: Phalangists overrun Palestinian camp of Dbayyeh.

January 18: Phalangists capture Qarantina and deport or massacre its inhabitants.

January 19: Syria sends PLA troops into Lebanon.

January 20: PLO-National Movement troops take Damour and kill a number of its civilians.

January 21: Syrian foreign minister, Abdul Halim Khaddam, arrives in Beirut to try to arrange a compromise.

February 14: Frangieh announces a programme of limited reforms.

March: Lebanese army disintegrates.

March 11: Brigadier Aziz Ahdab attempts a coup d'état.

March 13: Parliamentary deputies call for Frangieh's resignation.

March 27: Jumblatt meets Assad in Damascus. PLO-National Movement forces go on to the offensive in the Dhour Shuwair area.

May 8: Elias Sarkis elected as president designate. Jumblatt boycotts elections.

June 1: Syrian troops enter Lebanon.

June 22: Maronite forces attack Palestinian refugee camps in east Beirut.

July 1: Maronites capture Jisr al-Pasha.

August 12: Tal Zaatar is stormed by Maronite militiamen and its inhabitants massacred.

September 23: Sarkis succeeds Frangieh as president.

September 28: Syrians attack forces of the PLO-National Movement alliance in Dhour Shuwair.

October 13: Syrian army captures Bhamdoun from the Palestinians.

October 16: Riyadh mini-summit called by Saudi Arabia.

October 25: 19 Arab states approve the Riyadh resolutions at the Arab summit meeting in Cairo.

November 14: Syrian troops enter Beirut.

December 9: A cabinet of technocrats is formed under the new prime minister, Salim Hoss.

1977 *March*: The assassination of Kamal Jumblatt is followed by a Druze massacre of neighbouring Christians.

May: Menachem Begin wins the Israeli elections and forms the first Likud government.

July: Chtaura Agreement between the Lebanese government, Syria and the PLO.

1978 *March 11*: Fatah guerrillas launch raid along the Haifa-Tel Aviv highway.

March 15: Israel invades Lebanon and occupies the country as far north as the Litani river.

March 19: UN Security Council passes Resolution 425 calling upon Israel to withdraw from Lebanon.

April 7: Israel begins limited pull-back from Lebanon.

April: UNIFIL takes up positions in south Lebanon.

June 12: Israel hands over remaining slice of Lebanese territory to the rebel troops of Saad Haddad.

June 13: Phalangists attack Ehden and kill Frangieh's son Tony and a number of his followers.

July: Syrians shell Ashrafiyeh and do so again in September.

October: Beiteddine conference.

1979 *February*: Renewed fighting between Syrians and Phalangists.

April: Saad Haddad proclaims his Israeli-protected enclave as 'Free Lebanon'. Haddad shells UNIFIL's forces and prevents a Lebanese army unit from reasserting government control in the south.

June: Israel launches a number of attacks against Palestinian positions in southern Lebanon.

1980 *July*: Salib Hoss resigns as prime minister. Bachir Gemayel orders Phalangist militiamen to crush their former allies, the Chamounists.

October 25: A new government is formed with Shafiq Wazzan as prime minister.

1981   *March*: Haddad shells Nigerian troops of UNIFIL.

       April: Fighting breaks out in Zahle between Phalangists and Syrian soldiers. Syrians install Sam-6 anti-aircraft missiles in the Bekaa valley and Israel demands their removal.

       June 7: Israel destroys Iraq's nuclear reactor near Baghdad.

       June 30: Begin wins Israeli elections.

       July 17: Israel begins a series of air strikes against PLO positions in the south and bombs the Fakhani district of Beirut.

       July 24: Cease fire is arranged by American mediator, Philip Habib.

       August 4: Begin forms a government with Ariel Sharon as defence minister.

1982   *April*: Israel renews air strikes against Palestinian refugee camps.

       May: Further air strikes provoke PLO shelling of northern Israel.

       June 4: Anti-PLO Arab gunmen try to kill the Israeli ambassador to Britain.

       June 6: Israel invades Lebanon and four days later reaches the outskirts of Beirut.

       June 13: Israel begins the bombardment of Beirut.

       August 21: PLO forces begin their evacuation of Beirut.

       August 23: Bachir Gemayel is elected president.

       August 25: Multinational peace-keeping forces disembark at Beirut.

       September 1: President Reagan launches his Middle East peace initiative.

       September 10: Withdrawal of multinational forces begins.

       September 14: Bachir Gemayel is assassinated.

       September 15: Israel occupies west Beirut.

       September 16: Phalangist militiamen begin the massacres of Sabra and Chatila.

       September 21: Amin Gemayel is elected president of Lebanon.

       October–November: US Deputy Assistant Secretary of

State Morris Draper begins negotiations with Lebanon and Israel to discuss Israeli troop withdrawal from Lebanon.

1983 *January*: Israel and Lebanon agree on an agenda for joint talks.

February 8: Israeli commission of inquiry censures Defence Minister Sharon and senior officers for their role in the Sabra/Chatila massacres.

February 14: The Palestine National Council meets in Algiers.

April 10: King Hussein terminates joint PLO–Jordanian talks.

April 24: US Secretary of State George Shultz visits the Middle East.

May 17: Israel and Lebanon sign joint agreement providing for security arrangements and Israeli withdrawal from Lebanon. Syrian government denounces agreement and refuses to receive Reagan's special envoy, Philip Habib.

June: Syria backs Fatah rebels against PLO chairman, Yasser Arafat.

July 6: Shultz visits Damascus but fails to persuade Assad to accept Israel–Lebanese agreement.

August 2: Israelis order Phalangists out of their main southern base near Sidon.

August 10: Walid Jumblatt's Druze militia shell Beirut airport.

August 16: Israeli Defence Minister Moshe Arens visits Phalangist headquarters in Beirut.

August 29–31: Lebanese army goes into action against Shi'ite militiamen in Beirut's outskirts. Israeli army pulls back from the Chouf. Fighting between Druzes and Phalangists intensifies.

September: Druzes defeat Phalangists at Bhamdoun and in other parts of the Chouf. Reagan authorizes US navy to bombard Syrian and Druze positions near Souk al-Garb.

September 25: Announcement of a cease-fire and establishment of a National Reconciliation Committee.

October 23: Nearly 300 US marines and French paratroopers are killed in bomb explosions in Beirut.

October 31: National Reconciliation Committee holds its first meeting in Geneva.

November: The 25 September cease-fire gradually breaks down in many parts of the country. Druzes and Phalangists resume shelling each other's positions. Rebel Palestinian forces besiege PLO leader Arafat in Tripoli.

November 4: 60 people, half of them Israeli soldiers and the other half Arab detainees, are killed in a bomb explosion at the Israeli army headquarters in Tyre.

December 1: Sheikh Halim Takieddin, chief religious judge of the Druzes, is murdered in Beirut.

Maps

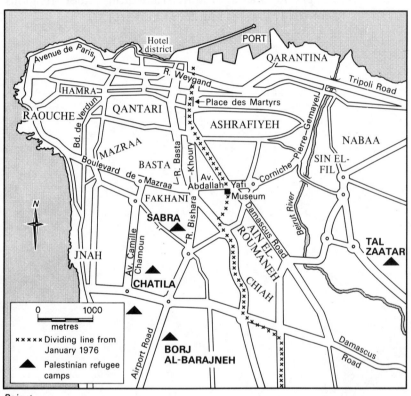

Beirut

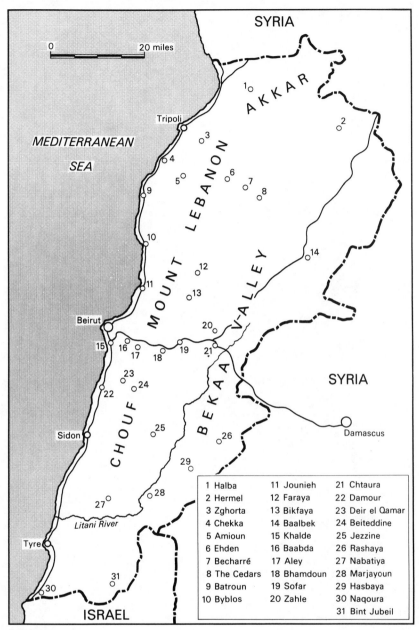

SYRIA

MEDITERRANEAN

SEA

Tripoli

AKKAR

MOUNT LEBANON

VALLEY

Beirut

SYRIA

Damascus

CHOUF

BEKAA

Sidon

Litani River

Tyre

ISRAEL

1 Halba	11 Jounieh	21 Chtaura
2 Hermel	12 Faraya	22 Damour
3 Zghorta	13 Bikfaya	23 Deir el Qamar
4 Chekka	14 Baalbek	24 Beiteddine
5 Amioun	15 Khalde	25 Jezzine
6 Ehden	16 Baabda	26 Rashaya
7 Becharré	17 Aley	27 Nabatiya
8 The Cedars	18 Bhamdoun	28 Marjayoun
9 Batroun	19 Sofar	29 Hasbaya
10 Byblos	20 Zahle	30 Naqoura
		31 Bint Jubeil

Lebanon

PART I

Lebanon on the Eve of the Civil War

Mount Lebanon . . . must form part of a new independent state which, without the incentives to territorial aggrandisement or the means of military aggression, shall yet be able to maintain its own honour and dignity and more especially to promote the great object for which it will be so eminently qualified, that of creating, developing and upholding a commercial intercourse in the East, which shall draw together and unite the hitherto divergent races of mankind in the humanizing relations of fraternity and peace.

Colonel C. H. Churchill *Mount Lebanon: A Ten Years' Residence from 1842 to 1852*

Pity the nation that is full of beliefs and empty of religion.

Pity the nation that wears a cloth it does not weave, eats a bread it does not harvest, and drinks a wine that flows not from its own wine-press.

Pity the nation that acclaims the bully as hero, and that deems the glittering conqueror bountiful.

Pity a nation that despises a passion in its dream, yet submits in its awakening.

Pity the nation that raises not its voice save when it walks in a funeral, boasts not except among its ruins, and will rebel not save when its neck is laid between the sword and the block.

Pity the nation whose statesman is a fox, whose philosopher is a juggler, and whose art is the art of patching and mimicking.

Pity the nation that welcomes its new ruler with trumpetings, and farewells him with hootings, only to welcome another with trumpetings again.

Pity the nation whose sages are dumb with years and whose strong men are yet in the cradle.

Pity the nation divided into fragments, each fragment deeming itself a nation.

Kahlil Gibran *The Garden of the Prophet* (1934)

1

Modern Lebanon

Beirut is unique among modern cities: it destroyed itself twice in a
generation, once by its own volition, once with the help of others.
The bulldozer and the pickaxe accomplished the first; bombs,
rockets and artillery shells the second. Both destructions were
methodical and yet at the same time uncontrolled, but there was a
peculiar irony about the second devastation. Beirut had destroyed
itself the first time so that it could be reborn, larger, richer and
more enjoyable. And it went again, unexpectedly, while the
prosperity was still rising. The dynamic, tolerant and lawless city
with its vulgarity and sham Western culture – the last Levantine
city in the Levant – was nearing completion. The Holiday Inn had
just been built, the Hilton was nearly ready, the cabarets and
nightclubs were in full swing. And it was all thrown away.

If you took a taxi from the airport to the smart hotel district
in the early seventies you would learn a good deal about the
character of the city. The first thing you reached at the end of the
airport boulevard was a low, dark wood of umbrella pine. Among
the trees on both sides of the road crouched rows of squalid huts
belonging to the Palestinian refugee camps of Chatila and Borj
al-Barajneh. At the edge of the wood, children in bare feet tried to
sell garlands of flowers to passing motorists. If you stopped at the
traffic lights, a beggar on crutches appeared at the car window.

Because of the traffic congestion in the centre of the city, the
taxi driver would now turn west past the Kuwaiti embassy and
join the corniche road by the sea. For the next three miles it was
impossible to see any sort of building put up before 1960. This
was Raouché, one of the smart new residential areas, a vast,
uneven development of high-rise apartment blocks dating mainly

from the 1970—72 building boom. You then passed the Pigeon Rocks and the popular bathing beaches before swinging east along the northern sea front. Up on the hill sat the American University, the best of its kind in the Arab world, for a hundred years a symbol of liberalism and progress in the region; at sea level the American embassy building, surrounded by tanks and barbed wire and machine gun posts — symbol of the United States' meddling and unpopular role in the Middle East.

Immediately afterwards the road twisted through the old quarter of Ain Mreissé, where some of the last Ottoman houses in the city were then being pulled down to make way for a dual carriageway. This demolition was a gradual process and the old stone houses, with their red roofs and arched, Venetian-style windows, stood for months, gutted and disfigured, before they were finally flattened.

By now you would probably have found yourself in one of Beirut's interminable traffic jams, for the Lebanese custom of going home for lunch produced four separate rush hours. Even these were made worse than they need have been by the number of enormous American cars, the lack of parking regulations, and the apparently optional observance of traffic lights. As most of the smart new buildings had been built without underground garages, cars were parked anyhow along the pavements and in the street, blocking both traffic and pedestrians. The noise level also was appalling since Beirut drivers considered, against all the evidence, that the only way to get the traffic moving was to keep their hands fixed firmly to the horn. Overhead the screech of incoming aeroplanes made matters worse, for the flight path to the main landing runway ran directly over the city centre.

As soon as the taxi driver had extricated himself from Ain Mreissé, you merely had to round the small promontory of Minet el-Hosn and then you were there, in fashionable Beirut, with the Vendôme and Phoenicia hotels, cocktails and water-skiing, and an army of people who earned their living by thrusting faked coins and Persian rugs on credulous tourists. Within five minutes walk you had the restaurants and cabarets of the Rue de Phénicie, with names like Lucky Luke's and the Crazy Horse Saloon; a little further off, the shabby brothels and pick-up bars of the Rue

Ahmed Chaoqui. This was the centre of what the Lebanese tourist office referred to as Beirut's 'pulsating, chromatic night-life'.

From the terrace of the Saint Georges Hotel (the most fashionable place in Beirut and the haunt of gossip columnists), you could see the port, crowded and vigorous, main creator of the country's wealth. Beyond was the slum area of Qarantina, a sight so disgusting that the government had built a wall in order to make it invisible to tourists on their way north.

In less than half an hour, then, you would grasp some of the main characteristics of Beirut: the Western outlook, the dynamism, the poverty and affluence side by side, and the chaos inevitably produced by an absence of planning. This materialism was undoubtedly successful, at least according to its own set of values. Lebanon's per capita income was higher than that of every Asian country with the exceptions of Kuwait, Israel, Singapore and Japan, and of every African country except for South Africa and oil-rich Libya. The material wealth of many Lebanese, and in particular the Beirutis, was considerable. According to one survey, which admittedly included neither the shanty towns nor the Palestinian refugee camps in its sample, a majority of Beirut homes possessed a refrigerator, a television and a washing machine, and nearly half of them also owned a camera, a car and a gramophone.[1] In other fields, malaria and smallpox had been completely eradicated, while the country's literacy rate, at around 80 per cent, was higher than in any other country in the Arab world.

This prosperity depended largely on trade and banking; industry and agriculture played minor roles, together contributing only a quarter of the country's income. Commerce was the historic occupation of the Levant coast, a consequence of its strategic position between East and West. This traditional role was extended by the link between the Arab oil fields and the industrial nations of Europe, the oil coming through the desert pipelines to Sidon or Tripoli before being shipped across the Mediterranean, while imports from the West were handled at the Port of Beirut before being transported overland to Saudi Arabia, the Gulf or Iraq. By contrast, banking was a more recent activity, Beirut replacing Cairo as the financial centre of the Middle East only after the Egyptian revolution of 1952. Subsequently, foreign investment and the expansion of banking services were greatly aided by the government's policy of non-intervention in the economy and by laws of secrecy more rigid than those in Switzerland. In 1951 there were 5 banks in Beirut; fifteen years later there were 93, as well as a large number of branches of foreign banks.[2]

Although Beirut has had a mercantile history for centuries, it became undisputedly the greatest port in the eastern Mediterranean only recently, achieving this position through the demise of its rivals. Tripoli went first, cut off from its hinterland, the Syrian interior, by the French in 1920. Haifa was the next to go, closed as an Arab port after the 1948 war and the establishment of Israel. It was soon followed by Alexandria which lost its Levantine spirit after the fall of King Farouk in 1952. Beirut received its biggest boost in 1967 when the closure of the Suez Canal blocked the direct route to the Gulf and left overland transport via Lebanon as the only real alternative to going round the Cape.

The country's second source of income was tourism and the Lebanese never tired of telling you that theirs was the only country where you could ski in the mountains in the morning and ski on the Mediterranean the same afternoon. Although Beirut itself was hardly a sight-seer's paradise, it profited from a lot of Arab tourism, particularly from the sheikhs of the Gulf who owned apartment blocks in the city and built large villas in the mountains. Industry's role in the economy of Beirut was subservient to commerce, partly because of a shortage of raw materials and partly because the free trade policy which suited commercial life effectively prevented many industrial ventures from getting off the ground. The Industrialists' Association fought hard for higher tariffs, but was invariably defeated by the far stronger commercial lobby. If there was a market for something in Lebanon, then it was imported, irrespective of the fact that Lebanese industrialists might be trying to manufacture and market a similar product. Nevertheless, in the years preceding the civil war, industry was managing to expand, especially in manufacturing, and nearly all of this expansion was taking place in or around Beirut.

The Lebanese liked to ascribe part of their success to genealogy. 'We are the spiritual descendants of the Phoenicians', they would say. 'Like them, our emphasis is on business. It is better to make money than to make war'. This was not in fact a dictum that the Lebanese always followed and Emile Bustani, a politician who personified the better side of the Levantine spirit, was to be proved sadly mistaken when he said, 'we have revolutions only about once a century.* The memory of how much they cost lasts that long'.[3] Nevertheless, in spite of the 1958 civil war, the country's economic performance since independence in 1943 had been impressive. During the 1950s the economy grew at an annual rate of 7 per cent and the average for the following decade was only slightly lower.

The post-world war boom was at its most visible in Beirut. For three decades the development of the capital took place at a prodigious speed and from the beginning it was unplanned. A man could build anything he liked wherever he could buy the land. And for those who could not afford land there was always public property. A large number of poor migrants from the south lived in a shanty town near the airport runway, and although this was illegal, the government did nothing about moving them, or about providing new housing. Nor did it make any attempt to control the city's development. It did not enforce restrictions on height, or use or architectural design. According to the Dean of Engineering and Architecture at the American University of Beirut, only 5 per cent of the architects putting up the new buildings were properly qualified.[4] Emile Yanni, a former governor of Beirut, complained that 'every notion of town planning . . . is destroyed by the pressure of individualism.'[5] As a result, it was the richer areas that were redeveloped the most, for there was no money in knocking down the slums. Thus, over half the houses in west Beirut were destroyed and nearly all the gardens eaten up in a matter of twenty-five years. By 1975, the campus of the American University was the last green space of any size left in the west of the city.

Property was regarded by the Lebanese as the safest form of investment and, since there was no development tax, nor indeed much tax at all, it also provided a large income. If a man made

---

* He was referring to the battles between Christians and Druzes in 1860 and the civil war of 1958.

some money, his first thought would often be to buy a site in the city and knock down the existing house. He would then wait for the market to improve (which it invariably did), perhaps in the meantime letting it out as a car-park, and eventually selling it to a bank, a foreign company or a hotel group. If you asked him why he had demolished the original house, he would smile and say either 'that's progress' or 'it was too old'. By 'old' he meant that it had been built before the Second World War. The real reason, though, was simply that new building land was immensely valuable and he was assured of making a fat profit.

The Lebanese were wholly undiscriminating about what they destroyed and so nearly everything of architectural value — save for a few museums — was swept away with a total lack of historical or architectural sentiment. Although you might occasionally hear a Beiruti complaining that he was unable to recognize his own city from one year to the next, a conservationist lobby barely existed. A majority of the Lebanese watched the eradication of the past with a certain pride in the achievement. For the tourist there were still scattered traces of previous civilizations — a few Roman pillars, a Byzantine chapel, some token Greek remains.

The human cost of all this was enormous. While the population of Beirut had increased tenfold since the 1930s, the actual city area was less than three times the size of the 1900 boundaries. The result was that by 1970 Beirut was one of the most overcrowded cities in the world, outside eastern Asia, and contained nearly half the population of the country.* Even before the construction boom of 1970—72, nine out of ten Beirutis were living in apart- ment blocks, more than 80 per cent of them built since the Second World War. By 1975, the idea of living in a house had practically disappeared from people's minds in most districts of the city. Moreover, since the government played no part in the construction industry, and the only stimulus to building was the prospect of a quick return on the investment, no attention was paid to environ- mental and community considerations. In several districts of Beirut the new blocks stood almost back to back.

*In 1973 the Lebanese population was estimated unofficially at 2,460,000 excluding Palestinian refugees and temporary Syrian workers. The last official figures were published in 1956, see p. 21.

Building was the most efficient Lebanese industry, but, like nearly everything else in Lebanon, it depended almost exclusively on the profit motive. Luxury flats and office blocks were the most profitable things to build. Public buildings such as hospitals, schools, prisons and libraries were ignored. Beirut, which called itself the intellectual capital of the Arab world and had four universities (three of them financed by foreign governments), as well as numerous institutes of higher education, was unable to boast of a single public library. More serious was the lack of cheap housing which both the government and the construction companies were reluctant to build. Remarkably, even after the building boom there was a shortage of housing. Although nearly half of all money invested in Lebanon in the decade before the civil war went into the construction industry, only six homes were built for every thousand people.[6] There were profits to be made in building villas and luxury apartments, not in providing cheap housing. Although, after pressure from the unions, Parliament had passed a law in 1965 ordering the construction of 4,000 low-cost housing units, nobody was very surprised when the project later collapsed.

Anybody who visited Beirut in the 1970s could see that the city badly needed public housing. Although the average standard of living was higher than in other Arab cities, there was also poverty as bad as anything to be seen in Egypt or Syria. The city enjoyed a spectacular post-war boom, but its profits were unevenly distributed and the benefits to many people were minimal. Beirut's chaotic development quickly showed up the real weakness, and in fact the main injustice, of the Lebanese economic system. For while it was capable of generating great wealth, the system had no means of ensuring that a substantial portion of the population caught more than a glimpse of it. There was little planning and a feeble welfare system. Consequently, since the country's wealth came from Beirut, it also stayed in and around Beirut — except for what was stacked away in London or Paris. It had no impact on the slums on the outskirts of the capital.

Since the Second World War, the inequalities in Lebanese society had been getting more pronounced and by 1960 the differences in wealth were enormous. While 4 per cent of the population disposed of 32 per cent of the GNP, half of the nation was apportioned only 18.3 per cent.[7] In other words, 50 per cent of the Lebanese had only slightly more than half the share of the GNP which the top 4 per cent enjoyed. Taxation, which could have been used to reduce this inequality, was in fact a means of strengthening it. The government raised more money by indirect taxation, which hit everybody, than it did by direct taxation which could have been aimed at the rich. Had large duties been imposed on Cadillacs or stereo equipment or other items of sumptuous expenditure, the system might have been fairer. Instead, the government preferred to put duties on commodities such as fuel, salt and tobacco. Income tax accounted for only one-tenth of the government's revenues partly because the rate was very low, partly because it was inefficiently collected and partly because there was widespread evasion. It was astonishing that people should have bothered to evade the derisory payments that they owed, but they did, and because of the banking secrecy law they got away with it. According to one economist, private business was evading three-quarters of its taxes while the men of the liberal professions were paying as little as a tenth of the money due from them.[8] The situation was scandalous and President Chehab (in office from 1958 to 1964) was right to warn: 'If the rich continue to maintain their privileges at everybody else's expense in this way, there will be a social revolution in Lebanon'.[9]

A glance at Beirut's slums made you wonder why there had not already been a social revolution. The cosmopolitan city of supermarkets and chic penthouses was enclosed by what people referred to as 'the belt of misery', a series of shanty-towns made of breeze-blocks and corrugated iron where perhaps one-quarter of a million people lived. In these places the mortality rate was two to three times the national average[10] and there were many homes without lavatories or drinking water. No Beiruti could have been unaware of their existence because you could not avoid them. Whichever road you took out of the city you had to drive past either the slums or the refugee camps.

Most of the people living in these areas were Palestinians or Muslims from the depressed regions of the country, driven from the land by their high birth rate and the government's neglect of agriculture. Another important factor, especially in the movement of the Shi'ite Muslims, was the Israeli policy of reprisals against the Palestinian guerrillas in the south. In fact, as the Israelis knew, these raids were far more damaging to the Shi'ite inhabitants than they were to the Palestinians, for every time they crossed the border they bulldozed houses and bridges, many of which had never been used by the guerrillas. The south was already the most underdeveloped region in the country and the Israeli policy made it in many cases impossible to go on living there.

So thousands of Shi'ites, resentful that the Lebanese army had made no attempt to protect them, came to Beirut and built themselves precarious shelters with whatever materials they could find. And just as the government had done nothing to help them in the south, so it did nothing for them once they had settled outside Beirut. It did not provide housing or employment — or unemployment benefit, since this did not exist. Nor did the Shi'ites, or indeed the other slum dwellers, have access to basic medical services. The former Minister of Municipal and Rural Affairs, Abdullah Mashnuk, once admitted that 'medical treatment is beyond the means of the poorest class.'[11] You only had to walk round the shanty towns to see for yourself that this was true. Many of the people had obviously never had adequate medical treatment in their lives; the most striking thing was the extent of eye disease.

In spite of the establishment of the National Social Security Fund in 1963, Lebanon's welfare system was very primitive and in any case half the population found itself excluded from it.[12] The situation was at its most absurd in the medical field: while Beirut had the best medical facilities in the Middle East, most of its inhabitants were unable to use them. Of the 48 Beirut hospitals recognized by the Ministry of Health in 1971, all but one were privately owned and charged fees which most people could not afford. Given these sort of conditions, the shanty towns naturally became potential revolutionary centres, and the Shi'ites, deprived of their traditional surroundings and leadership, provided recruits for the two communist parties, the Lebanese Communist Party and its offshoot, the Organization of Communist Action in Lebanon. The state's failure to do anything about all this had a simple explanation: the government, and therefore the public sector, was virtually powerless. Why it was so weak will be discussed in

Chapter 3, but the fact of it was obvious to anybody. By the 1970s, the Lebanese regime was unable to fulfill even basic functions of government. It could barely collect taxes and it was unable to organize the postal system properly. Even before the fighting, a letter took about ten days to get from one end of Beirut to the other. As for public transport, most of the buses were museum pieces which people avoided if they possibly could, while several of the locomotives employed by Lebanese Railways were constructed either in 1894 or 1905! A journey to Damascus, a matter of hours by car, would apparently have taken four days by train.

One obvious example of the government's ineptitude was its mismanagement of the Port of Beirut. The port was the country's principal money maker and one of the few things in Lebanon that were publicly owned. Yet it was poorly run, and had Tripoli or Latakia been viable alternatives, international shippers would not have hesitated to use them. Beirut's quays were too narrow and its equipment antiquated; there was also a shortage of labour. Worst of all was the congestion. If you looked out to sea on any day of the year, you would see 30 or 40 ships riding at anchor, waiting their turn to be unloaded; on average they had to wait three weeks. Yet the authorities made no attempt to enlarge the port by building a fourth basin, which was plainly needed if Beirut hoped to handle even a fraction of the traffic that formerly passed through the Suez Canal.

The inertia of the Lebanese government was sometimes put forward as an example of its 'moderate' policy. In fact it was nothing of the kind; the government seldom had a policy. Perhaps there would not have been much difference if it had because it did not in any real sense rule the country. Lebanon was run by 'interests' and 'lobbies' which demanded weak government and blocked legislation that threatened them. It was a system, or rather non-system, that functioned badly, and anyone could see why: everything depended on profits. Practically nothing ever happened in Lebanon, no measures taken, no reforms made, unless somebody, somewhere, was going to make a profit out of it.

The cosmopolitan features of Lebanon — the yachting marinas, the Casino, the great Baalbek festival — tended to obscure the primitive nature of the country. For all the glossy sophistication of Beirut and the smart resorts, most of the country remained socially and politically backward. Blood feuds between rival families or clans were still a feature in a Lebanon that possessed gossip columnists and imitation English pubs. In the summer of 1966 the army was even forced to intervene with an armoured unit to stop fighting between Maronite clans in the town of Zghorta. Violence, indeed, was easily accepted in a country which claimed to follow the traditions of the civilized Phoenicians, although a distinction must be made in this respect between the customs of the coast and those of the mountains. In the provinces of Mount Lebanon the emphasis on vengeance, the refusal to tolerate even the smallest insult, was particularly strong. If the family honour was insulted — a kinsman slain, a daughter seduced, or merely a sister wishing to marry a man of another religion — the stain could often be wiped out only by blood. If the insult was more offensive and embraced a whole community, the bloodshed was correspondingly greater. And there was no question here of the insulted party's response being limited to an eye for an eye. After the assassination of the Druze leader, Kamal Jumblatt, in March 1977, his followers took their revenge on the neighbouring Maronites and killed scores of them before the dead man's son could stop the fighting. Not that the Maronites themselves were any better. In December 1975 four of their number were found dead in the Metn region, in the mountains east of Beirut. Nobody had any idea why they had been killed, or by whom, and the Maronite leaders made no attempt to find out. Their militias immediately put up road blocks in Beirut and shot any Muslim who came along. In less than a day some 300 Muslim civilians were massacred.

Lebanese life revolved around the family and strict parental authority was still the rule in most communities.[13] Even in fashionable circles marriages were often arranged and it might be impossible to take a girl out to dinner without a formal introduction to her parents and their subsequent approval. Mixed Christian/Muslim weddings were illegal since there was no civil marriage (you had to go to Cyprus for that) and highly dangerous as well, unless both families agreed to it. Many couples eloped to the United States or Brazil to escape the vengeance of their families.

Once an acquaintance pointed out to me a girl walking down the street in Byblos and said: 'she is a Maronite and she wants to marry a Muslim. If she does, her brothers will kill both of them.' But the few mixed marriages that did take place were normally between Christian women and Muslim men since it was very unusual for a Muslim father to allow his daughter to marry into a Christian family.

As in most Mediterranean societies, the Lebanese family was dominated by the men. Among Muslims the sons inherited twice as much as the daughters, though a marriage between Shi'ite Muslims in the rural areas generally entailed a settlement on the bride in the form of land. A father's authority over his children extended practically until his death, sharing and sometimes collecting their wages, especially those of unmarried daughters. He would also be expected to choose their future wives or husbands, arrange the matter with the other family, and insist that his own accepted his choice.

Greater mobility, the emigration to Beirut, and the infiltration of modern ideas did, of course, do something to alter the structure of this highly traditional society. Polygamy, for example, although permitted by Muslim Sharia law up to a limit of four wives, was practically non-existent. Nor was it possible any longer to tell the status of a Shi'ite Muslim merely by his clothes: a white turban for sheikhs, a green one for sayids, the red fez for merchants and shop-keepers, baggy trousers and felt hats for the peasants. Nevertheless, few inroads had been made into the importance of the family as a social and economic unit. A Lebanese would know all his relations, even distant ones, would see them often and would know everything about them. He could count on elderly relatives to find him a job, probably in a family firm or business. If he was rich, he would take it upon himself to provide for poorer relations, and would even invite them to live with him. When the Palestinians were expelled from their country in 1948, the lucky ones were able to go and live with their Lebanese relatives.

The family's welfare role was of immense importance, especially as the state's welfare system was so inadequate. If somewhere in the family there happened to be a doctor or a lawyer, this would open up services to many people who otherwise might be unable to afford them. Perhaps the most influential role played by the family, however, was as a provider of employment, for a large majority of businesses, great and small, were family firms. In the 1955 Industrial Census it was shown that only one firm in fifty was a corporation.[14] Even in the 1970s a company dealing in insurance, engineering, advertising, printing or manufacturing was more often than not in the hands of one family. For those within the family circle, this obviously facilitated the process of finding a job, particularly as in Lebanon it was accepted without hesitation that a relative would automatically be chosen over a similarly qualified outsider. Even medical clinics and lawyers' offices might be operated along these lines.

Farming was a more difficult matter since, while there was almost limitless opportunity for the expansion of businesses like engineering and advertizing, particularly in the Gulf states, farm-holdings were generally becoming smaller. This was partly because of the increase in population and partly the result of the Muslim inheritance laws, which prescribed that every child must inherit some of the father's property. The economy of the region had traditionally rested on the merchant activity of the coast and the subsistence farming of Mount Lebanon. But the balance between them was disrupted by the government's lack of interest in agriculture. It did not carry out enough irrigation projects and it did not make an effort to encourage farmers by establishing state marketing boards – large piles of apples rotting by the roadsides for lack of markets was a common sight in north Lebanon. Nor did the government put forward proposals for agrarian reform. Consequently, while there were still large estates, principally in the Bekaa valley, over half the farmers owned less than an acre of land, and this was normally divided among several plots at differing altitudes. As a result, although there had been some increase in productivity, agriculture was depressed and Lebanon was unable to feed itself: agricultural imports were three times larger than exports.[15]

Some areas of agriculture were well-managed, however, particularly the citrus and banana plantations in the coastal regions. Hill farming too was intensive and fairly efficient and in recent years there had been some expansion of terracing and land reclamation by means of the Green Plan. But the government's more important scheme, the Litani river project, had been largely neglected. The project, which entailed building a dam in southern Lebanon, had a double objective: to produce electricity for much of the country and provide water for the irrigation of thousands of acres of arid land being worked by poor Shi'ite farmers. The dam was duly built and electricity produced but ten years after the plan's inauguration there was still no sign of irrigation. It was a typical example of government ineffectiveness. The country had a great deal of water underground and in rivers, and it was being wasted. Had it been exploited properly, Lebanon would have got much nearer to feeding itself. It would have also been able to avoid at least a part of the huge rural exodus to Beirut.

As with agriculture, the lack of government investment was one reason for the poor performance of manufacturing industry, though this was further hampered by the government's refusal to place sufficient tariffs on foreign goods for fear of offending the commercial lobby. Lebanese industry began under the disadvantage of few natural resources, the country's mineral wealth being confined to a small amount of iron ore in Mount Lebanon. It thus concentrated on manufacturing industries like textiles and in 1930 the big Arida cotton mills went into production outside Tripoli. Further expansion of industry was, however, effectively prevented by the attitude of the French Mandate authorities who regarded Syria and Lebanon as export markets for their own industries. After the Second World War, industry did make surprising progress, handicapped though it was by the rigid free trade system imposed on it. Yet even by 1972 it was still contributing less than one-seventh of the Gross Domestic Product.

Over two-thirds of this industry was in or around Beirut, with most of the remainder divided between Tripoli and Mount Lebanon. In other parts of the country — in the south or in the Akkar region in the north — there was virtually no industry at all. Even Tripoli, the second city of the country, had declined through government negligence. Apart from the Arida mills, a cement factory and an oil refinery, there was little industrial activity in this city that had been for most of its history a greater port than Beirut. Even the port itself had dwindled in importance, so that by the 1970s it was unable to handle more than a single vessel at a time.

It was the same story in Sidon, the third city in the land and, like Tyre, one of the greatest harbours of antiquity. Tyre, however, was beyond recall, its harbour long since silted up, most of its stone removed in the eighteenth century to rebuild Acre. The prophecy of Ezekiel had indeed been fulfilled and for centuries Tyre has been little more than 'a place for the spreading of nets in the middle of the sea'. But Sidon was the responsibility of the French mandate and the Lebanese republic. The port that had once harboured a hundred tiremes at a time was still, before the First World War, used regularly by Russian, British and Ottoman ships. By 1961 its depth did not in many places exceed one metre and only fishing boats and dinghies could use it.[16]

In the countryside, the problems fostered by neglect were also considerable. The growth of population, the agricultural depression and the attraction of Beirut produced such a huge emigration from the land that by 1975 nearly half the total population of the country was living in the capital. While the migrants often faced unemployment and appalling conditions in the Beirut slums, those who stayed on the land might also be condemned to poverty. While the standard of living in rural Lebanon compared well with that in Syria, Turkey or Jordan, there were some areas, particularly in the Muslim regions of Akkar and the south, with large-scale poverty. Even in the 1960s, the governor of the south could complain that 200 villages in his region had no running water, that over half the children received no education at all, that none of the 445 villages had electricity, and that the town of Bint Jubeil was lit by kerosene lamps.[17] A decade later, however, much of this had changed; primary education was available to most of the population, and electricity extended to nearly all the villages. Nevertheless, the standard of rural housing remained low: although houses were often large and solid, over half of them had no bathroom and more than one-third lacked running water.[18] Moreover, the basic problem, that of underdevelopment, remained and was aggravated by the Israeli raids. Indeed, the more the Israelis bombed the south, the less the government seemed to notice. It certainly made no attempt to help the new wave of refugees thus created.* If any help was given to them, it was done by various private organizations, usually schools. When the village of Kfar Chouba was destroyed by the Israelis, in full view of the motionless Lebanese armed forces, it was the National College of Marjayoun, not the government, which offered accommodation to the villagers. This purely private foundation also took in 66 pupils from Kfar Chouba, who, like the children from neighbouring villages that had been bombed, were not required to pay fees. The Vocational Training Centre at Borg Chmali, built with funds raised by the Shi'ite Imam Musa Sadr, was another foundation that did the work which should have been done by the government.

These schools were added evidence that what was best in Lebanon was privately run. The majority of the country's schools were in private hands, run by Americans, French, British, Italians, Germans, the Jesuits, the Lazarists, the Sisters of Charity, as well as the various Lebanese sects, both Muslim and Christian. Of the two best universities, the American University of Beirut was run by Americans and the St Joseph University by French Jesuits. The most woefully inadequate was the Lebanese University, founded by the government in 1953, and attended by those who were unable to afford the fees of the others.

Similarly, the 20 public hospitals were inferior in quality as well as quantity to the 123 private ones. This would not have mattered so much if the private hospitals had been adequately spaced throughout the country. Although there were 36 of these hospitals in the relatively prosperous region of Mount Lebanon, however, there was only one in the backward Bekaa province.[19] In the far north of the country the 200,000 inhabitants of the Akkar region had no local hospital at all.[20] Under these conditions, the better doctors inevitably stuck close to Beirut and looked for clients from the capital, whether Lebanese, Western, or from the oil states.

The basic problem in the country was exactly the same as in Beirut — an absence of administrative control. Neither the govern-

---

* The extent of this exodus obviously varied from one district to another. In some it was very great; the population of Majdel Zoum, some 8 km from the border, dwindled from 1,200 to 200 in a matter of months after Israeli raids during which the mukhtar and three other people were abducted. According to *Newsweek* (8 June 1970) Bint Jubeil lost 90 per cent of its inhabitants.

ment nor the bureaucracy were ever enthusiastic about planning, and both were in any case to idle and too inefficient to carry it out. The result was too much development in Beirut with consequent chaos, and too little in the rest of the country with consequent depression. This in turn produced the large-scale migration to Beirut for which the authorities were quite unprepared and which they then ignored. The resentment of the migrants, badly housed and often unemployed, living on the edge of one of the most prosperous cities in the eastern Mediterranean, was an important factor in the build-up to the civil war.

Although a Planning Board was set up in 1953 and a Ministry of General Planning the following year, these achieved little and received only token attention from the government. It was not until President Chehab's term of office that anybody took planning seriously, and then only briefly. One prime minister introduced a development plan with the words, 'Planning has become a scientific necessity in our age'[21] but neither he nor his successors were able to carry it out. Father Louis Joseph Lebret was commissioned to prepare several studies on the prospects of development,[22] but of all his recommendations, only part of the Litani project was attempted. Similarly, the development plans put forward in 1958 and 1965 (based on Lebret's studies) were both largely ignored, and their proposal that nearly half of Beirut should be allocated to parks, roads, public buildings and monuments, had become a bad joke by the 1970s.[23] The government's attitude towards planning can be assessed by its treatment of the National Development Bank. Although Parliament passed legislation for its establishment in 1962, the bank was not actually set up until 1973.

But even had the government so wished, planning stood little chance of success in Lebanon, for it would have threatened the commercial lobby and the big political bosses, the two most important power groups in the country. The politicians opposed the very idea since it would have inevitably lessened the almost total independence they enjoyed in their constituencies (See Chapter 3) and the commercial lobby was unwilling to divert investments away from its profit-making activities in Beirut. For there was no incentive to invest in the rest of Lebanon. Beirut was the boom city, and once a man had made his money, he put a good deal of it abroad. The fact that some 100,000 Lebanese were able to spend the greater part of the civil war abroad, in London, Paris, Cairo or Cyprus, many of them in great luxury, shows that they invested well.* But there was, therefore, little private capital for Lebanon itself, outside of Beirut. And since the government was so weak, and its financial resources so meagre, without that capital there was little it could do — even had it wanted to.

* This does not include the vast numbers who fled to Syria where conditions were much less luxurious.

2

The Religious Factor

The formula, right-wing Christian versus left-wing Muslim, has been often used to describe the line-up at the beginning of the Lebanese civil war. It is such an over-simplification that it is of little use as a serious explanation. If there was sectarian hostility, it was no so much between Christians and Muslims as between the different sects, or communities, within these religions. Throughout its history, both as an Ottoman province and an independent state, Lebanon has been a confederacy of different and distinct religious communities. Michael Hudson has described it as 'a collection of traditional communities bound by the mutual understanding that other communities cannot be trusted'.[1] Origins, traditions, history and environment have so moulded the communities that each has usually acted independently of its co-religionists. The land has always been divided, and frequently by war, but the division has never been made along simple Christian/Muslim lines. The Lebanese are not a notably religious people and conflict between different sects was usually the result of political rivalry.

The two main Christian communities in Lebanon are the Maronites and the Melchites, the latter being subdivided into Greek Orthodox and Greek Catholics. There are also about a dozen smaller communities of which the most important are the Armenian Orthodox, the Armenian Catholics and Protestants.*

*The last official estimate of population figures, published in 1956, divided the sects as follows:

Maronite Catholics	423,000	Sunni Muslims	286,000
Greek Orthodox	149,000	Shi'ite Muslims	250,000
Greek Catholics	91,000	Druzes	88,000

Others (including Armenian Orthodox, Armenian Catholics, Syrian Catholics, Syrian Orthodox, Assyrian Catholics (Nestorians), Chaldean Catholics, Roman Catholics, Evangelists, Baptists, Anglicans, Monophysites (Jacobites) and Jews) number 122,000.

For political reasons there has been no official census since 1932 but by 1975 it was generally recognized that the Muslims were in a clear majority and that the Shi'ites and possibly the Sunnis were by then numerically greater than the Maronites.

The principal Christian communities are products of the great schisms in the Church during the Byzantine Empire. In the fifth century, the Christian world was bitterly divided over the question of whether or not Christ had both a divine and a human nature, and it was from this quarrel that the sects originated. The Monophysite group, which had most of its support in Egypt, denied that Christ had a double nature and managed to impose this view on the Eastern Church at the Second Council of Ephesus. In 451 AD the Byzantine emperor reversed this decision at the Council of Chalcedon, and most of the Syrian* Church accepted the new decrees. They formed the Melchite Church, accepted the Byzantine rite, and later followed the Patriarch of Constantinople into schism with Rome (1054). Partly owing to the zeal of the Jesuit missionaries, however, the Melchite Church split at the end of the seventeenth century and a group of them formed a Uniate Church with Rome in 1727. They became Greek Catholics and the non-Uniate Melchites became known as Greek Orthodox.

The Monophysites, however, refused to accept the decisions of the Council of Chalcedon and by the seventh century the controversy had engulfed the whole of the Byzantine Empire. Since it then began to threaten the safety of the Empire itself, a compromise was attempted. This was the Monothelite doctrine, which affirmed that Christ had two natures but only a single divine will. Unfortunately, both the Eastern Church and the Monophysite heretics rejected the solution and at the Sixth General Council of the Church in 680 it was officially banned. However, it was enthusiastically accepted by one solitary group of Syrian Christians who became known as the Maronites.

The term 'Maronite' was first used by John the Damascene in the eighth century, and it may have originated either from a Syrian hermit, St Maron, or from John Maroun, the first Maronite patriarch. It referred to a Syrian group of Aramaic origin who had embraced the Monothelite heresy and were later persecuted on that account by Emperor Justinian II. A large number of Maronite monks were executed on the Orontes river by Justinian,

---

* Until 1920, Syria was taken to mean not only the territory of the present state of Syria but also that of Lebanon, Palestine and Transjordan. When dealing with events before 1920, the term is used in this book to denote the area of 'Greater' Syria.

their principal monastery near Antioch was destroyed, and a part of the Maronite community shipped off to Thrace in the seventh century. As a reaction to these events, and also perhaps to the encroachments of the Muslim Arabs, most of the Maronite population retreated to the northern mountains of Lebanon where they settled, and where many of them have lived ever since. According to the medieval bishop, William of Tyre, they formed a Uniate Church with Rome in 1182, although the union was not consolidated until much later, but they retained their Patriarch and their own liturgy in the Syriac language. During this period they were firm allies of the Crusaders, but after the European defeat they came under pressure again, this time from the Egyptian Mamelukes who invaded their territory on four occasions at the end of the thirteenth century. Nevertheless, they survived and gradually during the next four hundred years spread southwards and came to occupy much territory that formerly belonged to the Shi'ite and Druze communities. Until the eighteenth century, however, they remained politically weak and in close partnership with the Druzes, the dominant sect of Mount Lebanon at the time. By 1770 Druze hegemony was over and, in recognition of this, the Chehab emirs, who had ruled the Mountain since the extinction of the Ma'nid dynasty in 1697, were converted to Christianity and became Maronites. The Druze-Maronite alliance continued, however, until the middle of the nineteenth century when it was ended by civil war. After the end of the fighting in 1860 many Druzes emigrated to the Jebel Druze in Syria and the Maronites were able to consolidate their majority.

Until the 1960s the largest of the Lebanese sects, the Maronites were the most influential and privileged group in modern Lebanon. Traditionally, they are a fiercely independent community of mountain peasantry whose main ally in their conflicts with the feudal landowners has been the Maronite church. By contrast, the Melchites have usually lived in the coastal towns and larger inland villages, working as traders and artisans. Although politically less active than the Maronites, they have been the best educated and most economically successful of the Lebanese communities.

Comparatively recent arrivals among the Christian communities were the Protestants and the Armenians. The former, divided into

Evangelists, Baptists and Anglicans, were mostly converted from other Christian sects by American Presbyterian missionaries in the nineteenth century. The Armenians came to Lebanon in stages: in the wake of the 1895—96 massacres, in the 1920s as the victims of Kemal Ataturk, and in the late 1930s after the Turkish annexation of Alexandretta. Some of them settled in the Bekaa valley, but most went to live in Beirut and its suburbs. In 1924 the French authorities gave them Lebanese citizenship and by the 1970s there were believed to be about 150,000 Armenians in the country.

On the Muslim side, geographical divisions between the sects are also discernible. The predominant sect, the Sunnis, or orthodox Muslims, have worked mainly as merchants and traders in Tripoli, Beirut and Sidon since the Mameluke period, although there is also a large rural community in the Akkar region in the north. The Shi'ites, the chief minority sect of Islam, are the most scattered of the Lebanese communities. Traditionally, they are peasants from Mount Lebanon, the south and the Bekaa valley, although by the 1970s they also formed a large section of the 'belt of misery' around Beirut. They are the poorest of the Lebanese sects and, because of their high birth rate, have recently become the largest. A third Islamic sect, though to Orthodox Muslims they are heretics, are the Druzes. They practise a secret faith and only their men can be initiated into it. Among other things they believe in predestination, reincarnation and the divinity of the Fatimid Caliph al-Hakim (996—1021 AD). Although they read the Koran and believe that Muhammad was the prophet of God, they do not pray in mosques and have no public places of worship. Nor do they observe the fast of Ramadan or go on the pilgrimage to Mecca. They were for a long time the dominant sect of Mount Lebanon but now form a fairly small community based on the mountainous area south of the Beirut—Damascus road.

The relationship between the Sunni and the Shi'ite communities has always been an uneasy one, since for centuries the two sects disputed the leadership of Islam. The split occurred in the early days of the movement after the assassination of Ali, the Prophet's son-in-law, the Sunnis taking the side of the Ummayad family, the Shi'ites supporting the descendants of Ali, whom they called Imams and whom they claimed as the lawful successors of

Muhammad. There were twelve Imams and Shi'ites believe that the last one, who was also called Muhammad and who disappeared, will one day return to establish the true faith. However, although there are important differences in religion, the reasons for the historical antagonism between the two sects are political. While they have had their moments of power, notably during the Fatimid Caliphate based on Cairo, the Shi'ites are conscious of the fact that they have generally been a minority, and a barely tolerated one at that. A majority of the inhabitants of the Ottoman Empire were Sunnis and political life during the centuries of Turkish rule was dominated by them. Fear of being swamped by the Sunnis has been a constant factor in Shi'ite history, and has at times led them to side with Christian forces against their co-religionists.

Both Christian and Muslim sects, especially those based in the Mountain, have often made a point of remaining isolated from neighbouring communities. The differences between them have always been apparent and in the nineteenth century were encouraged by the European powers. The Russians set themselves up as the protectors of the Greek Orthodox, the French and the Austrians tried to outbid each other for influence over the Maronites, and the British, at a loss to know whom to support, finally championed the cause of the Druzes. Politically, the Americans were less interested and their educational achievements were undoubtedly impressive, yet the eagerness of their Presbyterian missionaries understandably irritated the other communities from whom they were trying to make converts. European meddling in Lebanon had generally unfortunate consequences, though there were few foreign agents who went as far as Father Maximilien Ryllo, a Lithuanian Jesuit who paraded round the countryside between 1837 and 1841, encouraging the Maronites to fight their Druze neighbours.

Different sects within the same religion have rarely been united. Indeed, alliances or friendships, when they have taken place, have normally been between sects from different religions: Maronites and Shi'ites against the Sunni Mamelukes, Melchites and Sunnis living in harmony in the coastal towns, the Druzes and Maronites in an alliance which was the mainstay of Lebanese stability until the 1830s. During the fighting between the Maronite and Druze communities in the middle of the nineteenth century, some Shi'ites fought for the Maronites while the Greek Orthodox assisted the Druzes. Religious persecution has been rare in Lebanon. When it has taken place it has usually been amongst co-religionists: Sunnis against Shi'ites or Maronites against the Greek Orthodox.

From 1516 to 1860, Mount Lebanon was a largely autonomous province of the Ottoman Empire, although the coastal plain was more firmly under the control of the Turkish authorities. Following the massacres in the Maronite–Druze war in 1860, the Ottoman government, compelled by the major European powers to do something, decided to bring the whole province under its control. A more centralized government was therefore created based on an administrative council consisting of members of all the religious communities. The governor, or *mutesarrif*, was a Christian from the Ottoman Empire (but not a Lebanese) and was directly responsible to the Porte. This system, which introduced the confessional principle into government, brought administrative and economic benefit to the country and survived until the collapse of the Ottoman Empire at the end of the First World War.

In 1920, the French achieved one of their imperialist ambitions and received a mandate for Syria and Lebanon at the San Remo Conference. In 1943, after a drawn-out struggle between De Gaulle's Free French on the one hand, and the Lebanese supported by the Churchill Government on the other, the country became independent. Having lived for centuries in varying degrees of isolation, the major communities now had to come together and find some acceptable basis for co-existence. Fortunately, for the first and almost the last time in its short history, the new state was able to produce men capable of doing so. The most important of these were Bishara Khoury, the new Maronite president, Riad Solh, the Sunni prime minister, and Michel Chiha, a Roman Catholic writer and financier.

The problems that faced them were considerable. Under the Ottoman Empire, the Sunni Muslims had been the most priviliged sect in the region but, with the arrival of the French, they lost this position to the Maronites. The alliance between the French and the Maronites had always been very close (see pp. 76–8) and with the establishment of the Mandate the richer Maronites tended to identify themselves increasingly with France and Europe. They spoke French, were educated in French, wore French clothes and went to French theatres. Before long, many of them had become openly contemptuous of Islam and the Muslims. The Maronite who most clearly represented these ideas was Emile Eddé, President of Lebanon under the Mandate from 1936 to 1941. Eddé had studied law in Paris and spoke French better than he spoke Arabic. His opinion of Muslims and of Arab aspirations was disparaging, and he refused to move outside Christian francophile society. To him, Lebanon was a Christian refuge, an outpost of European civilization in the backward East. Had he been succeeded by men with similar views, the Lebanese war would have started thirty years earlier.

It was the object of Bishara Khoury's administration (1943–52) to make sure that Eddé's attitude did not prevail among the Maronite community. Its guiding principle had already been set down by Khoury's brother-in-law, Michel Chiha, who had been one of the principal authors of the constitution passed by the Lebanese Representative Council during the French Mandate in 1926. To him, an equitable balance between the communities was vital, the only means of ensuring stability, for he knew that Lebanon was an artificial country with arbitrary borders chosen by the French. Within these borders resided six large religious sects and about a dozen smaller ones, all with different traditions, different cultures and different loyalties. The Maronites had close affiliations with France and the West, while the Sunnis, for instance, who had benefited little from the Mandate, looked to the East and the emerging power of Arab nationalism. They had little desire to stay in a Lebanon dominated by the Maronites and would have preferred to be incorporated by Syria, whose population was largely Sunni.

Co-operation between the communities, then, was the way to prevent Lebanon from falling apart. No single community must be allowed to antagonize the others, especially over foreign policy. The Maronites should not go all out for alliance with the West, the Sunnis should exercise restraint in their enthusiasm for pan-Arabism. This was the basis of the unwritten National Pact between the communities, and clearly implicit in the speech made by Riad

Solh to parliament in 1943: 'Lebanon is a homeland with an Arab face seeking the beneficial good from the culture of the West'.[2] Foreign policy was the main success of Lebanon's first independent government and Khoury managed successfully to observe both halves of the National Pact. In 1948 he committed Lebanese troops to the first Arab-Israeli war, a decision applauded by the Sunni Arab nationalists, and in 1950 he abolished the customs union with Syria, a move welcomed by Christian business circles.

As for co-operation in internal matters, the obvious method of ensuring that each sect did not receive more than its fair share was to create positions in the administration which could only be filled by members of a particular sect. The president was to be a Maronite, for example, the prime minister a Sunni Muslim, and the speaker of the Chamber of Deputies a Shi'ite. In Bishara Khoury's first government (1943) all the major communities were represented, and this pattern has generally been repeated since then. The principle that the distribution of posts should be accorded to the sects in rough proportion to their numbers was extended to the civil service, the army and the foreign ministry.

This system, though flawed, was probably the only one possible at the time. It did give the Christian sects, in particular the Maronites, a predominance which their numbers and political sophistication perhaps then justified. Towards the end of the Mandate, parliamentary representation had been fixed at a ratio of 6:5 in favour of the Christians, a compromise suggested by the British Minister, Sir Edward Spears, after the then Head of State, Dr Ayub Tabet, had tried to secure an even better ratio for the Christians. The 6:5 proportion, which Spears intended as a temporary expedient, remained after independence and has continued ever since, although no neutral observer would deny that the Christians have been in a minority for years. Apart from the presidency, the Maronites were also given the army command and the directorate general of public security.

Confessionalism thus became the basic principle in Lebanese life. Saeb Salam, one of the leading Sunni politicians and a former prime minister, once said that for the Lebanese religion serves as a passport, a cheque, a privilege and a certificate of competence.[3] He was not being unduly cynical. It is difficult to over-estimate the effect of a man's religion on his life and career in Lebanon. Because of the principle enshrined in the National Pact that each sect must have its fair share of power, confessional membership was often more important for someone applying for a state appointment than his actual qualifications. It was the same for a man looking for a career in politics. As a Protestant, Emile Bustani was unable to stand for election since before 1960 his sect was considered too small to merit parliamentary representation. Before he could be elected, therefore, he had to change his religion and become a Maronite. A man's religion would also determine which schools he was educated at, since the communities ran their own schools*, which youth and sports clubs he might join, since these too were organized on a confessional basis, and which law courts he might be tried in, since the sects even had their own courts and legal systems which were quite separate from the civil courts. A Sunni Muslim, for example, would be tried according to Sharia law, a code of law taken from the Koran.

The influence of the Islamic Society of Benevolent Intentions provides an example of the importance of the religious communities in the lives of their members. The Society was the principal Sunni charity in the country. It ran 19 schools in Beirut (most of them not charging fees), 85 schools in rural areas, a nursing school, a teacher-training centre and one of the best institutions in the city, the Maqasid hospital.[4] It gave grants to orphanages, training colleges and an old people's home. It also undertook the burial of Beirut's Muslims. In the lives of many Sunnis the Society played a more useful and important role than the government itself. Among the Shi'ites, a similar job was undertaken by the Amiliyah Islamic Benevolent Society.

In Lebanon a man's loyalty went first to his community. If he had to choose between that and the state, it was the state which generally lost. A striking instance of the strength of confessional loyalty occurred in an inter-Sunni quarrel in 1970 when the Mufti

---

*Article 10 of the Constitution states that 'the right of the sects to operate their own schools shall not be interfered with in any way, provided they comply with the educational laws issued by the state.' Barely a third of Lebanese schoolchildren went to state schools.

demanded the resignations of all the Sunni ministers in the cabinet. Since the prime minister was always a Sunni, this was tantamount to demanding the resignation of the whole government. And astonishingly, Rashid Karami, who was then prime minister, capitulated to the Mufti. Although a compromise was later engineered, Karami announced that he was prepared to resign. In a conflict of loyalties, the whims of his religious leader proved more compelling than the needs of the state.

Confessionalism, whatever advantages it might have had in 1943, clearly had its drawbacks. It was inefficient, cumbersome and tended to reinforce sectarian ties at the expense of national feeling. The National Pact was an attempt to reach a consensus whereby none of the communities would try to dominate the others. It was, in the words of one Arab writer, 'a form of mutual deterrence'[5] and it was little more than that. According to Michel Khoury, the son of the late president, 'the National Pact is a negative pact. The Christians abandon the idea of protection from a foreign power, and the Muslims agree not to merge with the Arab world, but this is merely negative . . . What we need is to create a new national consensus.'[6] What Lebanon needed was a new approach to the state, a national approach, and this was being prevented by the confessional system. Practically everyone in Lebanon called themselves nationalists of one sort or another but their ultimate loyalties usually lay with their communities.

Yet on only one occasion before 1975 did the confessional system break down and the country polarize behind the Maronite and Sunni establishments. This was in 1958 when the then president, Camille Chamoun, upset the balance of trust on which Lebanon has to exist. 1958 was the high tide of Arab nationalism, the year Egypt and Syria formed the United Arab Republic (UAR). In Jordan and Iraq, Arab nationalist pressure was building up against the pro-British Hashemite regimes. In Lebanon, Gamal Abdel Nasser was the hero of the Muslim population and the proclamation of the UAR was greeted with enthusiasm by Arab nationalists all over the country. It was against this background that Chamoun, with a strange lack of political judgement, tried to push Lebanon into an alliance with the West.

Chamoun was of course a Maronite, although his personal

affiliations were with Britain rather than France, and it was widely believed that he had worked for British Intelligence in the 1940–43 period. Although originally a supporter of Khoury, his views were closer to Emile Eddé. He believed that Lebanon was more European than Arab and he made little effort to conceal his hostility towards Islam and the Arab states. He particularly disliked Nasser and seemed to regard him, curiously, as a communist who was attempting to subvert Lebanon. At the time of Suez he had hoped that the invasion of Egypt by the combined forces of Britain, France and Israel would be successful and that Nasser would be deposed. Afterwards, when the invaders had withdrawn, Chamoun told the American journalist Drew Pearson: 'Your [the United States'] greatest mistake was not to let the Israeli army continue in Suez for another fourteen days.'[7] Thus the leader of an Arab country not only supported foreign aggression against another Arab country, but wished it had gone further. It was this contempt for Arab nationalist aspirations combined with the arrogance he displayed towards Lebanon's Muslims that brought about his downfall two years later.

The move that led to the 1958 crisis was Chamoun's acceptance of the Eisenhower Doctrine the year before. This declared that 'the United States is prepared to use armed forces to assist any nation or group of such nations [in the Middle East] requesting assistance against armed aggressors from any country controlled by international communism.'[8] The 'doctrine' was a typical product of American Cold-War thinking and owed far more to Mr Dulles' obsession with communism than to any understanding of the situation in the Middle East. For the United States the proposal was a failure: all the Arab countries except Lebanon rejected it and most of them ended up closer to the Soviet Union than they had been before. And for Chamoun to accept it, even before it had been approved by the US Congress, was an act of outstanding folly. It was a slap in the face to all the Muslims in the country who were outraged by his treatment of the National Pact and were determined to remain independent of the West. Worst of all, it was unnecessary. Nobody could think that Lebanon was threatened by communism. Its own Communist Party was the oldest party in the country but also one of the weakest and of little political significance. As for the UAR, against which this 'doctrine' was presumably aimed, it was surely impossible to pretend that Nasser was planning 'armed aggression' against Lebanon or that his country was 'controlled by international communism'.

The parliamentary elections of 1957 were fought in a highly unpleasant atmosphere with the government accusing its opponents of being 'the candidates of Abdel Nasser' and the opposition furious at the decision to accept the Eisenhower Doctrine. The result was a major victory for Chamoun who was helped by financial assistance from the CIA. In Beirut his allies or clients won 10 out of 11 seats; in Mount Lebanon they won 18 out of 20. Further-more, several of the leading Arab nationalists, two of them former prime ministers, were defeated. Although the opposition's accusa-tions that there had been a lot of ballot-rigging could not be proved, there had certainly been some gerrymandering which contributed to the defeats of Saeb Salam in Beirut and Kamal Jumblatt, the socialist leader, in the Chouf. Chamoun followed up his victory by making it clear that he intended to alter the constitution in order to allow himself a second term as president. Coming after the Eisenhower Doctrine and the elections, this was too much for his opponents and there was an uprising against the government. On July 14 there was a coup d'état in Iraq which overthrew the monarchy and this affected Chamoun so much that he panicked and appealed for American support. Some 15,000 American marines duly landed in Beirut, where they remained largely inactive, though their mere presence did much to reduce American prestige in the Middle East. There was clearly some puzzlement among the American forces about what they were meant to be doing in Lebanon, but their commander, Admiral Holloway, had a shrewd idea: 'that man', he said, referring to Chamoun, 'had the impertinence to call in American armed forces to protect his own personal interests'.[9]

As for the revolt, that was never crushed simply because it did not need to be. It was neither subversive nor communist. It was simply a reaction against Chamoun's behaviour and his disregard of the National Pact. In September 1958 Chamoun was succeeded by the army commander, General Chehab, and, after one last round of fighting, the revolt died down. For Chehab, like Bishara

Khoury, understood that Lebanon could only survive by com-
promises. To try to turn it into an American satellite would only
tear it apart. So Chehab turned the nation's foreign policy in a
neutral direction and the crisis passed.

The 1958 confrontation is normally explained by the old
Muslim versus Christian formula. As usual it conveys at best a half-
truth. It would be more accurate to say that it was a clash between
those Maronites who thought like Chamoun and Emile Eddé, and
the rest of the country, which included 'dissident' Maronites, the
majority of the Melchite population, and the Muslims. Even that
is not quite sufficient for Chamoun still retained the support of
a few anti-Nasser Muslims and some of the wealthier Melchites.
Among the Christians who opposed him were four former foreign
ministers, his predecessor Bishara Khoury, the army commander,
two future presidents and the Maronite Patriarch, Bulos-Butros
Meouchy. The last, in particular, made no secret of the fact that
he regarded the Muslim leaders and General Chehab as the saviours
of the country, and understood the folly of trying to align Lebanon
with the West against the Arabs. An alliance between the Americans
and the Christian Lebanese, he believed, would be disastrous for
both. American behaviour was driving the Arabs towards the Soviet
Union and destroying Lebanese co-existence. By its actions, he
said, the United States was putting a placard saying 'Anti-Arab'
on every Christian in the Middle East.[10]

3

Democracy: the Lebanese Version

Westerners often used to talk of Lebanon as the only democracy of the Arab Middle East, the one state with free elections and a free press, a shining contrast to the shoddy dictatorships of Syria, Egypt and Iraq. Such people saw only the form of democracy, perhaps no more than the blurred outline, and then went away satisfied they had found at least one Arab country on which the West could rely. Had they prodded at all, they would have found little in the content that resembled Western-style democracy. The Lebanese version was unique to Lebanon and only vaguely democratic. True, there were elections, though these could not be described as free any more than the resulting parliament could be described as representative. The political establishment was a closed and highly conservative club, whose members quarrelled bitterly among themselves, but who combined sufficiently to prevent the admission of newcomers. As one Lebanese journalist complained, the country was governed by *'la dictature d'un Club de Notables'*.[1] All the major Lebanese leaders on the eve of the civil war had been prominent politicians over the previous quarter of a century. Pierre Gemayel has been leader of the Phalangist Party since 1936. Sabri Hamadeh, who became a cabinet minister in 1972, had been a member of parliament ever since 1925 when the country's first elected assembly, the Lebanese Representative Council, was set up.

The crucial figure in this system was the za'im — originally, the holder of a fief or feudal office — who occupied an undefined but immensely powerful position both in the cities and in the rural areas. The za'im was a political leader who might not be a minister, might not even be a deputy, but whose power gave him control not only over groups of deputies but also over government ministers as well. In his own particular constituency, or 'fief', he would probably exercize greater power than the government itself.

A za'im generally owed his position to his ancestry, for the hereditary principle was revered in Lebanese political life. Politics was often treated like a family business and there are twenty families which have each contributed more than one cabinet minister since the establishment of the French mandate. The Eddé family has produced four ministers as well as the last president before independence. The Solhs, a family originally from Sidon which moved to Beirut, provided four prime ministers in 25 years. A glance at the parliamentary lists of the 1930s shows many of the same names that are prominent now — grandfathers, fathers and uncles whose positions and prestige were inherited by younger members of their family. Thus, Rashid Karami inherited his father's power base among the Sunnis in Tripoli and Saeb Salam succeeded his father in Beirut. After Emile Eddé's death, his son Raymond succeeded him as leader of the National Bloc, even though their ideas were radically different. In the case of the Druzes, the two most important leaders, Sheikh Kamal Jumblatt and Emir Majid Arslan, were directly descended from rival families that have led the Druze community for some four hundred years. When Jumblatt was assassinated early in 1977, his 28-year-old son inherited not only his father's position as leader of the Druzes, but also the leadership of the leftist alliance. He was elected President of the Progressive Socialist Party without opposition, although he had no political experience whatever and was most reluctant to accept. Yet another example was the election of Myrna Bustani as deputy. When the self-made Maronite za'im, Emile Bustani, was killed in an air accident, the Bustani family not only decided that his daughter Myrna should succeed him, but even had enough influence to ensure that her election was unopposed.

Pierre Gemayel and Camille Chamoun were two Maronite za'ims who had to create their own power bases without advantage of ancestry. Yet both of them did what they could to perpetuate the hereditary principle. From the middle of 1976 the militias of Gemayel's Phalangist Party and Chamoun's National Liberal Party, which formed the backbone of the 'Christian' forces, were commanded respectively by their sons, Bachir

Gemayel and Dany Chamoun. It was a ridiculous situation in a modern war, and hardly conducive to military efficiency. But it was all bound up in the cult of the za'im, the 'Godfather' figure with his cigars, his Cadillacs and his permanent retinue of bodyguards and hangers-on. Any tourist would be aware of this cult the minute he looked at his map: so many of the most important streets were named after living za'ims — the Boulevard Saeb Salam, the Corniche Pierre Gemayel, the Avenue Camille Chamoun and so on.

The attitudes and traditional independence of the religious communities made it difficult for a za'im to have much of a following outside his own particular sect. The only one who did manage it to any significant degree was Kamal Jumblatt, who became the principal spokesman of the Arab nationalist and left-wing groups. Yet until the civil war, his power rested mainly on his following among the Druzes, whose feudal chieftain he was. In any case, it was only the small, left-wing parties who might be prepared to follow a leader of another sect. The traditional groups, without exception, followed leaders from their own communities: Saeb Salam, Rashid Karami, or members of the Solh family for the Sunnis; Pierre Gemayel, Raymond Eddé and Camille Chamoun for the Maronites; Kamal Asaad, Sabri Hamadeh and, more recently, the Imam Musa Sadr for the Shi'ites.

But if a za'im's support was limited to members of his own community, it was also limited to a particular locality. Rashid Karami was the most powerful man in Tripoli, but in Beirut, unless he happened to be prime minister at the time, he had no supporters. The Sunnis in the capital were Saeb Salam's followers. This was equally true of the rural districts: support for the Eddé family came from their home district of Byblos, and for the Frangiehs it came from their native town of Zghorta. Every za'im had his 'fief', protected by his own gunmen, and, whatever his position in the country as a whole, in his 'fief' he was supreme. In Lebanon a prime minister could go back to his stronghold immediately after his resignation speech and publicly hand out rifles to his supporters.*

---

* Rashid Solh did precisely this in May 1975.

The 1958 insurrection demonstrated only too well the power of the za'ims in their strongholds. Tripoli was ruled by Karami, the Chouf region south-east of Beirut by Jumblatt, and over neither of these places did the government exercise any control whatever. In the Basta quarter of the capital supreme power was held by Saeb Salam who directed the revolt like a medieval baron under siege. His house even looked like a fortress with its grey castellated walls, and in its halls and ante-rooms the garrison lounged around with their weapons, waiting for the attack which the government had ordered but the army commander refused to carry out.

The za'im's role and responsibilities differed according to the region but they were rarely confined to politics. In the backward areas (mainly Shi'ite or Druze) where there still existed a more or less feudal social system, the political leaders were often the greatest landowners and, in the case of Kamal Jumblatt, the spiritual leader as well. Jumblatt's politics, an idiosyncratic and not very radical form of socialism, mattered little to his clansmen. He was their leader and because of that they gave him their votes. Jumblatt had given most of his land to his tenants and therefore the relationship between them was no longer strictly feudal. But this was not the case with the other great feudal houses. The Shi'ite community was dominated by two landowning families, the Hamadehs of Hermel and the Asaads of south Lebanon. Such was the strength of patronage and the client system in their constituencies that they nearly always managed to get themselves and their allies elected to parliament. Moreover, the heads of the two families, Kamal Assad and Sabri Hamadeh, were brothers-in-law and when they combined they were able to 'deliver' most of the Shi'ite community. If they joined forces with the old Druze chieftain, Emir Majid Arslan, the veteran member of twenty-four cabinets, they could make and unmake governments.

A za'im's main task was to please his clients and constituents — finding them jobs, settling disputes, persuading the government to provide a village with a mosque or a church or drinking water. If he became a minister he would be expected to favour them with new projects, and this is what Rashid Karami did as prime minister when he organized the Tripoli fair in the late sixties.[2] Kamal

Jumblatt described how his constituents consulted him about 'their personal problems, the projects they would like to carry out in the village, even their medical problems'.[3] As their za'im he was expected to do a lot for them: 'they rely on me to build this or that school, a particular road, a new water pipe: in short to deal with everything which concerns public services.' The role of the urban za'im was more complicated. Since his position was not based on inherited property, he could theoretically be unseated. The Sunni za'ims of Beirut thus had a more difficult job than the Shi'ite landlords of the Bekaa. They had no land and so no tenants and these disadvantages were not compensated for by a political organization or an electoral programme. Apart from his inherited position, the Sunni urban za'im had to rely, therefore, on his abilities and the strength of his personality. Saeb Salam, the leading Sunni politician in Beirut for more than thirty years, looked almost like a caricature of a za'im with a large cigar always in one hand and a carnation in his button-hole. But he needed more than his charm and ability to retain his 'street' or con-stituency. The Sunni za'im was the representative of the Arab nationalist tradition in Lebanon and no Sunni who collaborated with the French could aspire to be a successful politician after the mandate. Besides his ability as a fixer, therefore, a Sunni za'im was also required to have a political appeal and to make at least occasional concessions to ideology, especially since his followers were likely to be more sophisticated and politically active than those of rural za'ims. Thus, he would have to talk emotively of Nasser and Arab nationalism even if he did not wholly believe in them, just as his Maronite counterpart would appeal to his constituents in the name of *Libanisme* or Lebanese nationalism (see Chapter 5). If a Sunni za'im ignored the Arab nationalist movement he was unlikely to last long. Sami Solh, the Sunni prime minister who backed Chamoun in 1958, never again held political office. Nevertheless, in spite of this, the basis of the za'im's support was always the client relationship, the extensive use of patronage and also, at election times, strong-arm tactics.

Given the confessional nature of the country, national parties, with coherent political programmes, were practically out of the question. Religion, ancestry, wealth, strength of personality, managerial ability — in Lebanese politics it was more important for a man to have these than to have ideas. The system depended on bargains and alliances at every level, and a coalition between blocs in the parliament was more likely to be founded on the self-interest of the controlling za'ims than on any similarity of ideas. Often the za'ims behaved not like modern politicians but as clan chieftains resuscitating old grievances. The Druze community had been split for centuries between the Yazbaki and the Jumblatt factions. The rival groups, which were now represented by Kamal Jumblatt and Emir Majid Arslan (whose family had long supported the Yazbakis), continued the feud into modern times and Arslan habitually opposed any suggestion of Jumblatt's. In southern Lebanon the hostility between the Asaads and the Khalils of Tyre dated from the time when Kamal Asaad's grandfather brought about the execution of Abdel Karim al-Khalil by denouncing him to the Turks as an Arab nationalist.[4]

By contrast with the za'ims and their alliances, political parties were of minor importance. The largest party, and the only one that possessed an organization on anything approaching a European scale, was the Phalangist Party, and yet in the 1972 election it gained only 7 deputies out of a total of 99. At every election since independence at least 60 per cent of the deputies have not belonged to political parties, the Lebanese evidently preferring the simpler relationship between the za'im and his client which rarely involved complicated questions of principle.

There were many more party members among the Christian deputies than among the Muslims but nearly all their political parties were more or less sectarian. As one commentator put it, 'the party system is to a large extent a modern facade to the system of communities which lies behind it'.[5] Although the Phalangists have always claimed that they are not a confessional party, their membership has been almost entirely Maronite and in fact no party, except perhaps the Communists, has managed to attract significant numbers of supporters from different sects. For all their high-sounding names, the parties have usually consisted merely of the followers of a particular za'im. The National Bloc and the Constitutional Bloc were simply the respective names by which the supporters of Emile Eddé and Bishara Khoury chose to identify themselves. The second largest party in the country was Camille Chamoun's National Liberal Party. But it was not a political party in any real sense: it had little organization and no programme and it would go for years without issuing a policy statement. Moreover, the name could hardly have been more misleading. As the civil war was to prove, it was neither national (it was prepared to partition the country) nor liberal (it was right-wing and authoritarian) and it was less of a party than a collection of westernized Maronite families grouped around the most charismatic Maronite za'im.

Even at election time, these 'parties' refused to behave like most political organizations in other countries. They would change coalition partners at almost every election and sometimes they would ally themselves with a party in one constituency and then oppose it in another. In the Metn district in the 1960 elections the Phalangists and the Constitutional Bloc were in alliance against the National Liberals, but next door in Ba'abda the Phalangists joined Chamoun's men to defeat the Constitutional Bloc.[6] A study of Lebanon's electoral alliances indicates that almost every politician has at one time supported and at another opposed every other politician. Even Kamal Jumblatt, a man with reasonably consistent political views and, in Lebanese terms, on the left of the political spectrum, managed to be at different times the ally (as well as the enemy) of almost every right-wing politician. During thirty years of political activity his allies included Khoury, Chamoun, Gemayel and Raymond Eddé as well as Chehab, the *Parti Populaire Syrien* (PPS; see pp. 66–7), the Ba'ath and the Communists.

The Lebanese electoral system was based on multi-member constituencies, with the seats in a constituency being allotted to the different communities according to their numbers. For example, the constituency of Aley in the mountains east of Beirut returned two Maronite deputies, two Druzes and one Greek Orthodox. Everyone in the constituency, whatever their religion, would be entitled to vote for a candidate for each seat, but in this particular case only Maronite, Druze and Greek Orthodox candidates would be allowed to stand. In this example the local za'im was the Druze chieftain, Emir Majid Arslan, and therefore one of the seats would always go to him. And the chances were that the other seats would be filled by three of his Christian supporters and one of his Druze allies. Thus, the first thing an aspiring politician had to do was enlist the support of the za'im. In Aley he would generally hope to join Emir Majid's list but he might for political or other reasons prefer to stand with Kamal Jumblatt who submitted a rival slate for this constituency even though his own fief, where he was practically unbeatable, was further south in the Chouf.

There was no point in a candidate standing as an independent as he would be certain to lose easily. He thus needed first to attach himself to a za'im and then to find a large sum of money to fight the campaign, beginning with a deposit of a thousand dollars, though during the campaign itself he would have to spend a great deal more. One deputy for Aley said that he had spent US$66,000 in the two elections of 1957 and 1960. In the 1964 election, two candidates in Beirut were reported to have spent one-third of a million dollars between them.[7] These expenses would include the entertainment of a candidate's supporters, the bribing of newspapers and the hiring of *qabadayat* or muscle-men to disrupt the opposition and keep his own followers in line. A substantial portion of it would be allocated to vote buying which was a widespread and fairly open practice that took place not just in the backward parts of the country but even in Beirut.

Without personal wealth, or some financial backing, it was impossible to stand for parliament, and indeed there has never been a working-class deputy in Lebanon. Deputies were nearly always landlords, lawyers, bankers or businessmen, in most cases elected on account of their family's position or their relationship with the local za'im. And once elected, they were still in the za'im's power since he could withdraw his support at any time and ensure defeat at the next elections.

Such a system obviously did little for either the strength or the prestige of parliament. It was unrepresentative of the country and people recognized it as such. One of the main problems preventing any modern evolution away from the za'im—client system was the government's insistence that voters should be registered in their home town or village and not in the city where they might have been living for years.[8] A Shi'ite originally from the Bekaa, for example, might have migrated to Beirut in the early sixties and settled down there, found a job and become interested in politics. He might be attracted to the Ba'ath Party, one of the Nasserist movements, or even the Communists. At election time, however, he would be unable to vote for any of these parties but would have to vote in his home village where the choice might be between two conservative landlords. This arrangement clearly reinforced the political hold of the za'ims and at the same time made it difficult for modern, broadly-based political movements to emerge. The industrial working class, for example, was small enough in Lebanon but it might have had some political weight had its members been allowed to vote in Beirut. Dispersed all over the country, they simply became targets for the za'ims' election agents.

The za'ims' near monopoly of political power was also instrumental in keeping the standard of political debate at a low level. If it was practically impossible for someone to get elected without becoming a sycophant to a za'im, then it was hardly surprising that many able and decent men should have avoided a political career. Occasionally somebody would challenge the system but almost invariably without success. Not until the last elections in 1972 did a couple of complete outsiders triumph in the preserves of two traditional za'ims. But these upsets took place in Beirut and Tripoli; they could not have happened in the Bekaa.

It was perhaps odd that the za'ims should have been so eager to get into parliament because they did little enough when they got there. Although in theory the Chamber of Deputies was the legislature, in practice it did not legislate. Bills were prepared by the government and then sent to parliament to be passed. One political scientist looked at four sample years between 1950 and 1966 and discovered that the Chamber had not rejected a single one of the 384 bills brought before it.[9] In spite of all the fervour at election time, the Lebanese did not have much respect for their parliament. They knew it had been fixed and they knew that it did not represent them. In 1951, President Khoury was brought down by a coalition of opposition politicians. Yet he was not forced out of office by parliament but by strikes and demonstrations in the country. Parliament understood nothing of the popular mood. On the night of his resignation nearly 60 of the 77 deputies visited Khoury and pledged their support.

The most important single ingredient in the za'im—client relationship (and the element which cemented it) was patronage which, with its close relations, nepotism and corruption, existed at every level of the political and administrative 'systems'. Its use was considered entirely natural and acceptable and even the president was expected to give posts to his supporters, although there were limits beyond which he was not expected to go. Suleiman Frangieh, president from 1970 to 1976, exceeded these limits, and the extent of the corruption of his regime shocked even the Lebanese. Frangieh was a Maronite za'im from Zghorta who inherited his position and his 'fief' from his abler elder brother Hamid, a man widely considered as a future president in the 1950s who had later been forced to retire from active politics after a stroke. He was stubborn, narrow-minded and unteachable, triumphing in the 1970 election as the anti-government candidate. Immediately after his election, which he won by a single vote, he began to distribute the important offices of state among his friends. It was joked in Beirut that as long as you came from Zghorta you would get a good job. Iskander Ghanem, a close friend, became commander-in-chief of the army; Ramez Khazen, the Mayor of Zghorta and a strong supporter, became Director of the Ministry of Information. But by far the worst instance of this nepotism was the wholly undeserved favour he showed his son Tony. After the presidential election Tony Frangieh inherited his father's seat in Zghorta and before long he was promoted to the cabinet. As Minister of Posts and Telecommunications he was a disaster: the telephone system, which had admittedly never functioned very well, became almost unworkable, while the postal service practically collapsed. A quick visit to the central post office made you come out wondering how you received any letters at all. It was widely said that Tony Frangieh allowed this decay so that he could buy new machinery but that, since he demanded such exorbitant commissions from the foreign firms he approached, he usually failed to do so.[10] In spite of demands for his son's resignation, President Frangieh refused to have his son dismissed. When the government of Takieddine Solh resigned in the autumn of 1974, Frangieh called on Saeb Salam, the strongest of all the Sunni politicians, to form a government, but only on condition that certain people, including the irrepressible Tony, were included. Salam was the last man to accept this sort of restriction and refused. But eventually a minor Sunni politician was found who would form a government and include Tony Frangieh in it.

One astounding thing about Suleiman Frangieh, and one which not surprisingly puzzled foreign visitors, was that he was a suspected murderer. In 1957, some of his followers slaughtered several members of the Douaihy family who were attending mass at Miziara near Zghorta. The Douaihy clan were rivals of the Frangiehs in the region south-east of Tripoli and were shot on account of a feud between the two families. It has frequently been alleged that Frangieh himself was one of the gunmen, although he has denied it. After the killing he fled to Syria where he remained for a year or so before returning. But he retained his fondness for guns and in the 1970 election his supporters brandished their revolvers in parliament when it appeared that the Speaker was disputing his electoral victory.

It was extraordinary that a man like Frangieh should manage to get himself elected president in the first place. He was in fact a compromise candidate, the eventual choice of all the motley groups who were opposed to the then government, which was dominated by the supporters of General Chehab. This opposition agreed on only one thing and that was to get rid of *al-Najj al-Shihabi*, 'the Chehab method'. General Chehab was the only statesman produced by Lebanon since Riad Solh and Bishara Khoury. One of the few incorruptible politicians in the country, he had become president after the 1958 crisis and did much to keep the country together at that time. He warned the rich that their behaviour was likely to provoke a social revolution and introduced social and economic reforms designed to help the poorer areas. Practically all the improvements in public services in Lebanon — in water supply, rural electrification or public health — are due to Chehab's almost single-handed campaign for social and economic justice. But he also tried to strengthen the administrative structure of the state and to make the government at least partially effective. For a while he gained an ascendancy over the za'ims which no other politician has managed to achieve. But he was not able to change the system as radically as he intended and to create institutions that would be able to continue his reforms after him. He despised the za'ims — *fromagistes* or cheese-eaters as he called them — whose interests demanded that the state should be kept weak. But he could not disregard them entirely without setting up a dictatorship. So he had to make an alliance with some of them in order to implement his reform programme. It was an understandable decision but it put an end to his hopes for decisive political and administrative reform.

Ultimately, Chehab failed but he still made the system strong enough to annoy the *fromagistes* and at the 1970 election they all ganged up and managed to defeat the 'Chehabist' candidate, Elias Sarkis. The election offered one of the few crucial and clear-cut choices Lebanon had experienced. The deputies, who elect the president, had to choose between Frangieh — a feudal za'im with a dubious past likely to restore the za'ims' club to its former importance — and Sarkis — the Governor of the Central Bank and an advocate of Chehab's reforms. During the summer it seemed that Chehab would put himself forward as a candidate and had he done so there is no doubt that he would have won easily.* The za'ims were of course terrified and managed to put considerable pressure on Chehab to dissuade him from standing. Even the Maronite Patriarch strongly advised him not to stand. Shortly before the election Chehab announced that he would not be a candidate and his supporters put up Sarkis instead.

The anti-Sarkis coalition was an alliance of enemies, of za'ims who in some cases were not on speaking terms but were prepared to go to any lengths to stop Chehabism. It included the main participants of the 1958 civil war, including Chamoun, Salam and Kamal Jumblatt. How Jumblatt, a supporter of the Chehab reforms and a fierce critic of the za'im system, could have

---

*Chehab's term of office ended in 1964 so he was entitled under the constitution to stand again in 1970.

joined the *fromagistes*, remains a mystery. But he did and his role was crucial. Sarkis was defeated by a single vote.

Frangieh became the anti-Chehabist candidate for various reasons. To begin with, his career had not been important enough for him to have had much opportunity of antagonizing the Muslims. Besides, he had supported the anti-government movement in 1958, though in this he was motivated by personal differences with Chamoun rather than by any matter of principle. In the 1952 presidential election his brother Hamid had been an opponent of Chamoun who then supported a rival Zghorta clan in the parliamentary elections of 1957. Later, when Chehab refused to show him any favour, Frangieh made up his quarrel with Chamoun and remained a political ally. In the second place, for one reason or another, all the leading Maronites had too many enemies to secure nomination. Lastly Frangieh was well-known to be tough, a quality that appealed to many Lebanese in the aftermath of the 1969 disorders. In short, he was elected for purely negative reasons and for his muscle, rather than for any ideas or political ability he might have had.

Frangieh's election was a victory for the traditional za'ims whose one cardinal political principle was that the state machinery must at all costs be kept weak. Such a situation safeguarded the independence of the za'im in his fief, which was in many cases almost absolute. In the Chouf region south of the Beirut–Damascus road, Camille Chamoun was the most important Christian and Kamal Jumblatt the most important Muslim. If the government wanted to do something in the Chouf, and neither of these two liked the idea, then it wasn't done, because ultimately it was their authority which counted. Therefore they had to be represented in the government, or at least have some cabinet member whom they could control. And as every power bloc in the country demanded to be represented in one way or another, the government would be forced to include people with such conflicting views that it was practically impossible to get them to agree on anything.

The cabinet was not, therefore, a group of like-minded people intent on carrying out a specific programme. It was more a mini-parliament and the quarrels that took place in the Chamber were repeated in the cabinet. In 1960 Saeb Salam formed a cabinet whose eighteen ministers represented all the za'ims in the country except the disgraced Chamoun and in 1972 he again headed a government that included every major faction except, on this occasion, the Chehabists and Jumblatt. The formation of these cabinets was a complicated business and the prime minister designate had to be careful to balance competing interests. So many considerations — regional, political and of course confessional — had to be taken into account that a candidate's ability might be completely disregarded. The most absurd situations could arise as a result of the practice of allocating ministries to particular sects. In 1955, a Sunni ex-diplomat occupied the ministry of public works while a Maronite engineer became foreign minister.[11]

Although in theory Lebanese cabinets accepted the principle of collective ministerial responsibility, in practice ministers spent much of their time criticizing each other in public. In the early sixties Kamal Jumblatt and Pierre Gemayel regularly attacked each other through their party newspapers even though they were members of the same government.[12] Za'ims such as these two were too powerful and, therefore, too dangerous to leave out of the cabinet for long periods and so they had to be admitted even if their presence paralysed the government. Disagreement between ministers was in fact the usual way for a cabinet to fall. Governments were never voted out of office by parliament.

The paralysis of government suited the za'ims very well, and although habitually at each other's throats, they agreed that everything should be done to preserve this situation. The za'ims, or at least the majority of them, were united on only two occasions in the thirty years after independence, and each time it was to get rid of a government which was strong enough not to include most of them. The anti-Chehabist coalition has already been discussed. In the other case, the alliance formed in 1951 to oust the government of Bishara Khoury, many of the same people were involved: Chamoun, Gemayel, Raymond Eddé — the country's leading right-wing politicians backed by the Phalangist Party and the PPS (see pp. 66–7) — all lining up with Jumblatt in an alliance calling itself the Socialist Front! It hardly needs to be said that there was nothing socialist about them, and that their one policy was to force Khoury's resignation, which they soon did.

While the za'ims circumscribed the government's powers on one side, the various business interests and lobbies (often composed of much the same people) did the same thing on the other. Since the country's wealth had been made by its merchants and bankers, they consequently formed the strongest pressure groups. And naturally the one thing they demanded was a weak state and minimal intervention by the government in the economy. They achieved this, but only at enormous cost to the country. For instance, during the 1960s and '70s it became more and more obvious that money should be spent on the development of backward regions like the south or the Akkar region in the north. But this did not suit various commercial and banking interests, since it would have increased the scope of the government. In 1971 the Finance Minister, Elias Saba, realizing the need to put money into social and economic development, decided to raise customs duties on several imported goods. This move was supported by the Industrialists' Association, anxious for some means of stimulating local industry. But a strike of Beirut shopkeepers and businessmen, which lasted ten days, killed the proposal.[13] Thus the social and economic health of the nation was in practice regulated less by the government than by the commercial lobby. There were other, similar incidents to illustrate the point that even when the government was moved to do something about social welfare, it could be prevented from actually carrying it out. For example, in the government that Saeb Salam formed under Frangieh in 1970, the minister of health was Dr Emile Bitar, a man who by Lebanese standards was a reformer. One of the first things he decided to do was to cut the cost of medicines and so put some of them within reach of the poorer sections of the country. But the monopolists of the pharmaceutical industry, who included some of Frangieh's close friends, wouldn't stand for it and refused. Bitar then turned to the government for help, assuming they would force the measure through. Frangieh, however, declined to support him and he was forced to resign.[14] Once again it showed what little control the government actually exercized over the country.

The government was thus caught in a feeble and ridiculous

position, the economic interests ordering it about on the one hand, the *fromagistes* consistently sabotaging it on the other. There was even a third constriction on its activities: the bureaucracy. Anybody who stayed in Lebanon for more than a month would realize that the bureaucracy, over-staffed, underpaid, idle, corrupt and above all incompetent, could only hinder the process of government. The short trip to get your visa or driving licence renewed provided enough evidence of this: the endless offices you had to visit and the innumerable signatures you had to obtain, the interminable waiting while newspapers were read and gossip completed, the cups of heavily-sugared coffee you had to drink before anything was done. It could last a whole morning. The bureaucracy had been reformed and purged by Chehab and his successor Helou without seeming to make much difference even though 200 civil servants were dismissed.[15] The bureaucrats remained extraordinarily indolent with short office hours (mornings only) and long vacations (4 weeks plus 25 official and religious holidays) often extended without permission. The top officials were just as bad as their juniors. As one inspector of the bureaucracy reported, 'Although they [the senior bureaucrats] are expected to be leaders and pacesetters, their behaviour does not in fact differ from that of their subordinates, except that they sign more documents. They are not unlike postmasters indiscriminately shuffling paper from one official to the other.'[16] The problem was partly a lack of talent: although the Constitution stressed the right of the Lebanese to office on the basis of merit and competence, people were in fact appointed according to their confessional status. Moreover, because of the inadequate pay, the bureaucracy was unable to attract the best brains in the country who could earn far more in private business. Even those who did join rarely spent more than three or four hours in the office because they wanted to go out and do other jobs as well.

More important was the problem of attitudes. This was the Lebanese tradition of government and nobody who has tried to alter it has ever had much success. On his appointment as minister of reconstruction and of public works in 1956, Emile Bustani announced in parliament that he would receive visitors in his ministry from dawn until 8 a.m. after which he would work and

and see only those who had made appointments; that he would sack any civil servants who accepted gifts or even visits from parliamentary deputies; and that the money allocated for the rebuilding of villages shattered by a recent earthquake would not be distributed as presents to the distressed villagers but would be actually used to rebuild their houses.[17] Such an approach was of course anathema to the rest of the cabinet and consequently the most energetic minister the Lebanese have ever had was forced out of office within three months of his appointment.

Against a background of semi-feudal political barons, a selfish commercial lobby and a bureaucracy that could be counted on to destroy projects through inertia and red tape, the incapacity of the Lebanese government becomes understandable. No wonder it was unable to take important decisions or solve ordinary problems. No wonder it was unable to persuade people to pay their income tax even though the country had one of the lowest tax rates in the world. And no wonder that cabinets on average lasted less than ten months. Given the obstacles the government had to face merely to exist, little could be done about political or economic reform, or about the deplorable social situation, or even about the gangsterism in the cities and the general lawlessness in the country. Least of all could anybody be surprised by its inability to root out inefficiency and corruption in high places, since among the worst offenders were President Frangieh and his son.

While Lebanon was at peace it was possible to argue that its political system, though not ideal, did at least work. It may have been corrupt and inefficient but it did not prevent the economy from steadily growing and it was at any rate preferable to the endless round of dictatorships and coups d'état in neighbouring Syria. According to a popular view, the 'system' worked tolerably well as long as no outsiders interfered with it. But the real problem was that it did not actually *work* at all. It merely survived with the help of a growing economy. One Lebanese professor has written more accurately that 'the system was built for a liberal, mercantile epoch, not for an ideological or revolutionary one'.[18] Whether it was suited to any epoch is doubtful but it was certainly an anachronism in our own. Although it was kept going by economic success it was paradoxically challenged by the moderni-

Above: Beirut 1970, looking
towards Hamra and Ras
Beirut (MEPhA)
Right: Becharré, Mount
Lebanon: spiritual home of
the Maronite community
(A. Duncan, MEPhA)

Left: Bishara Khoury (President 1943-52)
(Keystone Press)
Above: Fuad Chehab (left) (President 1958-64)
with Camille Chamoun (President 1952-58) on the
day Chehab was elected (Keystone Press)
Below: Elias Sarkis (President 1976-82)

Maronite Leaders 1943-82

Above: Suleiman Frangieh (President 1970-76) and Camille Chamoun
Below left: Pierre Gemayel, Leader of the Phalangist Party since 1936
Below right: Bachir Gemayel, Commander of the Phalangist militia and
President-elect at the time of his assassination in September 1982

Top: Saeb Salam and Rashid Karami, political leaders of the Sunni community. Both men have been Prime Minister several times since the 1950s

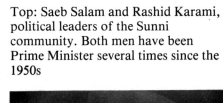

Lebanon's leading Druzes

Left: Kamal Jumblatt, President of the Progressive Socialist Party until his assassination in 1977 (SIPA-Press)
Above. Emir Majid Arslan

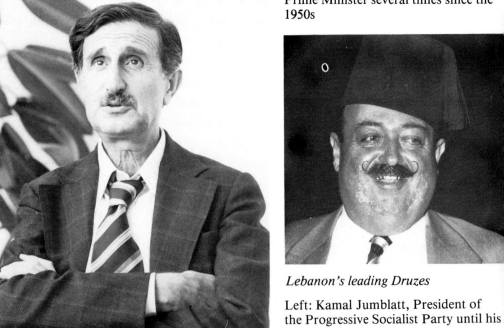

Top: President Assad of Syria and President
Frangieh of Lebanon
Above: Abdul Halim Khaddam, the Syrian
foreign minister, with PLO chairman, Yasser
Arafat (Associated Press)
Left: Raymond Eddé, leader of the National Bloc

The Place des Martyrs, Beirut: 4 stages in its history

Top Left: Before the First World War, when it was known as the Place des Canons (Gebran Tuéni)
Left: In the early 1970s, after most of the Ottoman buildings had been destroyed (Gebran Tuéni)
Below: November 1976, after the worst fighting in Beirut (MEPhA)
Bottom: June 1978, business in the rubble (MEPhA)

Metamorphosis of a Palestinian refugee camp:
Dekwaneh at Tal Zaatar

Above: Soon after the 1948 war. Christian Palestinian
children beside their tents and their church. (UNRWA)
Top right: About 1970, with Beirut in the background
(UNRWA)
Right: In 1976, after the massacre of its inhabitants by
Maronite militiamen (Myrtle Winter Chaumeny, UNRWA)

Above: UNIFIL troops with Israelis in south
Lebanon, April 1978 (Associated Press)
Top: Israeli tank crew at Ba'abda
overlooking Beirut during the siege of 1982
(MEPhA)
Right: Phalangist militiamen celebrate
Bachir Gemayel's election in August 1982
(Associated Press)

The aftermath of the 1982
Israeli invasion. Palestinian
refugees among the
wreckage of their homes
outside Sidon
(George Nehmeh, UNRWA)

Chatila, September 1982:
after the massacre
(George Nehmeh, UNRWA)

zation which that success brought with it. By the early 1970s the country was in chaos: as Kamal Jumblatt complained, it 'had lived too long on foggy liberalism without laws or frontiers, without moral or human restraints'.[19]

Lebanon needed a government to carry out reforms and other policies, a government of the type General Chehab at least partially succeeded in setting up. But the political club, that 'arrogant alliance of money and the feudal system'[20] as Georges Naccache termed it, rejected him. It wanted to have a government without policies, a government that would do little except maintain the old political and confessional structure of the country. Politics thus became a frivolous occupation, a contest among the various za'ims for jobs and influence. It became almost an end in itself, a game for jostling notables more concerned with the state of their own prestige than with the condition of the country.

PART II

Nationalism and Ideologies

'Neither Westernization nor Arabization': it is upon this double rejection that Christianity and Islam have based their alliance [in Lebanon].

What kind of unity can one derive from such a formula?

It is easy to see what half the Lebanese do not want.

And it is easy to see what the other half do not want.

But what the two halves actually both want — that one cannot see . . . .

This Lebanon which they have made for us is a country consisting of two fifth columns . . . .

The folly was in having elevated a compromise to the level of a state doctrine — in having treated an historical accident as an element of stability — in having believed that two Noes can, in politics, produce a Yes . . . .

A state is not the sum of a double negative.

Georges Naccache *Deux négations ne font pas une nation* (1949)

4

The Arab Nationalists

Few of the theories put forward to explain the great Lebanese divide in 1975 have been satisfactory, partly because such a large proportion of the country was forced into taking sides not through political conviction or religious loyalty but for other often unrelated reasons: the location of a man's house, the nature of his work, the politics of the local za'im, the traditional relationships with the neighbouring towns and villages, as well as casualties among his friends and relations or damage to his property. If you were a Greek Orthodox from Tripoli, you were likely to have friends among the Sunni population with whom you also did business; probably you would know few Maronites, who comprized only 5 per cent of the city's population, and whose violent brand of politics you distrusted. And yet if, along with a good deal of Maronite property, your shop was looted and your house gutted by left-wing Muslim guerrillas, your family threatened and forced out of the city — even if this was done by extremists whom your Sunni friends detested as much as you did, then you were unlikely to waste much time deciding which side you were on.

Even for the activists the theories don't really hold. It was not a war between Christians and Muslims, or between right and left, or between the bourgeoisie and the proletariat — though it contained elements of all these things. A more satisfactory explanation, though only as far as the activists were concerned, is that it was a clash, not between ideologies as such, but between different ideological traditions which produced conflicting concepts of nationalism. All the leading figures in the war, except the far left, regarded themselves as nationalists defending their traditional brand of nationalism.

In this chapter it is not possible to give a full narrative of the

Arab nationalist movement. But it is worth making a short excursion into its history because Arab nationalism, however romantic and ill-defined it has often seemed, has been at the root of political conflict in Lebanon since the declining years of the Ottoman Empire. For more than fifty years, from the First World War to the October War of 1973, Arab nationalism was the most potent political ideology of the Arab east, a creed that sought to unite all Arabs in an effort to rid themselves of foreign domination. It was the Arab nationalists who fought the Turks in Greater Syria and who afterwards opposed French and British rule in the Levant. It was they who swept away the conservative monarchies of Egypt and Iraq and took it upon themselves to curb the expansionist designs of the Zionist movement. But Arab nationalism was more than a liberation movement. It was also an ideological response to the challenge of the West. Threatened by the arrival of the European powers in the Middle East, and their political, economic and cultural penetration, Arab intellectuals tried to produce an ideology that would preserve the Arabic heritage and lead to a political and cultural regeneration of the Arab world.

The initial stimulus for the Arab nationalist idea was provided by the decline of the Ottoman Empire. This decline must have been evident to its Levantine subjects from the beginning of the nineteenth century onwards. While the administrative defects of the empire were becoming steadily more apparent, its credibility as a major power was being undermined by successive military defeats from the armies of Muhammad Ali, the Governor of Egypt from 1805 to 1847. Conversely, the vitality of the European powers, first demonstrated by Napoleon's Egyptian expedition and his march on Palestine, was increasingly obvious. British manufactured goods had penetrated the souqs of the Levant and a number of Manchester textile firms kept branches in Beirut. At the political level, the power of the European consulates in Beirut was growing rapidly. European influence was also increasingly evident in the way people lived, in the way they behaved, and in their art and architecture. They began to speak European languages, even among themselves, and to discard eastern customs. The men started to wear western clothes, rejecting all oriental dress except the fez. The houses too became more European with balconies, arched windows and red tiled roofs. These trends were most pronounced among the Greek Orthodox community, wealthy merchants of the coast, whose large, florid houses in the fashionable suburb of Ashrafiyeh owed much to Italian inspiration.

By the 1830s the Ottomans had lost control over much of the Arab world, and they only regained it in Syria because Lord Palmerston was not prepared to see Muhammad Ali establish Egyptian rule over the Middle East. Their tired and ineffectual regime was, however, bound sooner or later to collapse, and something had to be found to take its place. It was this realization that led to a lot of rethinking among Lebanese intellectuals, both Muslim and Christian, though at times they differed radically in their respective conclusions.

The position of the Muslims, particularly the Sunnis, was difficult for they practised the same religion as the Turks and played an important role in the administration of the empire. Moreover, they had little enthusiasm for the European powers. Nevertheless, by the middle of the nineteenth century there were signs of discontent among them and a minor movement towards the re-establishment of an Arab caliphate. In 1858, the British consul in Aleppo remarked on 'the hatred felt by the Arab population of this part of Syria for the Turkish troops and officials in general' and added: 'The Mussulman population of northern Syria hope for a separation from the Ottoman Empire and the formation of a new Arabian state under the sovereignty of the sharif of Mecca'.[1] However, no widespread nationalist movement among the Muslims was to emerge until the beginning of the twentieth century.

The position of the Christian communities was very different for nothing bound them to a clearly shaky empire. It was therefore natural that the initial moves towards a nationalist solution should have been made by Christians. Two Lebanese Christians who sought to promote an Arab 'consciousness' by a revival of Arabic culture, in particular of Arabic as a language, were Nasif Yazegi and Butros Bustani. In this they were helped unconsciously by the foreign missionaries, especially the American Presbyterians, who were active in the region from about 1820 onwards. Although their chief purpose was to proselytize, the missionaries aimed to do this through education, and the consequent establishment of the Syrian Protestant College (later the American University of Beirut), as well as various other institutions, and the publication of various text-books in Arabic, did much to encourage an Arab linguistic and cultural revival. At the same time, societies such as the Syrian Scientific Society and the Society of Arts and Sciences began to appear. Although at the beginning there was little political content to all this activity, by 1880 matters had begun to change. In that year a secret society began posting notices in the major Syrian cities expressing what amounted to an important political programme. Among other things, it stressed the unity of the Arab peoples and demanded autonomy for the whole of Syria (i.e. including Lebanon and Palestine) and the recognition of Arabic as an official language in the region.[2]

Until the early years of this century, however, the movement remained a minor one led by a small number of Syrian Christians. Few Muslims participated, partly because they distrusted the foreign missionaries, who were after all trying to convert them, and partly because of the pan-Islamic policy of the Turkish sultan, Abdul Hamid (1876–1908). Few rulers have come to power in such difficult circumstances as Abdul Hamid. His empire was weak and practically bankrupt, its population restless and its enemies swooping in from time to time to snatch pieces of territory. Within a few years of his accession, France had taken Tunis, the British had installed themselves in Egypt and the Russians were approaching Istanbul. Aware that his empire was disintegrating, Abdul Hamid hoped that a revival of Islam might hold it together. Thus he made a great effort to please the Muslim Arabs by repairing mosques and founding schools throughout Syria. Perhaps his master move was to build the Hejaz railway, which facilitated the pilgrimage to Mecca, as well as giving his army quick access to the heart of the Hejaz.

The Sultan's policy was successful in keeping the Syrians loyal to his regime and it was not until his deposition in 1908, and the subsequent emphasis placed on centralization and Turkish suprem-acy by the Young Turks, that many Syrian Muslims adopted a nationalist position. Nevertheless, even in the latter half of the nineteenth century, there had been a few Muslims, as well as Christians, demanding unity and independence for the Arabs —

with the difference that the Muslims were coupling these demands with a call for the regeneration of Islam. It was this new concept of Islamic nationalism, as advocated by Jamal al-Din al-Afghani in Egypt and Abdul Rahman Kawakebi in Syria, that was largely responsible for turning many Christian Arabs against the nationalist movement. Among the Melchite communities, however, in particular the Greek Orthodox, support for a secular nationalist solution remained strong. Their intellectuals believed that there existed a Syrian national identity which should be expressed not, as the Arab nationalists demanded, in a state embracing all the Arab peoples but in a single Syrian state. This state would be based not on the religious solidarity of Islam, but on the idea of Syria as a distinct historical, cultural and geographical entity — as in fact it is — which had been suppressed for centuries by the Ottoman occupation. Thus, they came to support the aims of those Muslim nationalists who were more concerned with the political success of the movement than with the idea of an Islamic revival. Nevertheless, after 1908 the nationalist leaders were generally Muslims and remained so. For example, when the Young Arab Society was founded in Paris in 1911, all of its initial members were Muslims. Likewise, of the 11 nationalists who were hanged in Beirut's main square (subsequently named the Place des Marytrs) in August 1915, every victim but one was a Muslim.

In that part of Syria which subsequently became the Lebanon, there was some hostility towards the Arab nationalists from the beginning. The Maronite community, although it had some members living in Syria, was firmly based in Mount Lebanon which had a long tradition of autonomy. It was unwilling to lose the privileged position it had enjoyed for centuries and be swallowed up in Greater Syria. The Maronites certainly wished to be rid of the Turks but the last thing they wanted was to become part of an Arab empire, and in this they received considerable support from the local Greek Catholic community. For them there was another solution: Europe. The European (particularly the French) connection with Lebanon was historically strong (see Chapter 5) and, mainly through the influence of the various missions, was becoming more so. In this respect, the French ecclesiastical missions, run by the Jesuits and Lazarists and subsidized directly by the Third

Republic, were of great importance, since they were intended to pave the way for the French government to step in and control things once the Turks had left. Thus, their primary purpose was to extend French influence through their schools and university. Unfortunately this policy was often tactlessly carried out. For example, the Arabic language, which was one of the foundations of the Arab movement, was dropped as the language of instruction in favour of French. Besides, the Muslims were largely ignored by this programme, the principle aim of which was to secure the friendship and support of the Maronite community. In this way the French began the process they later completed during the mandate of dividing the Lebanon into those who looked towards the West and those whose culture and outlook remained Arab.

The French had claimed to be the protectors of the Levantine Christian communities since the early Middle Ages. In 1250 Louis IX is supposed to have written a letter describing the Maronite community as 'a part of the French nation, for its love for France resembles the love which Frenchmen bear one another'.[3] Later in this epistle, which may never have existed but which has in any case become a part of Maronite mythology, he promised to give the Maronites protection at all times. Although the Franco-Maronite connection lapsed for a period it was revived in the early sixteenth century and was increasingly strengthened over the next four hundred years. Lamartine summed up the feelings of many Frenchmen when he described Lebanon as 'an admirable French colony, waiting for France'.[4] By the early years of the twentieth century, the French government had decided that Lebanon should wait no longer.

Of course, the nationalists knew about the French intentions and the Sharif of Mecca had delayed proclaiming open revolt against the Ottomans while he tried to obtain assurances from the British government that the Arabs would be granted their independence in all those territories liberated from the Turks.' . . . any concession designed to give France or any other Power possession of a single square foot of territory in these parts is quite out of the question',[5] he declared. Since the British replies on this point were vague and unsatisfactory, there might never have been an Arab revolt had not the Turks suddenly decided to wage a campaign of terror against a number of Syrians suspected of nationalist leanings. Certainly the Sharif's son, Feisal, was reluctant to begin a rebellion if the Arabs were merely going to exchange one set of oppressors for another.

What neither Feisal nor his father knew, however, was that even before the outbreak of the revolt Britain and France had signed a special agreement giving themselves possession of all the non-desert areas of the Middle East after the First World War.* Instead of the single Arab nation for which the nationalists were struggling, the Balkanization of the Middle East had already been prepared and was soon to be carried out by the imperialist powers: Iraq and Palestine to Britain, Lebanon and western (later all) Syria to France. In Beirut, the Arab government which was set up after the withdrawal of the Turks in October 1918 was turned out in less than a week by General Allenby and a Frenchman installed as the military governor. The following month, in order to allay the fears of the nationalists, a joint Anglo-French declaration claimed as its goal 'the complete and final liberation of the peoples who have so long been oppressed by the Turks.'[6] The final paragraph of the document opened with the declaration that Britain and France were 'far from wishing to impose this or that system upon the populations of those regions.'

The Maronites, however, were not fooled by this piece of window-dressing and saw that events were running their way. Hence they sent off delegations to the peace conference at Versailles to press for a French mandate over Lebanon. For they realized that they needed the French as much as the French needed them: they would thus be preserved from the ambitions of the Arab nationalists, and in turn would provide support for France to fall back on once it had alienated the rest of the population by opposing Arab nationalism. The first delegation was headed by the Maronite Patriarch himself who met Poincaré and Clemenceau and outlined the Maronite aims. These included the independence of Lebanon and the enlargement of its borders to be achieved with the support of France. Clemenceau wrote to the Patriarch to tell

---

* The Sykes-Picot Agreement, negotiated in the spring of 1916 by Sir Mark Sykes and M. François Georges Picot.

him that France agreed with the Maronite objectives but pointed out that although Lebanon would have *'un Gouvernement autonome et un Statut national independant'*, there would not be full independence.[7] In fact, as both of them knew, Lebanon was not going to be independent at all but under French control. The country's 'independence' would merely be from the rest of the Arab world. The decision of the San Remo conference (which followed Versailles) was never in doubt. France was a victorious power and Feisal, who had recently been acclaimed King of Syria, was not going to be allowed to obstruct its ambition.

In April 1920 France was offered the mandate for Syria and Lebanon. It was an absurd arrangement, like the parallel one dealing with the British mandates — the product of hypocrisy, greed and shortsightedness. The Covenant of the League of Nations, in discussing populations under a foreign mandate, pompously declared 'that the well-being and development of such peoples form a sacred trust for civilization. . . .' But the fact that the most advanced peoples of the region were put under foreign domination while the primitive tribal areas of Arabia were given complete independence exposed the lie that the mandates were actually for the good of the people. Their main purpose was clearly different. As General Sir Edward Spears, later to become British Minister to Syria and Lebanon, wrote: 'the French and the British . . . satisfied each other's appetites after the First World War, by serving up strips of the Arab lands to each other'.[8]

It was not only the Arab nationalists who were vigorously opposed to the establishment of the French mandate. The only representatives of a Western power who bothered to go to the Middle East and find out for themselves what sort of governments would be suitable for the area, declared that the very worst thing would be a French mandate. At the end of the war President Wilson set up a commission of enquiry consisting of two Americans, Dr Henry C. King and Mr Charles R. Crane. Wilson had originally proposed that France and Britain should also supply commissioners. But both countries knew very well what the likely outcome of such an enquiry would be and soon found excuses to opt out. In the event the Americans went alone and, after interviewing a great many people, they reported that 'the feeling of the Arabs of the

East is particularly against the French'.[9] Of the petitions received by the commission, less than one-sixth asked for a French mandate,[10] most people preferring either the United States or Britain as the mandatory power. The year before, the League of Nations had produced its Covenant in which it declared that the wishes of the people should be 'a principal consideration in the selection of the Mandatory'. However, when the League came to award the mandate, it evidently did not feel compelled to follow the guidelines it had laid down only shortly before.

The people's wishes were also disregarded over the question of boundaries. Four-fifths of the petitions called for a united Syria and only a small minority wanted to see a Greater Lebanon carved out of Syria.[11] The commissioners therefore recommended that

> 'the unity of Syria be preserved, in accordance with the earnest petition of the great majority of the people of Syria. The territory concerned is too limited, the population too small, and the economic, geographic, racial and language unity too manifest, to make the setting up of independent states within its boundaries desirable, if such division can possibly be avoided. The country is very largely Arab in language, culture, traditions, and customs . . . Lebanon has achieved a considerable degree of prosperity and autonomy within the Turkish Empire. She certainly should not find her legitimate aspirations less possible within a Syrian national state.[12]

I have quoted at length because this advice was totally ignored by the Western powers — the Report was never published and it was many years before the text leaked out — and because the consequences of their actions are with us still. Most of the modern problems of the Middle East, including the Arab-Israeli wars and the Lebanese conflict, stem directly from the decision to divide Syria and distribute the pieces between Britain and France. From the beginning of history Syria has been recognized as a single geographical unit. To the Greeks, to the Romans and to the Turks, Syria meant the same thing: that area bounded by the Mediterranean, the Taurus mountains, the Euphrates and the deserts of Arabia — natural boundaries, thought Napoleon, as good as one could find anywhere. Until 1920 Lebanon had no national existence; it was merely a semi-autonomous area of Syria and was recognized as such. The American University of Beirut was founded in 1860 as the Syrian Protestant College; when the Jumblatt family received letters at their home in the mountains southeast of Beirut, the address on the envelopes was Moukhtara, Syria.

For the Arabs, 1920 became known as the Year of Catastrophe. The French occupied Beirut, where they proclaimed the state of Greater Lebanon, and Damascus, where they ejected Feisal. Their programme in the mandated countries opened with a sustained attack on the Arab movement, partly because they knew the nationalists would resist the spread of French culture in Syria, and partly because a successful nationalist movement in the Middle East might have had repercussions among the French colonies in North Africa. Thus their first action was to increase the size of Lebanon (i.e. Mount Lebanon or the former Ottoman sanjaq), which was largely anti-nationalist, at the expense of Syria, which was almost entirely nationalist. In addition to Mount Lebanon, the new state received the Bekaa valley, the Akkar region in the north, Tyre and Sidon in the south, and the two most important Syrian ports, Beirut and Tripoli. A new nation was thus created, at the behest of the Maronites, with artificial borders which had no basis in history. It was a selfish and self-defeating decision, which ensured that in the long run the Christians became a minority in the state they had created for their own benefit. While they were a majority in Mount Lebanon itself, the Maronites comprized less than a third of the population of Greater Lebanon — because the new areas, which they had insisted on, contained large Muslim majorities. This enlargement made sense economically, for Mount Lebanon and Beirut would not have been self-sufficient by themselves. But by other standards it was short-sighted, as the Arab nationalists deeply resented it and clamoured for federation with truncated Syria. Besides, although they themselves had determined that the Muslims would total nearly half the population of the country, the Maronites seemed intent on emphasizing that Lebanon was to be a country controlled by the Christians.

The most vehement opponents of the Greater Lebanon idea were the Sunnis. They were accustomed to being the majority sect in the Ottoman Empire and many of their leaders had recently acquired a pan-Arab, sometimes pan-Islamic, outlook. Understandably, they were horrified by the prospect of being relegated to a subordinate position in a tiny state dominated by Maronites and Europeans. Many of them simply refused to recognize the Mandate: during the entire inter-war period the Sunni inhabitants of the Beirut district of Basta refused to fly the new Lebanese flag. In Tripoli the Sunni citizens repeatedly asked to be annexed by Syria.[13] Within the new borders they felt constricted and cut off from their natural hinterland. They could not understand why Lebanon should have been awarded the two major ports of the Levant coast while Syria had to make do with Latakia.

Most of the other sects opposed the new state but with less vehemence than the Sunnis. The Shi'ites, the most backward of all the communities, had not yet developed a clear political consciousness. Although their leaders were generally supporters rather than opponents of Arab nationalism, the Shi'ites were unable to work up much enthusiasm about joining a country dominated by their Muslim rivals where a Shi'ite population barely existed. There were more Druzes and Greek Orthodox, however, in Syria than in Lebanon and large numbers in each sect were opposed to the setting up of an artificial division between them. The Druzes, who had been masters, then enemies and finally junior partners of the Maronites in Mount Lebanon, had close links with their compatriots in the Jebel Druze in Syria and rallied to their support when the Syrian Druzes rose against the French in 1925—26. For their part, the Greek Orthodox — who had lost their traditional protectors in the Russian revolution — had little desire to live under Franco-Maronite rule and most of them advocated union with Syria.

Throughout the Mandate, in both countries, the French continued their policy of opposition to the Arab nationalists, who were watched and obstructed by the police. French became an official language, it was taught compulsorily in all state schools, and was also used in the law courts — thus weakening one of the major bonds of the nationalist movement, the Arabic language. France also encouraged the growth of separatist tendencies among the Syrian minorities, and furthered this policy by dividing the country into three more states: an Alawite one based on Latakia, a Druze one centred on Suwaida and a dismembered Syria in the rest of the country. In Lebanon, the government of the country revolved around the French authorities and the Maronite community. The other communities had few political traditions and, with the exception of the Greek Catholics, they were unwilling to co-operate with the French. The Sunnis were the only people accustomed to government but since they continued to deny the legality of the new borders, few of them could be persuaded to play any role in the administration of the state.

With the Middle East firmly under the control of Britain and France, the nationalist movement made little headway in the inter-war years. In Lebanon the nationalists continued to demand that the predominantly Muslim areas of the north, the Bekaa, and the coastal towns be transferred to Syria and in 1936 Sunni notables organized a 'Conference of the Coast' to publicize their demands. On several occasions there was violence in Tripoli and Beirut between their supporters and those, mainly Maronites, who were now calling themselves Lebanese nationalists. These outbursts led to the creation of a militant youth organization called the Najjadeh. Later a political party with strong Arab nationalist leanings, it found its supporters mainly in the poorer Sunni quarters in Beirut. In the late 1930s, along with other nationalist groups, it adopted an increasingly hostile attitude towards the French, who seemed only interested in supporting their Maronite friends, and whose grip on the country was symbolized by the design of the national flag — as laid down in the 1926 constitution, it was to be the Lebanese Cedar with the French Tricolour as background.

But the period also brought forward more radical groups such as the Egyptian Misr al-Fatat (or Green shirts) and the PPS, which borrowed some of the style if not the ideology of European fascism. The PPS was founded in 1932 by Antun Sa'ada and included among its members a large number of Greek Orthodox, some Protestants and a few Muslims. Like the Christian Arab nationalists of the nineteenth century, the party believed in a Syrian national identity which should be expressed in a non-confessional state. It was opposed to the Arab nationalists who dreamt of a single Arab state from Muscat to Marrakesh, and wanted to return to Greater Syria within its natural borders. Because of its violent methods, however, the party suffered repression under the French and subsequently remained underground for much of the post-war period.

In November 1936 the Franco-Lebanese treaty was signed, closely following a similar treaty between France and Syria. France thereby recognized the independence of the two countries, subject to various conditions intended to ensure her continued influence over the area. But by the outbreak of the Second World War three years later, the French still had not ratified the treaty. General Spears, a fervent Francophile until he was posted to Beirut in 1941, observed that this 'was due to the inability of the more conservative [French] politicians to realize that these countries, of very ancient civilization, were neither colonies nor conquered lands and that the mandates, themselves arbitrary impositions of the victors against the Turks in the 1914–18 War, were not meant to involve either annexation or permanent control'.[14] The country thus came under the rule of the Vichy authorities and remained so until June 1941 when British and Free French forces took possession. Immediately the British put pressure on De Gaulle to end the mandate, Churchill declaring in the House of Commons that there was 'no question, even in wartime, of a mere substitution of Free French interests for Vichy French interests'. But although De Gaulle's delegate-general, General Catroux, formally proclaimed the independence of both Lebanon and Syria, it soon became clear that the French had every intention of staying put. Only under pressure from Britain did De Gaulle agree to hold elections, which resulted in an overwhelming defeat for the supporters of French policy. The victors included members of all sects, even Maronites, who had decided that it was time to bring the mandate to an end. The new government, led by the Maronite Bishara Khoury and the Sunni Riad Solh, quickly proclaimed a series of constitutional amendments to this effect that were passed unanimously.

But the French were not prepared to accept independence. They had only got to the Levant in the first place on the coat-tails of Allenby's army in 1918. In 1941 the Free French had again to rely on British arms to get themselves back there. To be told to leave by the British only two years later was no doubt very galling for them, particularly since the British were then showing no sign of relinquishing control of Palestine. In any case, after consultation with the Free French leaders in Algiers, the new Delegate-General, Jean Helleu, returned to Beirut in November 1943, whereupon he arrested the leading members of the government, including President Khoury and Prime Minister Solh, and confined them in much discomfort in the old castle of Rashaya. He also suspended the constitution and placed Emile Eddé, now regarded as simply a French stooge, as head of a puppet government.

The folly of the French behaviour alienated even their Maronite friends and brought about a unity among the Lebanese factions that was unfortunately never to be repeated. The Arab nationalists, who had always opposed the French mandate simply on the grounds that there was no justification for its existence, were joined by many of the Maronites who believed that the French had now exhausted their usefulness. According to the British Minister in Cairo, the Grand Mufti of the Lebanon declared that 'years of oppression by the French had forced the people almost unanimously to vote against all those suspected of being friends of the French'.[15] The Minister also reported in his telegram to London that the Maronite Archbishop of Beirut had spoken in similar terms: 'They had previously been friends of the French but they could stand no more. Spoke with great heat of the years of growing exploitation by the French and of his conviction that the French now had to go finally.'[16] Indeed, the unity of Lebanon at that moment was such that the great Sunni leader of Tripoli, Abd al-Hamid Karami, was able to declare that people should talk no longer of Christians and Muslims, but only of Lebanese.

But the spirit did not last. Finally the French did go, though their evacuation was not completed until 1946, and they were unable to resist, as a parting shot, the bombardment of Damascus which left about 500 Syrians dead. But the dilemma the French mandate had posed still remained: should Lebanon look East or West? For notwithstanding the conciliatory government of Bishara Khoury, the Maronites and the Arab nationalists remained deeply distrustful of each other. The Maronites had lost their protectors, and in spite of the way the French had governed, many soon regretted their departure. On the other hand, the nationalists, though more or less reconciled to the 1920 enlargement of the Lebanese frontiers, had achieved few of their objectives. The country remained dominated by the Maronites, orientated towards the West, and little interested in the affairs of the other Arab states. Furthermore, their hopes that the Arab League, founded at the end of the war, would be able to induce at least a degree of Arab unity soon proved illusory.

The achievement of independence in Lebanon, then, did not greatly further the aims of the nationalists. Nor were they much more successful elsewhere since most of the other governments in the Middle East were still in large measure subservient to Britain. The military defeat in Palestine in 1948 emphasized the disunity, corruption, and ineffectuality of the Arab governments. But it drove many people to realize that, if the Arabs were to make any progress, they must start doing things by themselves and cease relying on the West.

The man who put this idea into practice was Gamal Abdel Nasser, who came to power in Egypt shortly after the revolution of 1952. For the first time a convinced nationalist, who believed in the pan-Arab idea, was the leader of a government and within a short time he had become the symbol of Arab nationalist aspirations throughout the Middle East. His support for anti-colonial movements, his denunciation of the Baghdad Pact, and his nationalization of the Suez Canal, won him large bodies of supporters in all Arab countries, particularly those where there still existed pro-Western governments. In the two years following the Suez crisis a wave of nationalist sentiment broke over the Middle East. The pro-British regime in Iraq was swept away, while the Syrian nationalists united their country with Egypt. In Jordan the nationalist strength was such that Britain landed troops in Amman in order to keep King Hussein's regime alive.

In Lebanon the strength of nationalist feeling was demonstrated by the 1958 uprising against President Chamoun. After decades of frustration, and in the face of Chamoun's attempt to align Lebanon firmly with the West, the nationalists finally revolted. Nasser was their hero, and the Lebanese Sunni leaders, Saeb Salam and Rashid Karami, freely echoed the pan-Arab pronouncements of the Egyptian president. But they understood they could not go the whole way with Nasser, as Lebanon's peculiar circumstances required that everything must be decided by compromise. When the revolt was brought to an end by the judicious statesmanship of General Chehab, Lebanon returned to its previous policy of friendship but not alliance with the West, and alliance but not union with the Arab countries.

The Sunni establishment might respect the special nature of Lebanon, but there were many who increasingly did not. The social problems were partly responsible for the increasing radicalism of the Arab nationalists. Although the wealth of the country was growing all the time, the inequalities in society were getting worse. With the inspiration of Nasser before them, the new generation of nationalists began to demand a fairer share of political and economic power. It was time, they believed, to finish with the antiquated 'system' imposed by the National Pact. Confessionalism, which served to maintain the Maronite domination, was an inadequate way to run a modern country.

The Arab defeat in the 1967 war with Israel further radicalized the Arab nationalists. For many years they had put their faith in the Egyptian president but now it was clear that Nasserism was not enough. The remaining areas of Palestine, a part of Syria and the Egyptian Sinai had been conquered by the Israeli army in a matter of days. Their recovery would require more than the old nationalist rallying call of 'unity'. More radical, even violent, solutions had to be looked for. As a symptom of the change, the Arab Nationalist Movement, a pro-Nasserist organization formed in Jordan in 1953, split into different factions, two of them becoming revolutionary groups prepared to use terrorism in the fight for the liberation of Palestine.

The 1967 catastrophe had repercussions in Lebanon even though the army refused to take part in the war. In the 1948 campaign their performance had been unimpressive, but Lebanese soldiers had at least engaged the Israelis. In 1967 the commander, General Bustani, refused to send his troops into action even though he had been ordered to do so by the prime minister. Bustani's decision was no doubt wise because his army's involvement could have had no serious impact on the campaign and would probably have led to an Israeli occupation of southern Lebanon. But it angered the Arab nationalists who felt humiliated by yet another show of Arab weakness in the face of the Zionist enemy. They reacted to the defeat by drawing closer to the Palestinians. Just as they identified with Nasser's struggle against the West in the 1950s, so now they identified themselves with the Palestinians' struggle against Israel.

This new radical mood inevitably dug into the positions of the older nationalist leaders like Saeb Salam and Rashid Karami. In 1958 they had understood the popular mood and the followers of Nasser had been able to support them. By the 1970s this was no longer true. They were too old, too conservative, too much part of the system to appeal to the new radical forces which demanded immediate action. In the 1972 elections candidates supported by Karami and Salam in their 'fiefs' of Tripoli and Beirut were defeated respectively by a Ba'ath socialist and a radical Nasserist. The traditional za'ims of the Shi'ite community were also finding their positions eroded, principally by the charismatic religious leader, Imam Musa Sadr, who founded the Movement of the Deprived. He attacked the greedy establishment, accused the conservative Muslims of being indifferent to social problems, and threatened to loot the houses of the rich. He also promised to train Shi'ite militias to defend south Lebanon if the government persisted in refusing to do the job itself.

The man who most closely represented the Arab nationalist position in Lebanon in the 1970s was the Druze leader and socialist, Kamal Jumblatt. With the untidy appearance of an absent-minded academic, Jumblatt was the strangest and most unpredictable of

Lebanese leaders. He was an intellectual and a mystic who travelled frequently to India where he claimed to have understood his own religion from the teachings of the *vedanta advaita*. Although he affected to despise politics, Jumblatt was one of Lebanon's leading politicians for thirty years. He was the *enfant terrible* of Lebanese politics, provocative and iconoclastic, the only za'im to advocate the abolition of confessionalism and the za'im—client system.

After toying with the idea of joining the PPS, Jumblatt founded his Progressive Socialist Party in 1949 and led it until his death in 1977. Although he was fond of revolutionary rhetoric and was frequently calling for a revolution in the critical spring of 1976, Jumblatt was not in fact a revolutionary. His socialism owed more to the British Labour Party than to Marx. He opposed collectivism and advocated small farms and co-operatives: one of the party's slogans was, 'Every Lebanese a landowner'.[17] Jumblatt did not say 'Property is theft' but 'Property equals social function'[18] and he used it to help his Druze followers. He was a paternalist, an enlightened landowner and other things besides, but he was not a Marxist.

The Progressive Socialist Party, a group of genuine socialists backed by Jumblatt's Druze supporters, became the leading organization of the new radical alliance which took shape in the late 1960s. Calling itself the National Movement, it attracted a host of small groups eager to jump on the radical band-wagon. They included the communist parties, various Nasserist and other Arab nationalist groups, the Lebanese branches of the Syrian and Iraqi Ba'ath, Sadr's Movement of the Deprived, Islamic groups and the PPS which had recently abandoned its neo-fascist style.

But although it was a coalition of radicals, Jumblatt understood that there was no possibility of persuading the Lebanese to accept a radical programme. He once said that his programme was designed to save Lebanon from radicalism and it was a fair claim.[19] Had it been accepted, much of the social tension would have gone and Lebanon would have moved towards a Western style of democracy. As Georges Hawi, the Communist leader, said, 'the reforms we are seeking aim at transforming our sectarian feudalistic system into a secular, democratic, liberal system which would maintain the production relationships of capitalism.'[20] The main plank of the National Movement was nothing more revolutionary than the abolition of sectarian representation in government, which it saw rightly as an obstacle to political and administrative reform. It also advocated proportional representation, the removal of sex discrimination, some degree of regional development, and an end to electoral corruption. In principle, few of its opponents disagreed with any of these objectives, and indeed the Phalangist Party had originally been the first to suggest proportional representation and the abolition of the confessional principle. But there was one point in the Arab nationalists' programme that their opponents could not accept, and which later led them to reject all the others: the nationalist support for, and increasing identification with, the cause of the Palestinians. It was this issue which caused the final rupture between two groups whose co-existence had always been uneasy — the Arab nationalists, inspired by Arabic language and Arab history, and the so-called Lebanese nationalists, the vast majority of whom were Maronites, with history and traditions which turned them towards the West.

5

Libanisme and the Maronites

To Pope Leo X the Maronites were 'a rose among thorns', but they themselves have demanded more heroic comparisons and their mythology is deeply tinged with Crusader symbolism. They see themselves variously as descendants of the Phoenicians, defenders of the only true democracy in the Arab world, and the one Catholic 'nation' of Asia. By their enemies, however, the Maronites are regarded as little better than Zionists, and their chief organization (the Phalangist Party) as brazenly neo-fascist.

The Maronites are of Aramaic origin and until the eighteenth century they spoke Aramaic in its Syriac form rather than Arabic. For over a thousand years they have inhabited the northern regions of Mount Lebanon, gradually spreading southwards since the later Middle Ages over former Druze and Shi'ite territory. In the mountainous stretch north of the Beirut–Damascus road they still formed, in 1975, the overwhelming majority of the population. Conversely, in Sidon, Tyre and the south of Lebanon, and in Tripoli and the northern region of Akkar, the proportion of Maronites among the inhabitants was very small.

Mount Lebanon is a beautiful, largely barren landscape which in many places is inaccessible except on foot. One of its most striking characteristics is the sheer quantity of churches and chapels; another is the extent of agricultural activity in such unpromising terrain. In some parts the terraces are piled almost on top of each other. Life on the Mountain has always been hard and the priests and sheikhs have had to work on the land with the peasants — a thing considered degrading in more prosperous regions. Consequently many Maronites have emigrated in the course of the present century, some only as far as Beirut, others to Brazil, West Africa, Australia and North and South America. For those who stayed there were compensations, since the Maronites enjoyed considerable economic privileges under the French mandate and came to rival the Greek Orthodox as the wealthiest of the communities. In independent Lebanon trade and industry have been very largely dominated by Christian businessmen.

Writing of the Lebanese mountains in the eighteenth century, Baron de Tott remarked that 'the steepest places have been at all times the asylum of liberty.'[1] Certainly the Maronite peasants, helped by a powerful church in their struggle against the landowners, lived under a weaker and less oppressive form of feudalism than the other mountain communities. And certainly they have always acted vigorously to maintain their independence. According to Istfan Douaihy, a Maronite Patriarch of the seventeenth century, 'the Maronite community's history is a continuous struggle to maintain national and religious identity in a dominant Muslim environment.'[2] It is a community very conscious of its history and it remembers the repeated attempts of Byzantines, Mamelukes and Ottomans to control it. Religious and historical symbolism play a vital role in the Maronite community. Their civil war militias, for example, had strange religious titles, evocative of the Crusades: the Knights of the Virgin, the Wood of the Cross, the Youth of St Maron. Phalangist gunmen often went into battle wearing crosses over their uniforms.

Kamal Jumblatt once referred to the Maronites as 'that minority obsessed with their sense of being a minority',[3] and it is a reasonable comment. The Maronites are a suspicious and aggressive community. They have been living in their mountains for thirteen centuries and their political and ecclesiastical traditions are long and unbroken. Lebanon is the only country where they have an important presence and this has given them an outlook quite unlike that of the Druzes or Greek Orthodox who are spread over other countries. The Maronites regard themselves almost as a separate people and consider Lebanon as their particular homeland to be defended against all intruders. It is this feeling that Lebanon belongs to them more than to the other communities which has made them so intolerant of other ambitions.

Isolated in their region, the Maronites had to look for allies elsewhere, and they chose Europe, which practised the same religion, and which during the Middle Ages was already over-taking the East in technological and industrial achievement. The clergy, which probably entered into a rather loose union with the Roman church in the latter part of the twelfth century, did much to establish close links with Europe. Maronite priests were sent to Italy to study during the Renaissance and in 1584 the Maronite College was set up in Rome. Since then there have been several Maronite librarians in the Vatican. By the seventeenth century Jesuits, Capuchins and Franciscans were already active in Lebanon, where they advised the Maronite Patriarch, and where they later set up schools. In 1734, the Jesuits founded the St Joseph College of Aintoura, the oldest of its kind in Lebanon, and in the following century they established schools in Beirut, Zahle, Bikfaya and Ghazir. The concordat of 1736 brought the Maronite and Roman churches still closer together. By its terms the Maronites recognized the Pope and agreed that their bishops would wear mitres. How-ever, they retained their own saints and feast days, their own Syriac liturgy, and they did not insist that their priests should be celibate on taking orders.

Trade brought further links with Europe, although the merchant activities of the Maronites were on a small scale and did not compare with those of the Melchite or Sunni communities. Beirut and Alexandria were the two most important ports in the world for the Venetians from the fourteenth to the sixteenth century, and in 1585 some 4,000 Venetian families were living in the Levant. In the same period Lebanese traders are recorded as far afield as London, Timbuktu, Seville, Lisbon, Lwow and Amsterdam.

But from the Maronites' point of view the most important visitors were the French, who monopolized the trade at Sidon and whose trading posts were organized by Colbert. French interest in the area went back to Charlemagne, who was granted the protectorate of the Holy Places by Haroun al-Raschid. After the failure of the Crusades the connection lapsed, and it was not until 1535, when a treaty was signed by Francis I and his ally, Suleiman the Magnificent, that the French were able to establish a strong position for themselves amongst the Christians of the Levant. Of all the communities of the region, it was the Maronites who most welcomed this development. They regarded France as their protector, and referred to her as *umm al hannoune*, 'the nourishing mother'. The French relished the role and from 1655 their consul in Beirut was often a Maronite sheikh. When Napoleon met a Maronite delegation in Palestine in 1799, he is supposed to have told them: '*Je reconnais que vous êtes francais de temps immémorial*'.[4] Although the Emir of Lebanon wisely decided to remain neutral between Bonaparte and the Ottomans, the Maronite Patriarch ordered a Maronite force to help the French at the siege of Acre.[5] In 1860, France sent a military expedition to restore order after fighting between the Maronites and the Druzes and by 1915 the relationship was so close that the Maronite Patriarch openly proclaimed his country's gratitude to France, in spite of the fact that Lebanon, as part of the Ottoman Empire, was actually at war with the Third Republic. When the French occupied the region in 1918, their chargé d'affaires declared in public that the principal reason for the French presence was the protection of their friends the Maronites.[6]

The setting up of the mandate and its purpose have already been discussed. Its legacy is still with us: nobody who visited Lebanon before the civil war could have failed to appreciate the extent that French attitudes and French culture had penetrated the country, even if to outward appearances American influences often seemed to predominate. Two Lebanese out of five could speak French, and in the cities the proportion was much higher. Many of the Christians also had French first names: the leaders of the three main Maronite parties, for example, were called Camille, Raymond and Pierre. Not so the Muslims, whose three leading representatives had the Arabic first names of Rashid, Saeb and Kamal. French was usually the first language of wealthier Maronites, many of whom spoke Arabic badly, and it was easy to appreciate the nature of Lebanon's problems if you went into a shop and heard a smartly-dressed woman speaking French to her children and addressing the shop assistant in bad Arabic. If they could afford it, the Christians might send their children to French schools and universities, though some of them preferred to send their sons to English or Scottish public schools. A majority of Lebanese cabinet ministers have been educated at French or Franco-Lebanese schools.[7] As for dress, traditional Lebanese costume had long since been discarded, and their clothes were either the products of smart new boutiques in Beirut, or from frequent visits to Paris or London, where many of them owned flats. The interior decoration of their apartments in Beirut was likewise imported. In most of them it would have been difficult to find anything actually manufactured in Lebanon.

French food, however, had made curiously little impact. Although there were a few French restaurants in Beirut with pictures of Notre Dame on the walls and Edith Piaf as background music, these were undistinguished and the Lebanese usually preferred the heavily-spiced food of the eastern Mediterranean. Strangely enough, American influences were increasingly evident in this sphere and the Wimpy Bar civilization had successfully enslaved the modern quarter of Ras Beirut. American films also enjoyed enormous popularity in a city reputed to have (after Hong Kong) the highest per capita film attendance in the world; similarly, American detective serials like 'Cannon' and 'Kojak' were shown on television several times a week.

Beirut 'society', however, which was mainly though not exclusively Maronite, conducted itself in French, adopting French invitation cards and protocol. It was also extremely formal, for the Lebanese took their social life very seriously and their appetite for parties was enormous. Apart from huge, very smart dinners and cocktail parties where the same people inevitably met each other night after night, this society frequented the Saint Georges Hotel and swimming pool, the night clubs, the smart ski-resorts at Faraya and the Cedars, the yachting marinas, the Casino du Liban, and in the summer the large villas in the hills. It was so ostentatious that a swarm of gossip columnists was able to make a living from the adventures of *'le tout Beirut'*. Even after the devastation caused by two years of civil war, the magazine *Monday Morning* could entertain its readers with page after page of identically-coiffured debutantes.

The first thing that must have struck anybody was the vulgarity of this society. There were simply more night clubs, faster cars, bigger jewelry, longer swimming pools and more luxurious apartments than in other places. The fact that jewelry and precious metals comprized the biggest single item in the country's import bill (nearly 30 per cent of all imports in 1970) is indicative of these people's priorities.[8] Besides, it was a society which, as it became richer, paid less and less attention to those outside it. In fairness, though, the Maronites formed only the greater part of this society; it also included Melchites, a few Sunnis and members of smaller Christian communities as well. Furthermore, the Maronite wealth was unevenly distributed and many Maronites remained what they had always been: peasant farmers working their terraces on the slopes of the Mountain.

The Maronites did not consider that either they or their country were really Arab. As one historian has suggested, they viewed Lebanon 'not so much as the western frontier of the Arab East but as the eastern frontier of the Christian West.'[9] Many Maronites vigorously denied their Arab ancestry. If you referred to them as Arabs, you were likely to be met with the furious retort — 'we are not Arabs, we are Lebanese' — followed by an unconvincing and indeed entirely fanciful explanation that they were the descendants of the Phoenicians.

'Phoenicianism', the attempt to link the civilization of 5,000 years ago with their own, was one method used by Maronite writers to distance themselves from the Arabs. It was complemented by 'Mediterraneanism' whose prophet, Michel Chiha, claimed that Lebanon and the Near East 'belong in the first place to the Mediterranean world whereas the Middle East properly speaking belongs primarily to the world of the Indian Ocean'.[10] Maronite intellectuals such as Chiha and Charles Corm thus promoted the idea that Lebanon belonged to an older and superior civilization to the Arab world. According to them, Lebanese history stretched back for millenia while Arab civilization had lasted a mere thirteen centuries. This was the language talked also by Pierre Gemayel and other Phalangists who believed that Lebanon, like France, had a *mission civilisatrice*. Some of the claims they made for their civilization sound somewhat ridiculous. Gemayel once declared that 'the faithfulness of Lebanon to its mission and to its heritage have never been denied over the last six thousand years of history'.[11] Such a view inevitably entailed a certain denigration of the Arabs whom they regarded not only as culturally different but racially distinct as well. This is not a tenable view because all the main Lebanese communities, except the Armenians, are in fact Syrians who easily assimilated their Arab conquerors but who, for the most part, adopted Arab culture and religion. Nevertheless, the Maronites persisted in thinking they were somehow different even though their own connection with Lebanon (dating from the seventh century) is no older than that of the Arabs themselves. Lebanon, they claimed, is thus essentially non-Arab. According to a Phalangist Party manifesto, 'Lebanon is a soul, a spiritual principle' with a mission 'incompatible with that which the Arabs aspire generally to realize'.[12]

The Maronite outlook, then, has been conditioned by a turbulent history, the friendship with France and its attitude towards the Arab world. This combination has produced the Maronite creed, or *Libanisme*, a word that can only be translated into English by the ugly 'Lebanonism'. Its ingredients include an emphasis on individualism and self-sufficiency, rejection of Islam and the Arab world, identification with the West and some Western values, and insistence on the survival of Lebanon as a Christian and democratic heartland in the Middle East. Professor Maxime Rodinson has described Maronite Lebanon as *'un pays phénicien, hellénisé, romanisé, croisé, chrétien, tout ce qu'on veut, mais pas pays Arabe . . . rêvant parfois encore, s'ils n'osent plus en parler, au bastion sionisto-chrétien appuyé à la Méditeranée contre le déferlement de la poussée arabo-musulmane.'*[13] As the last remark implies, there were many Maronites who sympathized with the Zionists. Perhaps their ideologies had points in common. Certainly *Libanisme* was as intransigent as Zionism, and the more uncompromising Maronites tended to see similarities between the Israeli position and their own. In 1947 the Maronite Archbishop of Beirut sent a memorandum to the UN Conciliation Commission on Palestine in which he suggested the establishment of a Christian state in Lebanon, as well as a Jewish state in Palestine: 'Lebanon as well as Palestine,' he declared, 'should remain permanent homes for the minorities in the Arab world'.[14]

There were of course degrees of *Libanisme* and it is possible to identify a clear division among Maronite leaders — between those who held to a rigid and uncompromising *Libanisme*, and those whose attitudes to the Muslims and Arab nationalists were conciliatory. The only two presidents with any claim to be considered statesmen represented the second strain of political Maronitism. Bishara Khoury set out his policy in June 1942: 'Lebanon wants its complete independence within its present boundaries; and we want, on this basis, to co-operate with the Arab states to the greatest possible extent.'[15] He was a Lebanese nationalist, like all Maronites, and he wanted Lebanon to retain the borders the French had arranged a couple of decades before. But he also understood that Lebanon would not survive without close co-operation with the Muslims both inside and outside the country's frontiers. Fuad Chehab came to power in even more difficult circumstances than Bishara Khoury. His job was to unite the country after the 1958 troubles, which meant persuading the Muslims that the country did not exist simply for the benefit of the Christians, and persuading the Maronites that it was not to be aligned with the West against the Arab nationalists. As we have seen, Chehab made the first and practically the last moves to develop the backward regions inhabited mainly by the Druze and Shi'ite communities. In foreign affairs he was conciliatory towards Nasser and the Arab world, although at the same time he maintained close ties with Europe.

By 1975, both men were dead and the Maronite leadership was largely in the hands of the old, intransigent leaders — former President Chamoun, Phalangist leader Pierre Gemayel and the president, Suleiman Frangieh. But one man of the conciliatory 'school' remained, Raymond Eddé, the leader of the National Bloc, outspoken, honest and democratic. He opposed the Phalangists because of their militarist and authoritarian tendencies, and he opposed Frangieh because of the blatant corruption of his regime. He had no use for those Maronites who saw Lebanon as a Christian bastion and who in 1976 would have partitioned the country rather than come to terms with the opposition groups. 'I do not want a new Israel,' he declared in February 1976. 'I do not want the Christians to live in a ghetto.'[16] But because he was a liberal and a democrat, Raymond Eddé had supporters but not gunmen, and when the civil war began he was powerless.

Surprisingly, Raymond Eddé was the son of Émile Eddé, the most unbending of all Maronites, and a man who made little attempt to disguise his contempt for the Arab world. Unfortunately it is he and his followers who have represented the dominant strain in political Maronitism. Its chief representative in recent Lebanese history has been Pierre Gemayel's Phalangist Party. Gemayel himself is an unimaginative man with fixed ideas, a clear if narrow vision of the Lebanon he wants to create, and a distaste for the unprincipled manoeuvring of other politicians. He founded the *Phalanges Libanaises* in 1936 after visiting Germany for the Berlin Olympics, a fact that has subsequently given his enemies the opportunity to brand him a Nazi. In fact there is no evidence to suggest that Gemayel was inspired by Nazi doctrines. What most impressed him was the discipline of the Germans — 'the perfect conduct of a whole, unified nation' — which he believed would be good for 'an unruly and individualistic people' like the Lebanese.[17]

Beginning as a Christian youth organization closely modelled on similar groups then in vogue in Europe, the *Phalanges* was authoritarian, paramilitary and puritannical. Like Vichy France, its motto stressed the importance of family and the fatherland; it also adopted the fascist salute as well as much of the flag-waving paraphernalia of fascism. Founded in response to the disorders following the Franco-Lebanese treaty, it was intended to be an organization dedicated to the defence of the Maronite view of Lebanon. 'The *Phalanges Libanaises* does not constitute a political party,' said Gemayel. 'It is neither for nor against anyone; it is for Lebanon.'[18] According to its basic laws, it believed in 'an ordered and disciplined democracy'.

After independence, the *Phalanges* went into politics to combat the Arab nationalists but not until 1958 did it become a serious political party. A decade later it was the largest in the country with nine deputies and a membership of 50,000 people, nearly all of them Maronites. As a party, it retained its militarist and undemocratic character, with a strong militia and an authoritarian party structure. Nevertheless, it had evolved from being something of a boy-scout movement to being a leading political organization and it even advocated a number of social democratic policies. When Gemayel was a minister during Chehab's presidency, he was responsible for passing the social security bill. At the same time the party suggested the abolition of the confessional character of the administration which it saw as an obstacle to the modernization of the country.

The two remaining leaders of Maronite Lebanon differed very strongly from Gemayel in at least one respect: they were widely regarded as politicians without any principles at all. Both Camille Chamoun (1952—58) and Suleiman Frangieh (1970—76) ended their presidencies in civil war and both were largely responsible for precipitating the violence. Camille Chamoun's actions in 1958 have already been discussed. Frangieh's role in the later war was less pivotal and more complicated. The charge against him is not that he provoked an uprising like Chamoun but that he abused his office in a number of ways that undermined the presidency and helped to divide the country into its natural and mutually antagonistic components. To begin with, his administration achieved nothing in the fields of social and economic reform. The economic plan (1972—77) aimed 'to reduce income inequality' but it did not specify how it was going to do this. In fact nothing was done and the reforms which Chehab had put through and Helou had to some extent continued came to a halt with Frangieh. According to one French commentator, the Frangieh regime did not undertake a single public works project during its entire term of office.[19]

This failure was perhaps merely a result of the regime's idleness and incompetence. More serious was the cavalier way it treated the National Pact. Two of the most important guarantees of co-existence were a neutral army and a good working relationship between the Maronite president and the Sunni prime minister. Frangieh made no attempt to preserve either. By purging the military intelligence unit, the Deuxième Bureau, he undermined the prestige and effectiveness of the army; by appointing hardline Maronite commanders who used force against the Palestinians in 1973 and against demonstrators in Sidon in 1975, he helped destroy its reputation for impartiality. His treatment of the Sunni politicians was equally far-reaching. After Saeb Salam's resignation in 1973 Frangieh chose in succession four weak Sunni leaders to head the government and thus antagonized the Sunni establishment at the precise moment when it was finding its own power eroded by the new radical movements. Frangieh's insulting attitude towards the Sunnis merely drove many of them into the radical camp. In this way he was very largely responsible for polarizing the country between the radicals and the intransigent Maronites. Indeed, he eventually split the country so decisively that even his elder brother Hamid, a former foreign minister, told him to resign in order to safeguard Lebanese unity.

Camille Chamoun was the most charismatic of Lebanese leaders and the real hero of the Maronite mountain. Gemayel was popular and respected but he was not revered. Chamoun had the charm and the ability to attract adulation, and in Mount Lebanon religious pictures were printed depicting him side by side with the Madonna.[20] Chamoun was originally a supporter of Bishara Khoury, but later formed a coalition against the Khoury government with the aim of forcing the president from office and installing himself in his place. He achieved this without difficulty but during his term of office he seemed to go out of his way to alienate the Muslim leaders. To begin with, he simply ignored them. Later, as we have seen, he chose to disregard their Arab nationalist sympathies by accepting the Eisenhower Doctrine. He was then surprised when an armed insurrection followed which put an end to his dreams of amending the Constitution and securing a second term of office. Like Frangieh many years later, he seemed unable to grasp that the survival of Lebanon depended on the participation of the Arab nationalists in the running of the state. As he grew older, Chamoun understood less and less the changing nature of Lebanon. He became increasingly reclusive, reactionary and obstructive, and his organization, the National Liberal Party, seemed to have no policies at all beyond those of denouncing all proposals of reform and upholding the prerogatives of the Maronite community.

Every time the Lebanese have had a President of the uncompromising Emile Eddé strain, there has been a disaster or near disaster. Emile Eddé himself ended up a solitary puppet of the French, unable to form a government, escorted out of a country on the point of revolt. Camille Chamoun invited an insurrection which only ended when he left office. And Suleiman Frangieh was more responsible than anyone for the polarization of the country which brought on the civil war. Whenever there has been a president of the conciliatory Bishara Khoury strain, there has been something approaching peace and co-operation between the communities. Khoury himself was the architect of Lebanese independence and the man who made the state possible. Fuad Chehab restored order after 1958 and retained the support and goodwill of the Muslim communities. It was disastrous for Lebanon that in the presidential election of 1970, Elias Sarkis, a disciple of Chehab and a man of unquestionable integrity, should have been defeated so narrowly by Suleiman Frangieh.

6

The Palestinian Presence

The Palestinians came to Lebanon in 1948, driven from their homeland by the forces of the new Zionist state. Some came by boat from Jaffa or Haifa but most were villagers from the Galilean hills who fled on foot across the Lebanese border. By the end of the war there were some 800,000 Palestinian refugees, of whom about 140,000 had arrived in Lebanon. They were joined after the 1967 war by Palestinians who had been chased out of the West Bank and in 1970 by refugees fleeing from the Jordanian civil war. By 1975 there were perhaps 350,000 Palestinians in Lebanon, of whom one-third were still living in refugee camps distributed around the country.

The United Nations Partition Plan of 1947, which proposed the partition of Palestine into a Jewish and an Arab state, also divided the Galilee. The western half was designed as part of the Arab state and the eastern half was allocated to the Zionists, although the population of the whole area was overwhelmingly Arab. In the event the Israelis seized both halves in the summer of 1948 and drove out the greater part of the population. In the words of Yigal Allon, the Israeli commander of the operation and later foreign minister, 'we saw a need to clean the Inner Galilee . . . to cause the tens of thousands of sulky Arabs who remained in Galilee to flee.'[1] The method suggested by Allon 'to clean' the area of its natural inhabitants was intimidation; the main cause of the exodus was a number of calculated atrocities in about a dozen Galilean villages which spread panic among the rest of the population.[2]

Thus the Palestinians left, snatching a few provisions and the keys to their houses because they all thought they would be going home, whether their side won or not, after the fighting. Throughout that terrible parched summer, long columns of refugees struggled across the Lebanese border and camped out a few miles from their homeland. Some from the most northern villages stayed close to the border so they could return to their homes by night to recover a few of their possessions or pick the fruit from their orchards. Others, desperate for food and water, walked on to Tyre and Sidon. But the Lebanese authorities did not want a large Palestinian conglomeration in the south so they dispersed half the refugees around the country, to camps in the Bekaa valley at Baalbek and Anjar or around the cities of Beirut and Tripoli.

In Lebanon, seventeen refugee camps were established with the help of the United Nations Relief and Works Agency (UNRWA). They were set up on any available land, sometimes on old camp sites once used by the French and British armies. At the beginning the refugees were herded into barracks, several families to a room, or packed closely in tents donated by the Red Cross and similar bodies. Just as the summer of the exodus had been insufferably hot, so the first winter of refugee life was miserably cold and wet. Musa Alami, a Palestinian notable from Jerusalem, recalls that fearful winter and remembers seeing twelve people with their heads in a tent and their legs in the rain outside. For a number of years most of the refugees remained in tents surviving on rations which an UNRWA report described as 'enough to ward off starvation, little more'.[3] Later they moved into small huts built by UNRWA and varying in floor space from 9 to 12.5 square metres.

Wavell camp was situated in the Bekaa valley near the great Roman temples at Baalbek. It was an old army barracks surrounded by refugee shelters, a neglected and desolate spot. A Palestinian woman recalls the living conditions there: 'Each section of the barracks had six families. Separating us there was only a thread and a blanket. Everything took place in public, eating, washing, sleeping. Those who had six children wouldn't have place to spread their feet at night.'[4] Little improved for the camp's inmates over the next three decades. In 1975 there were still no doors to the building or to the latrines and the roof leaked in several places. The blankets and thread had gone but they had only been replaced by cement blocks and pieces of cardboard. The rooms were still the same size and an entire family, no matter how large it was, lived in each of them. In some cases people had lived huddled together in the same room for fifteen years. They received basic rations of flour, sugar, pulses, rice and fat, and nothing else. The children were undernourished and often sick; in the camp there was nowhere for them to play. For the men there was no work either there or at Baalbek, and it was a long journey to any major town.

During the fifties and sixties many refugees followed the poor Lebanese to Beirut in search of work. They moved into the five refugee camps on the southern and eastern outskirts of the capital or into the spreading shanty-towns where their neighbours might be Kurdish immigrants or landless Shi'ites from the south. Some would be living in UNRWA huts, others in sheds which they built themselves from breeze-blocks and squashed petrol cans. Although the Beirut camps became dangerously overcrowded through migration and natural increase, living conditions improved slightly in later years when UNRWA brought electricity and water to many of the inmates. The refugees themselves built a few stores and workshops and the Palestine Red Crescent, an arm of the Palestine Liberation Organization, erected a number of medical clinics and hospitals.

Although officially welcomed by their host governments and assured that they would be returning to Palestine, the refugees soon found that they were not popular in their new countries. This was particularly true of Lebanon where many Christians resented their presence because most of the refugees were Sunnis and therefore natural allies of the Lebanese Muslims and because their presence further tilted the demographic balance in favour of the Muslims. The Palestinians learnt early on in their exile that refugee life entailed degradation and the humiliation of being exposed to the mockery of local inhabitants. Fawaz Turki, a Palestinian writer who grew up in Lebanon, remembers a street entertainer in Beirut who told his monkey to show the crowd 'how a Palestinian picks up his food rations'.[5] Another camp dweller recalls jeering Lebanese children who asked him to show them his tail. The Ain el-Hilweh camp near Sidon was even referred to by local inhabitants as 'the zoo'[6] although southern Lebanon in the 1940s was more primitive than northern Palestine.

In Jordan the refugees were given citizenship and although this was denied them in Syria they were allowed to enter the army and government service there. The discrimination against the Palestinians in Lebanon was much worse. There they were regarded neither as nationals nor foreigners but simply as 'non-nationals'. They were barred from working for the government in either a civilian or a military capacity and their children were not in general accepted in Lebanese state schools. Palestinians in Syria, Jordan, Gaza and Egypt were given places in state schools but in Lebanon refugee children at the primary and preparatory levels were confined to schools run by UNRWA; at the secondary level most of the schooling in Lebanon was private and, although UNRWA subsidized places in both state and private schools, the provision fell far short of that available in the other host countries.

Some of the 1948 refugees had Lebanese relations and with their help they were able to adjust to a new life. If given the chance of a good education they often became doctors, engineers and teachers. Sometimes they emigrated to America or the emerging countries of the Arabian Gulf where the oil industry provided employment. But most Palestinians had no such opportunities. The men of the camp population in Lebanon were usually farmers or labourers from Galilee and it was difficult for them to find work in a country where agricultural jobs were so scarce — although a number of them, with experience of 'Jaffa oranges' and other fruit, were able to find employment in the citrus plantations in the south. Most of the rest had to look for other jobs for which they were usually unqualified and for which they were supposed to get a work permit. The best they could hope for was unskilled work in the construction industry, but even if they got a job on a building site there were problems. Since the Lebanese authorities often refused to give work permits to the refugees, employers felt they were justified in paying them low wages on a daily basis. Three-fifths of refugee workers were paid daily and thus had no job security.[7] Very few of them were permanently employed, a large majority having to make do with seasonal or part-time work. A job for many of them would consist of hawking fruit from a barrow or selling lottery tickets.

In spite of their degrading refugee status, the Palestinians retained much of their social cohesion. Their village and family ties survived outside Palestine and so did many of their customs. Their camps were organized so that refugees who had once been neighbours in their village in Galilee were again neighbours in Ain el-Hilweh or Borj al-Barajneh. This has helped to preserve the Palestinian identity even in the most unpromising conditions. Contrary to the hopes and expectations of their enemies, who believed the refugees would quickly lose their identity and be absorbed by the Arab world, the sense of being Palestinian has actually increased during the long years of their exile.

The refugees' life in Lebanon was probably more miserable than anywhere else yet, strangely enough, Beirut was perhaps the city in which the Palestinians were most successful. Many of them, particularly if they were Christian and managed to acquire Lebanese nationality, became successful bankers and businessmen while others became professors at the American University. Two of the most remarkable banks which operated from Lebanon, the Arab Bank and the Intra Bank, were founded and directed by Palestinians. In addition, Beirut became the intellectual capital of the resistance movement. The Institute for Palestine Studies had been founded in the sixties in the Avenue Clemenceau beside the French embassy and other organizations such as the Palestine Research Centre and the Lebanese Association for Information on Palestine soon followed. Most important of all, the city became the headquarters of the Palestine Liberation Organization after its defeat in the Jordanian civil war of 1970–71.

At the beginning of their exile the refugees' leaders were Palestinian notables, sheikhs or mukhtars from the villages of Galilee. Although they did not usually live in the camps themselves, the organization of the Palestinians according to district and village enabled them to retain considerable influence over the refugees. Gradually, though, they were superseded by new leaders from the camps themselves but it was not until the sixties that the resistance organizations emerged and began to assert themselves as the leaders of the community. The Palestine Liberation Organization (PLO) was set up in 1964 after an Arab Summit Conference in Cairo declared its intention of approving 'practical resolutions . . . to organize the Palestinian people to enable them to carry out their role in liberating their homeland and determining their destiny.'[8] The Conference asked Ahmad Shuqairi, a Palestinian who had been head of the Saudi Arabian delegation at the United Nations, to visit the countries of the Palestinian diaspora and prepare the ground for a Palestine National Council. This body duly met and proclaimed the PLO with Shuqairi as the chairman of its executive committee.

The PLO claimed immediately to be the true representative of the Palestinian people but it was several years before it earned the loyalty of the refugees and only then after Shuqairi and the rather ineffectual collection of Palestinian notables who sat with him on the executive committee had departed. Many Palestinians were suspicious of the new organization because they saw it as an official body inspired not by the Palestinians themselves but by the countries of the Arab League. To them it was clear that Shuqairi and the PLO would have no real independence and would always be subjected to the pressure and demands of the Arab governments. Those Palestinians who distrusted the intentions of the PLO were divided into a number of different groups, small both in influence and in membership at that time but later to take over the Palestinian movement. Two such groups were the radical Arab Nationalist Movement led by a Christian medical doctor, George Habash, and the Palestine National Liberation Movement, known by a reversal of its Arabic initials as Fatah (conquest). It was from these organizations that the Palestine Resistance emerged. Fatah, led by Yasser Arafat and other Sunni Muslims, became the main guerrilla movement and concentrated on a strictly nationalist and non-ideological approach to the liberation of Palestine. After the 1967 war Habash took most of his followers into a new grouping, the Popular Front for the Liberation of Palestine (PFLP). This Marxist organization and two of its offshoots, the Democratic Front for the Liberation of Palestine (DFLP) and the PFLP-General Command, became the extremist wing of the Resistance and later, after the 1973 war, Habash headed the Palestine Rejection Front.

In the eyes of the Palestinians, the sweeping Zionist victory in the 1967 war discredited the Arab states and, by extension, the PLO as it then existed. The Palestinians finally realized that the

Arab armies were incapable of defeating the Israelis by conventional methods and so they turned increasingly to guerrilla warfare. In the aftermath of the defeat, thousands of them joined Fatah and the PFLP which had set up their headquarters in Jordan. Both organizations carried out numerous commando operations in the Israeli-occupied territories of the West Bank and Gaza and, in March 1968, they fought a pitched battle with Israeli troops at the Jordanian village of Karama. The Israelis suffered heavy casualties and the guerrillas emerged from the encounter with enormous prestige, although their success was in fact largely due to the support of the Jordanian army.

The rise of the guerrilla movements inevitably resulted in a temporary decline of the PLO. Ahmad Shuqairi, whose leadership had been bombastic but ineffective, resigned in December 1967 and his successor, Yahya Hammouda, realized that, if the PLO wanted to retain any support among the Palestinians, it would have to bring the guerrilla movments into the organization. In March 1968 an agreement was reached between the PLO, Fatah and the PFLP, according the guerrillas representation on the Palestine National Council. During the year the guerrillas, particularly Fatah, were able to extend their influence over the organization and in February 1969 they established control by electing Arafat as chairman of the PLO's executive committee.

Besides Jordan, from where the guerrillas could launch their operations into the West Bank, their other important base was Lebanon. When the Israelis took Gaza and the Sinai peninsula in 1967, the Palestinians lost their few bases in Egyptian-controlled territory. In Syria they were organized into a special force, Saiqa, and placed under Syrian army control. But in Lebanon, where the government was too weak to prevent it, the Resistance was allowed to do what it liked. On the establishment of the Palestine Liberation Army (PLA) as the military arm of the PLO in 1964, the Lebanese government had stipulated that it would not be permitted to have bases in Lebanon. After the 1967 war the situation changed. Every inch of Palestine was now in the hands of the Zionists, and the Resistance had nowhere else to operate from except the territory of neighbouring Arab states.

Following the battle of Karama in the Jordanian valley the guerrillas enjoyed such support in the Arab world that it was impossible for the Lebanese government to restrict their activities without incurring strong criticism from both other Arab states and the radical Arab nationalists inside Lebanon. By October 1968 guerrilla activity from southern Lebanon had rapidly increased and skirmishes between the commandos and the Israeli forces were taking place several times a week.

This development caused considerable anxiety to the Lebanese because they had witnessed the implacability of Israel's retaliatory policy against Jordan. Besides it was well known that Israel was short of water and had long looked covetously at the under-exploited waters of the Litani river. Israeli ministers such as Ben Gurion and Moshe Dayan had been planning to annex the Litani basin for many years (see p. 146) and Dayan had remarked ominously after the 1967 war that all of Israel's borders were now ideal with the exception of the frontier with Lebanon. This was one reason why the Lebanese were anxious not to give Israel an excuse to invade the country. In the event, however, the Israelis decided not to annex the area at that time but contented themselves with hitting back at selected targets inside Lebanon. This retaliation was by no means limited to the Palestinians and their refugee camps though these were the usual targets of Israel's reprisals. The most spectacular operation took place at the end of 1968 when troops landed by helicopter at Beirut International Airport and blew up thirteen civilian airliners belonging to Middle East Airlines.

The Lebanese authorities were also worried that the activity of the Resistance, and the retaliation which it provoked, were likely to have a disastrous effect on the uneasy relations between the Maronites and the Arab nationalists. The radicals were of course eager to strike back and accept the consequences. Palestine was the cause of all true Arabs and they demanded the removal of restrictions on the movements of the commandos. Their views were echoed by the prime minister of the day Abdullah Yafi, who declared in public that the guerrillas should be allowed total freedom to conduct any operations they liked. It was a foolish remark for a prime minister to make, one that was bound to provoke strong protests from the Maronite side and thus threaten the country's delicate confessional balance.

The Maronites viewed the battles in the south with apprehension. They claimed that Lebanon had traditionally avoided taking part in Arab struggles and argued that since the Israelis were by far the strongest force in the region, it was suicidal to go on provoking them. They also complained that there were parts of Lebanon that were no longer under effective Lebanese sovereignty. One such area was the Arqoub in the south-east of the country which was nicknamed 'Fatahland' on account of the large number of guerrilla bases there. To Maronite leaders it was intolerable that the Palestinians should be allowed to usurp an area of Lebanese territory and still worse that they thereby invited retaliation not only against themselves but also against thousands of Lebanese villagers. They therefore demanded the restoration of Lebanese control over the Arqoub and an end to the guerrillas' skirmishes with the Israelis. As Pierre Gemayel argued, with some justice, at a Phalangist Party conference: 'If the Resistance was capable of protecting the frontiers and protecting itself, or if we, along with the Resistance, or even along with all the Arab forces, were capable of protecting them, we might perhaps be willing to surrender this area to the Resistance. But the fact that the Resistance should insist on the right to dispose of our frontiers, when all of us together are incapable of protecting them, is something very strange indeed.'[9]

The Maronites demanded that the army should be used to control the Palestinians and thus they forgot one of the basic rules governing Lebanese co-existence: that the army should never be used without the consent of both halves of the National Pact. If one side used it against the other, or in this case against the allies of the other, the army would split and the most stabilizing element in Lebanon would become useless. General Chehab had obeyed the rule in 1958 and for that reason he had refused to use the army on behalf of President Chamoun.

In the difficult years of 1968 and 1969 the government realized that it was impossible to take decisive action against the commandos in the way that King Hussein was to do the following year. Yet it knew that if it did nothing at all, Israel was bound to step up its retaliatory operations against Lebanon. In its usual manner, therefore, the government muddled its way through the dilemma, ordering the army to take limited action against the commandos. Predictably this was followed by uproar in the country and large demonstrations in support of the Palestinians. One illegal demonstration in Sidon was put down in a heavy-handed way by the army and a number of people were killed. Clashes between the army and the guerrillas then spread to Beirut and Tripoli and continued intermittently from spring to November 1969. The Lebanese government meanwhile was paralysed and without a prime minister for most of the year, Rashid Karami resigning in April and refusing to participate in an anti-Palestinian policy.

Hesitant and divided as it was, the last thing the government needed was a flood of unhelpful criticism from the Arab states, which denounced Lebanese attempts at restricting the commandos. There was much hypocrisy in this: the Arab governments which urged Lebanon to give the Resistance a free hand, would never have entertained a similar idea in their own countries. The Syrians, for example, refused to allow any guerrilla activity from their territory and had placed their local commandos firmly under the orders of the army. Yet they were the ones who protested loudest when the Lebanese army tried to do the same thing. As the journalist, Edouard Saab, pertinently asked, 'Why do they want what is not permitted in Syria to be allowed in Lebanon?'[10] Egypt too, since it had lost Gaza in 1967 and no longer had a substantial Palestinian population under its control, felt free to criticize any move against the guerrillas. One sanctimonious message from the Egyptian National Assembly during a later round of fighting, stressed 'that protection of commando action is a sacred duty required of every Arab citizen of every Arab country, and that in fighting the battle for Palestine the Palestinian commandos are in fact also fighting the battle for Lebanon'.[11]

A compromise clearly had to be sought and so in November 1969 General Bustani, the army commander, and Yasser Arafat, the PLO leader, went to Cairo to work out an agreement. As the subsequent Maronite protests indicated, the compromise was clearly one-sided and in effect legitimized the Palestinian position. The government agreed that any Palestinian in Lebanon would 'be permitted to participate in the Palestinian revolution' and it even offered 'to facilitate commando activity' by, among other things, 'safeguarding the road to the Arqoub region'. Strangest of all, and particularly irritating for the Maronites, the government affirmed that 'the Palestinian armed struggle is an activity in the interest of Lebanon.' The concessions required of the Palestinians were minor by comparison and in some cases impracticable. The agreement stated that 'the Lebanese authorities . . . shall continue to exercize all their prerogatives and responsibilities in all areas of Lebanon in all circumstances', which sounded firm enough but was in fact contradicted by the clauses which effectively gave the Palestinians full control of the refugee camps as well as of the Arqoub. Another clause stated that the Palestinian leadership 'shall undertake to control the conduct of the members of its organizations and [to ensure] their non-interference in Lebanese affairs'[12] but this was another meaningless stipulation because it was well known that Arafat was unable to control the PFLP or the other extremist groups. The only concrete concession the Palestinians had to make was to remove a small commando base at Jirun which they seldom used anyway.

The Maronite Reaction

The road from Tripoli to the Cedars is one of the most spectacular in Lebanon. From the coast it rambles through groves of fine olives before reaching the foothills of the Mountain. Instantly the landscape changes, the slopes of the hills are stony and barren, the cliffs of a ravine emerge. The road winds along one side of the Qadisha gorge, past red-roofed villages which show what building skills the Lebanese once possessed. Terraced fields and orchards of apple trees appear, then the famous wild flowers of the Lebanon. An enormous number of chapels and anchorages are perched on the most unapproachable places, on the edge of cliffs, on remote spurs of the Mountain. At the head of the gorge stands the town of Becharré, the spiritual home of the Maronites and in Ottoman times the political capital. It has been a stronghold of Christianity since the seventh century. From Becharré with its vast churches, the road twists up on its last lap to a nasty skiing village containing a series of garish chalets with names like *La Dolce Vita*. A few hundred yards off you can see a small patch of cedars, the pitiful remains of the great forests where Solomon once sent 80,000 men to hew wood.

The cedar is the emblem of Lebanon. It is on the currency and the national flag. It is also the symbol of Maronite independence and is used on the posters of the right-wing political parties. For thirteen hundred years the Maronite community has lived on the Lebanese Mountain, defending with determination its independence and way of life. It has consciously turned its backs on the great plains and deserts to the east, choosing its allies, as we have seen, from across the Mediterranean. Its people's most enduring characteristic has been their refusal to compromise with anyone who threatens, or is perceived to threaten, their freedom — Byzantines,

Mamelukes, Turks or Arabs. The Cairo Agreement, which gave recognition and support for the Palestine Resistance, seemed to them just one more invasion of their independence. The hardline Maronite leaders opposed it from the beginning and Pierre Gemayel wrote to the prime minister complaining that the agreement amounted to a loss of sovereignty. If the authorities refused to do their duty, then the Maronites believed they should persuade them to change their mind. The Phalangists and the National Liberal Party decided to prepare themselves for the clash which many people already regarded as inevitable. Weapons were therefore bought and training camps set up. By the early seventies the peacefulness of the mountain road to Becharré had changed. You were likely to see dark military jeeps and young men in uniform. At times you would catch the unmistakeable sound of gunfire — carried down the Mountain from the training ground near the Cedars.

In the confrontation between the army and the Palestinian guerrillas in 1969 the Phalangists took part in the fighting on the outskirts of Beirut. But in March of the following year they engaged the Palestinians by themselves. Rashid Karami and Kamal Jumblatt were by then prime minister and minister of the interior respectively, and since they refused to order the army into action against the guerrillas, the Phalangist militia appointed itself the guardian of Lebanese sovereignty. In February 1973 the Phalangist Party submitted a memorandum to the President of Lebanon which said: 'We thank God that the state has decided to take firm action to meet this challenge, and we support you and support your stand. But should the state fail in its duty or weaken or hesitate, then Mr President, we shall ourselves take action: we shall meet demonstrations with bigger demonstrations, strikes with more extensive strikes, toughness with toughness, and force with force.'[1] After another round of fighting in that year, however, the Maronite leadership realized their militias were as yet no match for the Palestinians and they would have to build up their forces if they hoped to contain the guerrillas. Over the following months, large consignments of arms were landed at the Port of Beirut and the Jounieh Yacht Club. Their destinations were the training camps of the Maronite party militias.

Meanwhile the situation on Lebanon's southern border deteriorated as Israel stepped up the level of its retaliation. This had been high enough in 1968 and 1969 but after the Cairo Agreement it was increased and the exodus of Lebanese villagers to Beirut began. Air raids were directed against refugee camps and villages suspected of being friendly to the Palestinians. Assaults by land usually led to the blowing up of houses and bridges, the destruction of roads and crops, and the seizure of villagers who were often taken back to Israel for interrogation. It was easy to see the logic behind the Israelis' actions. They were 'encouraging' the Lebanese to take the same action as King Hussein had done in 1970 when he ordered his army into the refugee camps in Jordan to destroy the guerrilla forces. But even when the commandos began to conduct their operations from outside the Arab countries, the Israeli reprisal raids against Lebanon increased. After the terrorist attack on Israel's Lydda airport in May 1972, the Lebanese suffered the consequences, though the president rightly complained: 'How can Lebanon be held responsible for an act by foreigners who were transported to Israel on a foreign airline from a foreign capital?'[2] Lydda was followed by an air strike, which was followed by the Munich massacre, and this was in turn followed by a vengeance air raid in which four hundred people were killed. At this ratio, Israel's eye for an eye policy was working out at about twenty eyes for an eye. Yet even when the Palestinians agreed to stop their attacks across the border in 1974, the retaliatory policy continued. Israel was in effect telling the Lebanese not only to stop the Palestinian operations but to get rid of the guerrillas altogether.

Even if it was not obvious at the time it has since become clear that the Israelis wanted to create an upheaval in Lebanon and they knew that the best way to do this was to stir up the antagonism between the Maronites and the Arab nationalists. One incident in 1973 gives an idea of how they set about it. On 9 April an Israeli terror squad arrived in Beirut by boat and murdered three Palestinian leaders (including the poet Kamal Nasser) as well as a number of other people. The Israelis controlled an area of Beirut for several hours and even directed the traffic. Yet the Lebanese army did not fire a shot, or in fact do anything at all, although it was ordered into action by the prime minister Saeb Salam. Huge demonstrations were immediately held to protest against the army's ineptitude. Salam himself demanded the dismissal of the army commander, General Ghanem. But Ghanem was a friend of Frangieh and the president refused to sack him. Salam then resigned and a major political crisis followed. Three weeks later, fighting broke out between the commandos and the Lebanese army for the first time since the signing of the Cairo Agreement.

Israel's policy, which displaced tens of thousands of Shi'ite villagers from the south and also stimulated the mutual dislike between the Maronites and the Palestinians, led in addition to an erosion of confidence in the Lebanese state. For six years Israel attacked the south and the government made no attempt to respond. It neither defended its own people nor looked after them once they were made refugees. When the Israeli army attacked across the border, Lebanese soldiers were ordered by their officers not to fire because they knew that if they did not interfere no harm would come to them. Reduced to a state of humiliating impotence, it was scarcely surprizing that the government should lose the respect of its citizens. As the refugees made their way to Beirut, the Maronites complained vigorously that Lebanese citizens should be made homeless on account of a conflict that did not concern them. 'We welcomed the Palestinian refugees and gave them homes,' wrote one young Maronite. 'Then, having allowed the commandos to do what they please, we have to welcome our own refugees, chased from their lands because of Palestinian aggressions against Israel.'[3]

The Maronites' chief objection to the Palestinian Resistance was probably that it became a magnet for a large number of radical Lebanese groups. Traditionally, the radicals had had little influence in Lebanese politics, but now the alliance between Jumblatt and Arafat offered them an opportunity to assert themselves. They flocked to the PLO and the National Movement, an ill-assorted coaltion of Ba'athists, Nasserists and communists who had only one thing in common — they wanted to change the political 'system'. The Maronites immediately took fright and claimed that the National Pact and the country itself were in danger. It is true that there was a strong left-wing movement in the universities and that a number of people were trumpeting about revolution. But it was hardly a serious threat and even Jumblatt regarded his new allies with derision: 'certain left parties and small groups of every variety panicked and started rushing about calling for class struggle in a country which has barely 70,000 industrial workers, a great many of whom were fighting on the other side'.[4] The main left-wing force, the National Movement, was making no revolutionary demands but campaigning for a number of mild reforms: the abolition of confessionalism, proportional representation and so on. But these and any other proposals were rejected by the Maronites out of hand. Politically on the defensive, aware that their numbers less and less justified their privileges, the Maronites were unable to understand where their real interests lay. They adopted, quite needlessly, a 'backs against the wall' position and came to see the alliance between radical Arab nationalists and Palestinians as a plot of the international left.

Maronite objections to the Resistance were sometimes valid. Gemayel's complaint that the 'Palestinian camps have become the meeting place not only for all the outlaws of the Arab world but also of all the bandits of the world'[5] was obviously exaggerated but it was a widespread view. Under the terms of the Cairo Agreement, the Palestinians were meant to respect Lebanese sovereignty and not to interfere in the country's affairs. Yet the guerrillas insisted on making their presence felt by wandering around Beirut armed and in uniform. It was easy to understand the annoyance of a Lebanese who found himself stopped at an illegal roadblock and made to wait while commandos arrogantly inspected his identity card. The Palestinians did themselves no good by antagonizing the Maronites and thus reinforcing their anti-Arab and anti-PLO prejudices. In the months before the civil war it was difficult to mention the word Palestinian to a Maronite without evoking a passionate response. The Palestinians, you would be told, were thieves, communists, murderers and rapists. The Lebanese had given them food and houses and places to work; in return they were strangling the country and turning it into an armed camp. Invariably the unruly behaviour of a few commandos would be blamed on the whole Palestinian community. If an incident took place on the outskirts of Beirut — and many did, though these were not always begun by the commandos — you were liable to be shouted at: 'Would you allow this sort of thing to happen in your country? Do you let bandits stand at roundabouts and shoot you as you go by?'

For many Lebanese — and not only Maronites — the Palestinians became the scapegoats for almost everything that went wrong in Lebanon. Every incident, every problem, every evil, was blamed on the Palestinians. A party statement made later by the National Liberals reflected the frenzied state of Maronite opinion: 'the Palestinians by their irresponsible machinations, have proved that they have renounced Palestine and transferred their battle to Lebanon which welcomed them and bandaged their wounds. They are set upon the destruction, the demolition, and the assassination of Lebanon . . . We have always been the biggest supporter of the Palestinian cause. Our sacrifices for the Palestinian people have surpassed those of the Palestinians themselves.'[6] Although it is difficult to think of a single sacrifice made by Chamoun or his party for the Palestinians, the statement was typical of the Maronites' irrational and emotional, but not wholly unjustified, reaction to the activities of the Resistance.

The Maronite hatred of the Palestinians soon reached obsessive proportions and produced a 'them or us' attitude personified by the Chamoun family. The Maronite leaders did not hold identical views on the Palestinians. Pierre Gemayel, for instance, supported the Palestinian cause in general partly because he believed it was just and partly because a resolution of the Palestine question would obviously ease Lebanon's own problems. Camille Chamoun was different: he had no sympathy for the refugees and disliked them. His son Dory, the secretary-general of the party, held similar views and in private he referred to the Palestinians as a race of cowards whose refugee existence was no more than they deserved. 'If it's necessary', he once boasted, 'we will chuck the Palestinians into the sea. They will pollute it but that's too bad.'

The Maronites' over-reaction to the Palestinian presence led to a deterioration in Christian-Muslim relations and a revival of sectarian rivalry. Unquestionably, the Maronites were responsible for this. They seemed deliberately to be stirring up the old animosities, flaunting their ancient anti-Islamic prejudices and talking emotively of the superiority of the cross over the crescent. The Phalangist

Party, which had only recently emerged as a respectable, reformist party, quickly reverted to its old vigilante, goose-stepping days, attempting to galvanize its supporters by adopting an heroic, crusading pose. The party that had claimed to defend Lebanon was now more than ever championing the purely Maronite image of the country.

During the 1970s many Maronites managed to convince themselves that the PLO and its Lebanese allies were plotting to take over the country. One Maronite writer claimed that the Palestinian aim was 'the physical and political liquidation of the Lebanese resistance, and the setting up of a popular republic dominated by the Palestinians of Fatah and their Marxist allies'.[7] This was pure fantasy and it is doubtful whether even many Maronites believed in this kind of propaganda. What possible objective could the Palestinians have had in following a course of action that had already ended disastrously in Jordon? The reputation of the PLO was at a high point throughout the world following Arafat's UN speech in November 1974 and there was nothing the Palestinian leader wanted less than a war in Lebanon, as his caution and diplomacy all through 1975 showed.

But the Maronites refused to listen to reason. They pointed to the activities of a small extremist group outside the control of the PLO or to provocative remarks by one or other of the guerrilla leaders and claimed these to be official PLO policy. They decided that the entire Palestinian people were the enemies of Lebanon and insisted that there would be no peace until they left. Some Maronites, such as President Frangieh, said that Lebanon had too many refugees and proposed that other Arab countries should take some of them. Extremists such as the paramilitary organization, the Guardians of the Cedars, demanded that every Palestinian must leave Lebanon.

A Maronite plan was thus gradually revealed: the guerrilla organizations were to be suppressed and at least some of the refugees were to be removed. Lebanese control over the entire country would then be restored and Israel would no longer have an excuse to pound the southern villages. As a further consequence of the Palestinians' departure, the radical Arab nationalists would find themselves isolated and thus their agitation for economic reform could more easily be ignored. Maronite supremacy would then be easy to reassert.

The Maronites realized, however, that the war must be presented as a conflict between the Lebanese and subversive foreigners who threatened the future of the country. They needed to convince the other Lebanese that they should all stand together against the 'Marxist' Palestinians and their motley band of Lebanese fellow-travellers. If they succeeded in doing so, the Maronite militias could unite with the army and destroy the Resistance. If they failed, the conflict would become just another version of the Maronite—Arab nationalist antagonism.

The Maronites were in effect asking the other communities to forget their own history. The Sunni commitment to Arab nationalism, the Shi'ite resentment of the treatment their people had received in the south and in Beirut, the Druze and Greek Orthodox antipathy towards the Maronites — all this was to be shelved so that the country could stand firm against the cuckoo in its nest. As usual the Maronites were seeing Lebanon exclusively in their own terms. They insisted that the country was being threatened by the alliance between the PLO and the Lebanese radicals and it never occurred to them that other communities might actually agree with the reforms which that alliance was proposing. The Phalangists could claim that they formed 'the nucleus of the Lebanese resistance against foreign occupation and aggression'[8] but to other communities they were merely the nucleus of Maronite resistance against a series of political and social reforms which the country badly needed.

Maronite propaganda thus concentrated on the unity of the Lebanese and even Camille Chamoun, who of all people must have learnt that unity was at best skin-deep, felt able to claim that 'in spite of foreign interference which promotes the conflict, nothing can prevent the entente between the Lebanese'.[9] The ploy failed. Maronite propaganda was simply too far-fetched for most people to believe. It was no good claiming they were merely fighting foreigners and communists when everyone could see this was not true. The war the Maronites unleashed on their country soon proved that their version was both mendacious and absurd. It was never really a war between Lebanese and Palestinians; in origin it was simply a renewed civil war along the lines of the 1958 confrontation but with one crucial difference. In 1958 the Palestinians were not an issue and took no part in the fighting; in 1975 they were the catalyst. The conflict of 1975–76 had little or nothing to do with a 'communist offensive'[10] (Gemayel) or 'a plot of the international Left . . . under orders from Moscow' (Dory Chamoun). In spite of all the conspiracy theories and the interventions – real or imagined – of outside powers, the war was something far more traditional: yet another round in Lebanon's elemental struggle between the Maronites and the Arab nationalists.

PART III

The War and Beyond

Thou wast perfect in thy ways from the day that thou was created, till iniquity was found in thee.

By the multitude of thy merchandise they have filled the midst of thee with violence, and thou hast sinned . . . .

Thine heart was lifted up because of thy beauty, thou hast corrupted thy wisdom by reason of thy brightness . . . .

Thou hast defiled thy sanctuaries by the multitude of thine iniquities, by the iniquity of thy traffick; therefore will I bring forth a fire from the midst of thee, it shall devour thee, and I will bring thee to ashes upon the earth in the sight of all them that behold thee.

Ezekiel XXVIII, 15—18

8

Civil War

Civil wars usually begin with an 'event' — a revolt, a secession or a military uprising. Lebanon was different. There were any number of events but it is difficult to show that one in particular was the starting point of the confrontation. The massacre in Ain el-Roumaneh on 13 April 1975, when Phalangist gunmen ambushed a bus and killed 27 of its Palestinian occupants, is often put forward as the crucial incident and perhaps it was. With hindsight it does seem that Ain el-Roumaneh was a decisive moment and that afterwards there was no turning back. But it was not obvious at the time. The massacre was not a lone crime that shattered the confidence of a society at peace. Lebanon had been witnessing scenes of violence for years. Less than two months earlier there had been fighting in Sidon in which 16 people had been killed, and a case can be made for dating the beginning of the civil war from this incident.

Ain el-Roumaneh was a straightforward attack by the Phalangists on their principal opponents in a Beirut suburb, but the Sidon incident was more complicated. It began as a local issue and ended by polarizing most of the country at either end of the Maronite–Arab nationalist axis. It was a dispute between Lebanese, a conflict of economic interests between rich and poor, and between Christian entrepreneurs intent on profitable innovation and Muslim fishermen intent on preserving their traditional way of life. It epitomized the deep divisions in Lebanese society. A dispute over fishing rights was seized on by radical Muslim groups and a large demonstration in Sidon was organized on 26 February in support of local fishermen who felt threatened by the creation of a new fishing consortium under the chairmanship of Camille Chamoun. The protest demonstration was intercepted by an army detachment and in the

clash that followed Marouf Saad, mayor of Sidon and a supporter
of the fishermen, was mortally wounded. A further demonstration
three days later led to a battle between soldiers and gunmen belonging to left-wing Muslim groups supported by extremist guerrillas
of the Palestinian Rejection Front. After a short bombardment
of Sidon, ordered by the Maronite army commander, General
Ghanem, a cease-fire was arranged and the army withdrew from
the city. Five soldiers and eleven civilians had been killed in the
affair.

The involvement of the army in Sidon and the astonishing
decision of its commander to train his artillery against the country's
third city produced a barrage of protests from all over the country.
Even the Sunni establishment, conservative and ineffectual though
it usually was, demanded the urgent reorganization of the army
structure. The Muslim Higher Council and six former prime
ministers insisted that there should be equal representation between the sects in the army command because they realized that
it was vital to keep the armed forces neutral. Lebanon had managed
to survive the 1958 crisis principally because the army commander,
General Chehab, had refused to commit his troops to either side.
By acting as he did, he had been able to reassure the Muslim
communities that the army was a genuinely neutral force and not
merely the protector of the Maronite community. During the
1970s, President Frangieh and his protégé, General Ghanem, did
much to destroy the impartial image of the army, and its credibility as a national institution was further weakened by the role
it was ordered to play in Sidon. Saeb Salam and the other Sunni
leaders understood how important it was to restore that credibility, and for this reason clamoured for reforms and the dismissal
of Ghanem.

The army had never been intended to be a strong force capable
of acting outside Lebanon's borders. Although it had played a
brief and undistinguished role in the 1948 war, it had since been
used simply for internal operations and its commanders had usually
done all they could to avoid any kind of confrontation with Israel.
At full strength the army consisted of 19,000 men of whom a
slight majority were Muslims. Two-thirds of the officers, however,
were Christians and so were most of the twenty-four battalion

commanders.[1] Furthermore, Christians always occupied the two most important posts, the Commander of the Armed Forces and the Chief of Military Intelligence. In these circumstances it was understandable that the Muslims should accuse the army of a pro-Maronite bias.

While the Sunnis and the National Movement charged the army and the Maronites with collusion, the Phalangists and other hardline Maronite groups seemed determined to prove that their opponents were right. They arranged noisy demonstrations in east Beirut and paraded across the city proclaiming their support for the army. As far as the Maronites were concerned, there could be no question of reform. They claimed that the army was a national institution and argued that as their political parties were also national institutions pledged to defend the same ideals, it was entirely logical that they should all be on the same side. The Maronites were in effect claiming the state as their own and telling the other Lebanese that they and the army would stand together against all those who threatened the Lebanese system. They thought they were constructing a solid front against the menace of the Palestinians and the radicals, but the arrogance with which they assumed their role as upholders of the nation merely antagonized most of the rest of the population, particularly the Sunnis, most of whom had consistently observed the spirit of the National Pact.

For a few days at the beginning of March, barricades of burning tyres were set up in Muslim districts of Beirut in protest at the Sidon incident and people talked about the chances of a new 1958 confrontation. But then the demonstrations ended and life in the capital became normal once more. In spite of all the bitterness and the political problems, few people believed in the inevitability of civil war. There had always been bitterness and political problems and it was generally believed that they would be solved by the usual makeshift formulas. The Lebanese, momentarily stirred by the reappearance of traditional animosities, returned to their priorities: their jobs, their pursuit of profit, their families, their leisure and their food. Beirut society entertained as lavishly as it had always done and denunciations of the Palestinians became a still more regular feature of its dinner tables. Some of its more serious members, embarrassed by the lack of musical achievement in what was supposed to be a civilized society, discussed proposals for setting up a national symphony orchestra. Others returned to the spring routine of cocktail parties in Beirut and skiing weekends at the Cedars.

This complacency was upset by the news of Ain el-Roumaneh. The massacre took place on a Sunday and many Beirutis heard about it on their car radios as they returned to the capital that evening. Barricades were going up all over the city and the traffic jams stretched for miles in each direction. The next morning, on 14 April, the battles began. It was a matter of suburb against suburb, Maronite district against Palestinian refugee camp. Commandos from the camps of Tal Zaatar and Borj al-Barajneh fought with Phalangists from Dekwaneh and the fashionable quarter of Ashrafiyeh. In the centre of Beirut, the district of the souks and the main banks, and in the prosperous district of Ras Beirut by the American University, there was no fighting, but the sound of mortar fire a couple of miles off could be heard distinctly. Every so often a car screeched along the smart Hamra boulevard, its occupants firing indiscriminately into the air. They were not trying to kill anybody and you could not know to whose militia they belonged. They were just telling us they were there and it was their show.

All over the city the shops were closed and the streets deserted. The American University was almost silent. Only in the pubs of Ras Beirut was life much the same. In the Wellington pub Georges the barman went on serving draught Whitbread beer as if nothing had happened. Huge and imperturbable, he wore his tartan jacket and bow tie throughout the fighting. The Western journalists were usually there too, each with his own particular piece of news, although they were also enthusiastic patrons of the Pickwick and the Cock and Bull nearby.

The battles went on for a week and most of the population remained in their apartments, many of them discovering what was happening in their country from the World Service of the BBC. It was usually the third item, because the news from Cambodia and Vietnam was more dramatic, but it was always reported. By the end of the week the official death toll was put at 150, though people knew they had to multiply that number several times before they got the true figure. The streets of the city were at most times empty except for the queues of women outside the bakers' shops. Each day the piles of rubbish on the street corners grew larger. Each day the cats grew a little bolder, so that in the end they became the main inhabitants of the street. In the distance the shooting went on. Every quarter of an hour or so, the windows rattled as a bomb went off somewhere in the centre of the city. A bank or an office had been gutted, but nobody knew who had done it. Most people blamed third parties, no doubt with some reason. There were a lot of outsiders who had an interest in making Lebanon unstable, as the rest of the war was to prove. Depending on which side a man supported, he was likely to claim the bombs were planted by Iraqis or the Israeli secret service. In the middle of the fighting the Prime Minister, Rashid Solh, declared that more than 200 Israeli agents had entered the country with false passports in order to play the part of *agents provocateurs*.[2]

After three days of fighting a cease-fire was announced but it did not hold. On that same evening there was a heavy thunderstorm but it could not drown the noise of gunfire in different areas of the city. The following day the main participants stopped fighting but still a return to normal life was prevented by unknown gunmen shooting from rooftops in downtown Beirut. Although the government claimed that they belonged to a hostile third party, most people believed that the snipers had been sanctioned by the president or the Maronite parties or both. The fact that the gunfire came from Christian areas and that the identity of the gunmen remained undisclosed even after the security forces had shot or captured several of them, seemed to indicate that the Maronites had no interest in ending the fighting. Their opponents believed that the Maronite parties had already decided to escalate the conflict so as to force the army to join the fighting on the side of the Phalangist militia.

The Ain el-Roumaneh massacre naturally had an immediate effect on the political situation. The Phalangist Party found it impossible to deny the role played by its own gunmen in the ambush but claimed they had been provoked by commandos of the Rejection Front. Pierre Gemayel pointed to an incident earlier on the same day when gunmen in a car with covered number plates had driven up to a nearby church and killed four people, including two Phalangist Party officials. Although he did not deny the involvement of his own militia in the subsequent massacre, Gemayel said that the arrival of a bus-load of Palestinians in a Christian area shortly after the earlier killings was bound to lead to trouble. Few people, however, were convinced by his explanation. The very efficiency with which the massacre was carried out, the high death toll and the fact that Gemayel refused to condemn it, suggested that there had been some planning before-hand.

The Maronites' political opponents reacted to the event by attempting to proscribe the Phalangist Party. Kamal Jumblatt and other leaders of the National Movement immediately demanded the dismissal of both Phalangist ministers in the cabinet and two weeks later Jumblatt announced that his parliamentary bloc would not support any government which included members of the Phalangist Party. It was an ill-judged move which led to a further polarization of the country as the Maronite community rallied to the defence of the Phalangists. The Maronite Patriarch, the monastic orders and the National Liberal Party of Camille Chamoun all declared that Jumblatt's veto was unacceptable. Gemayel, who realized that the Sunni leaders and even the Palestinians themselves were uneasy about the Druze leader's intransigence, decided to force the issue. On 7 May his ministers resigned and were joined by three ministers of Chamoun's party and Emir Majid Arslan, the elderly Druze chieftain who could be counted on to oppose any proposal of Jumblatt's. In these circumstances it was impossible for the government to continue and a week later the prime minister resigned.

As negotiations for a new government began, there was an almost total collapse of law and order in many parts of the country. On 18 May serious fighting once again broke out in the capital. But the conflict was no longer simply between Phalangist militia-men and Palestinian guerrillas from the Rejection Front who refused to heed Arafat's demands that the Resistance should stay out of the battles. Camille Chamoun's militia, the 'Tigers', had also joined in alongside the Phalangist units and on the other side a rag-bag of small radical groups had taken to the streets. In some areas the fighting had turned into a straightforward social conflict as Shi'ite and Kurdish slum-dwellers, backed by the communists and other radical parties, attacked Maronite forces in the more prosperous suburbs.

President Frangieh, meanwhile, was trying to find some way of forming a government. The Maronites and the Arab nationalists had tacitly agreed at independence that both of them should always be represented in the government. In 1957 Camille Chamoun had managed to exclude the Arab nationalists not only from government but in some cases from parliament as well and a disaster had followed. Now Jumblatt, the foremost Arab nationalist politician in Lebanon, was vetoing the presence of the strongest Maronite organization in the new cabinet. To many people, it was a dangerous and unnecessary piece of obduracy.

Frangieh, who had no sympathy with Jumblatt's position, first had to find someone willing to take on the job of prime minister. The two most obvious choices were the tough, respected Sunni leaders, Saeb Salam and Rashid Karami, who had both been prime minister several times since the early 1950s. Yet it was not clear how either of them would be able to solve the problem set by Jumblatt. Besides, Frangieh had shown that he was adverse to appointing strong and able prime ministers over whom he could exercise little control. In the previous two years he had chosen three relatively unimportant Sunni politicians to head successive governments rather than accept Salam or Karami. It was, thus, hardly surprising that he should hit on a scheme to avoid them once again. On 23 May the radio announced the formation of a military government headed by a retired brigadier of the gendarmerie, Nureddin Rifai, and including only one civilian — Frangieh's relative, Lucien Dahdah, who became Minister of Finance and of Foreign Affairs.

The President's decision was bewildering because it was surely predictable that Chamoun and Gemayel would enthusiastically back the plan, just as it was predictable that practically everybody else would reject it. The Sunnis, the Shi'ites, the National Movement and the liberal Christians of Raymond Eddé's National Bloc were unanimous in their refusal to co-operate with the military

government. The Maronites' close alignment with the army and
the appointment of General Ghanem — of all people — as minister
of defence, made it impossible for them to do so. Three days
after its formation the new government resigned and reluctantly
Frangieh agreed to invite Rashid Karami to become the next prime
minister. Negotiations over the composition of the new cabinet
took more than a month and in the meantime the security situation
deteriorated. Throughout that hot, sticky summer there were
bomb explosions, murders and kidnapping, and occasional bouts
of savage fighting. There were gun battles in the north between
Tripoli and Zghorta and around the towns and villages lying on the
coast road between Beirut and Sidon. Towards the end of June
violence again broke out in the capital, principally between the
Maronite forces in Ain el-Roumaneh and the Shi'ites of Chiah.
By the end of the month the Lebanese authorities were admitting
that the fighting was the most violent in the country's history. In
Beirut's suburbs men and women, nearly always innocent civilians,
lay dying in the streets, for the gunfire was too insistent and too
ferocious for the ambulances to be able to reach them.

The main obstacles to the formation of a new government were
the old za'ims who had been squabbling over the country for
thirty years. But recently their quarrels had got worse and no
za'im was on speaking terms with all the others. Some of the
nation's leaders had not spoken to each other for years. Karami
and Chamoun, for example, had not acknowledged each other
since 1958, a particularly serious obstacle since one of them was
the prime minister designate and the other the key Maronite
figure. Eventually they were reconciled after the intervention of
the Syrian foreign minister.

The Syrian government, whose role in the Lebanese war will
be discussed in the next chapter, had for some time been dis-
turbed by events across the border. It had made its first move
the day after the formation of the military government when the
Syrian president, Hafez Assad, and three of his colleagues held a
meeting and decided to send a delegation to Beirut. The Syrians
realized that Rifai's government would not work and would only
lead to more fighting so they sent their foreign minister, Abdul
Halim Khaddam, to Lebanon to persuade Frangieh — a friend

of the Assad family since his youth – to change course. Khaddam was successful in his mission and he also managed to convince the Lebanese president to choose Karami as the next prime minister. A month later, after endless discussions between the za'ims had still failed to produce a government, Khaddam returned to Beirut where he was again successful. Within two days a cabinet had been formed and its two principal members were the now reconciled old za'ims, Camille Chamoun and Rashid Karami.

It would be difficult to claim that the new six-man cabinet was the one needed to rescue Lebanon from its troubles. Its members were mainly old and conservative – half of them had been cabinet ministers as far back as 1943 – and one of them, Majid Arslan, was joining his twenty-fourth government. Nevertheless, in the circumstances it was an achievement to have put together a government at all. Jumblatt had been adamant that no Phalangist should be included in the cabinet but he had been sufficiently flexible to let it be known that he did not insist on representation for his own party. In the end it was the Maronites who gained from Jumblatt's veto, because although the Phalangists had been excluded, they knew that their interests would be well served by their ally Chamoun. There was no-one in the cabinet, however, who would represent the interests of Jumblatt and the National Movement. Karami himself, who had been on the same side as the Druze leader in 1958, now deeply distrusted Jumblatt's motives and regarded him as ambitious and irresponsible.

Karami retained the Ministry of Defence himself and was thus in a position to reject Maronite demands that the army be used against the Palestinians. But the crucial appointment was Chamoun's because his position gave him control over the internal security forces. The decision to bring the former president back into government was widely welcomed at the time. Even the radicals and the Palestinians had high hopes of Chamoun, for they saw him as an old Christian statesman of sufficient firmness and prestige to control the Phalangists. Blinded by distrust of Gemayel and his party, they seemed to have forgotten Chamoun's role in 1958. Their optimism over his appointment was quickly shown to be misplaced. As Minister of the Interior Chamoun soon indicated his aversion to compromise solutions and over the following months he moved his party to positions where it became more intransigent than the Phalangists themselves.

For the first seven weeks of the new administration there was relative calm in the country and it even seemed that Karami might be successful. Certainly, life in the capital returned to a familiar summer routine. The offices closed at two o'clock and their occupants rushed down to the beaches, crowding on to every patch of sand and rock between the port and Bir Hassan. In the evenings the Lebanese went for their usual stroll, like any other Mediterranean people. I remember well the long promenade at Raouché on a humid summer evening, with the smoky smell of the corn-on-the-cob stalls all along the sea-front, and Lebanese families in hundreds parading up and down before eating in one of the numerous fish restaurants close by. It was a most inappropriate setting for a civil war.

The great Hamra boulevard also returned to life. At each outbreak of trouble the nightclubs and street cafes were instantly closed down for fear of bombs. The fancy boutiques too were shuttered and padlocked. But after a cease-fire Hamra immediately resumed its character as the Fifth Avenue of the Middle East: the Wimpy Bars re-opened with the shops and the cinemas and the airline agencies. At night it became once more a wilderness of flickering lights and traffic jams. At these times it would have been impossible to tell that the country was fighting an intermittent civil war had it not been for the posters pasted on walls by local militias and Palestinian groups to commemorate their dead.

The opening rounds of the war produced mainly puzzlement among the Lebanese themselves, accompanied by a feeling that it would not last. Whenever a cease-fire was announced, it was greeted with almost universal optimism. People flocked back to the beaches and the restaurants, convinced it was all over. The leaders would not let it happen again, they assured you. The Lebanese were not fighters, it was not in their blood, and soon they would go back to making money. And so they would return to their businesses, absurdly over-optimistic, until the next round began.

Sometimes, however, one had the impression that subconsciously the Lebanese did know that their way of life was coming to an end. There was a sort of desperation in the frenzied way they set out to enjoy themselves as if they had only a limited time to play with. That summer the Lebanese way of life became almost a parody of itself. Only in Beirut could you hear gunfire from one end of the city while you watched people water-skiing at the other. Only in Lebanon could the foreign minister — during a serious government crisis — attend a smart lunch at the Holiday Inn to launch the new office of Blakoe International Products, a company planning to market sex aids in Lebanon.[3]

The resilience of the Lebanese and their constant reassurances that the fighting was over provided strong evidence that the vast majority of the people had no desire to continue the war. Even more than in most wars, this one was kept going by the extremists. The international press reported endlessly on the Christian-Muslim divide and the sectarian hatred in the country. It was an appalling over-simplification and the huge, multi-confessional peace march in October 1975 indicated as much. The majority in all sects, whatever their history and traditions and however much they may have distrusted each other, had no intention of taking part in a war, and for months they stayed out of it. The early battles were fought between members of a neo-fascist organization and its allies posing as the saviours of the country, and an alliance of radicals, Nasserists and Palestinians outside the control of the PLO. Most people wanted nothing to do with them. It was only by stages, and against its will, that the Lebanese majority was dragged into the war. (The same was true of the Palestinians who identified themselves with Arafat and Fatah rather than with the extremists of the Rejection Front.) By the end, most of the Lebanese had taken sides, but only because they were forced to do so. Eventually the civil war became what people had wrongly claimed it always had been — a confessional war. When the extremists had begun to kill people simply because they belonged to a different sect, when the thugs of one side or the other put up barricades, examined the identity cards of passers-by, and put to death all those of the opposite religion — then, and only then, did the men of different faiths come to hate each other to an extent that seemed to justify the continuation of the war.

After forming his government on 30 June 1975, Rashid Karami's first priority was the restoration of law and order. For a few weeks he was successful and the country enjoyed its last period of peace for many months. But even during that time the militias were busily arming and training new recruits for what Jumblatt already referred to as 'the fourth round'. And if the security situation had improved, the country was no nearer solving its political problems. The Phalangist Party and the National Movement were still at loggerheads, with neither of them willing to make concessions to the other's point-of-view. Jumblatt, who announced his programme in mid-August, insisted that the new government must push through a series of urgent reforms, the most important of which were the abolition of confessionalism and the restructuring of the army command. The Phalangist Party was not in principle opposed to either of these reforms and, as we have seen, had itself proposed to end confessionalism many years earlier. But in the summer of 1975 the Phalangists were not prepared to accept any suggestions from Jumblatt, even if they agreed with them. They refused absolutely to discuss any reforms until the violence in the country had subsided. It was a short-sighted and illogical decision because the Phalangists knew perfectly well that the country needed those reforms. It was hypocritical also to demand an end to the violence when much of it was being committed by their own militia.

Throughout the autumn, Rashid Karami strove courageously to effect a national reconciliation between the quarrelling za'ims. In September, with the help of the Syrian foreign minister, he was able to set up a Committee for National Dialogue in which both Jumblatt and Gemayel agreed to sit. But it was unable to achieve much as Jumblatt refused to talk to the Phalangist leader and insisted on discussing his own programme. Later efforts by Karami to set up a Security Board and then a Higher Co-ordination Committee in which all factions would be represented foundered for similar reasons. Most of the za'ims could not be bothered even to attend the Security Board. In the midst of the nation's worst crisis, its traditional leaders continued to behave like prima donnas.

Perhaps the worst instance of all was the behaviour of the president, who following the failure of the military government adopted a sort 'Neroesque' attitude towards the fate of the country of which he was head of state. The appointment of Karami as prime minister, to which Frangieh only agreed after heavy pressure from the country and the Syrian foreign minister, was regarded by the president as a personal insult as well as a political defeat. He reacted by retiring in a huff to his villa at Ehden in the mountains and taking no part in the government of the country. When he was finally persuaded to come back after several weeks he seemed determined to frustrate Karami's attempts to reassert administrative control. An example of his attitude was provided by the arrival of a ship at Jounieh which Karami believed was carrying arms for the Maronite forces. The prime minister therefore sent a detachment of the security forces to search the ship, only to find that it was being defended by units of the Phalangist militia whose presence on the beach had been organized by the president.[4]

From the middle of the summer Frangieh was in fact behaving not like the president of the country but as just another Maronite leader. Although he did agree to one of his opponent's demands by dismissing General Ghanem and replacing him with a less obviously partisan Maronite, his presidential achievements were minimal. At a time when he was meant to be the impartial head of state his son Tony was in the north organizing the Frangieh supporters into a militia calling itself the Zghorta Liberation Army. From his presidential palace at Ba'abda outside Beirut he plotted with the other Maronite leaders. He even set aside a part of his palace for Camille Chamoun to live in after he had become minister of the interior. For the rest of the war many of the crucial army decisions were taken in Ba'abda by Frangieh, Chamoun and the new army commander, Hanna Said. Karami, who was thus seldom consulted about military matters even though he happened to be minister of defence as well as prime minister, was understandably angry and in parliament he attacked both Frangieh and Chamoun for their refusal to co-operate. By September the partisanship of the president had become so blatant that moderate politicians such as Saeb Salam and the Maronite, Raymond Eddé, both of whom had voted for him in 1970, were demanding his resignation.

The fourth round began at the end of August and for more

than a year there was scarcely a pause in the fighting. By September the battle lines had been drawn and the factions on each side were in the process of organizing military alliances. On the Maronite side, where the groups entered a coalition calling itself the Lebanese Front, the position was fairly straightforward. The dominant force was the Phalangist Party militia which at this stage possessed some 10,000 men, while Chamoun's Tigers and Frangieh's Zghorta Liberation Army totalled perhaps 5,000 militiamen between them. There were a number of smaller groups dispersed around the country including the sinister Guardians of the Cedars whose slogan was 'Not one Palestinian left in Lebanon'.

While the weapons supplies of their enemies were fairly straightforward and could usually be traced to Eastern Europe or the USSR, the Maronites collected arms from every corner of the world. Christian businessmen traversed the continents to raise money and buy armaments; expatriate priests beseeched their congregations to contribute to the cause. Although they too received arms from Warsaw Pact countries such as Bulgaria and Czechoslavakia,[5] the Maronites are also reported to have received supplies from the Mafia, the CIA and some conservative Arab states. Their supplies were generally unloaded at night at the Aquamarina cove near Jounieh. By early 1976, according to one of their commanders, Dany Chamoun,[6] their largest supplier was Israel, which sent convoys of boats carrying Russian weapons captured from the Syrians and Egyptians in 1973 as well as American super-Sherman tanks.[7]

The military leadership of the Maronite alliance was in the hands of the Phalangist Party, but the political leadership was shared by Gemayel, Chamoun, Frangieh and the militant Superior of the Maronite Monastic Orders, Father Charbel Kassis. Of these four, the only one who made any attempt to co-operate with Karami was, somewhat ironically, Gemayel. Although responsible for much of the fighting, his political vision was often clearer than that of his Maronite colleagues. As the war dragged on, he became more amenable to the idea of a compromise and supported attempts by the Syrians and others to mediate. Alone of the Maronite forces, the Phalangists were prepared to work seriously with Karami on the Higher Co-ordination Committee. And their militia was the only one which did not try to wreck the mediation attempts by France and the Vatican.[8]

Within a short time of his appointment as Minister of the Interior, Chamoun had established himself as the most hawkish of the Maronite leaders. Like the president, he was meant to be a servant of the state and, like the president, he was more concerned with the fortunes of his own militia than with the affairs of government. During his tenure of office his principal aim seemed to be to sabotage the policy of a government of which he was one of the two key members. At every stage he refused any suggestion that might lead to a compromise with the other side. He denounced all offers of mediation and he managed to prevent Gemayel from opening negotiations with Jumblatt. In October 1975, when Karami was trying to convene parliament, he even refused to send security forces to defend the deputies. His attitude often infuriated Gemayel and led to considerable tension between the two men. Five years later the Phalangists moved against the much smaller Tigers militia and broke Chamoun's power. But in the years of the civil war, when the Lebanese Front was often on the defensive before the combined forces of the National Movement and the Palestinians, it was impossible to do so. Besides, Chamoun was still the pre-eminent and most charismatic leader on the Maronite side.

Compared to the Lebanese Front, the political and military organization of the National Movement was chaotic. The spokesman and arbiter of their coalition was Jumblatt but as he possessed little military strength himself he was not able to exercise much control over the different militias which made up the movement. In contrast with their Maronite opponents, the National Movement had no ideological cohesion. It was a rag-bag coalition of very different political parties held together by little more than their opposition to Maronite domination of Lebanon. The heterogeneity of the movement brought obvious political problems. As Jumblatt himself later complained, ' . . . we had to secure the agreement of thirteen different parties before we could take any decision of the slightest importance.'[9] As many of these parties were backed by rival Arab states and as some of them would have been fighting each other had the battleground been elsewhere in the Middle

East, the National Movement not surprisingly lacked the discipline of the Lebanese Front. As Jumblatt pointed out, ' . . . we always had to take into account so many tendencies, vagaries, the different Arab backers of the different groups . . . some of the main problems we faced were due to the rivalries, secret composition and, occasionally, outright antagonism between the parties that made up the alliance.'[10]

The principal party in the National Movement was Jumblatt's own Progressive Socialist Party which drew its strength not from the country's scattered number of socialists but from Jumblatt's Druze followers in the Chouf. But the most dynamic parties in the coalition were the two communist parties, both headed by Christians, and the PPS, now more generally known as the Syrian Social Nationalist Party. The movement also included five Nasserist organizations, three of them in Beirut, the Lebanese branches of the Syrian and Iraqi wings of the Ba'ath Party and the Shi'ite Movement of the Deprived.

The scale of Jumblatt's problems in keeping this coalition together can be imagined if one considers the position of the Lebanese branch of the Iraqi Ba'ath party, whose secretary-general was one of the deputies for Tripoli, Dr Abdel Majid Rafei. At that time, the Iraqi government was fighting its Kurdish population, imprisoning its communists and preventing the Shi'ites, who were a majority in the country, from participating in political life. It was also as usual on bad terms with the Syrians. But in Lebanon its representatives had to take part in a movement in which all these groups — Kurds, communists, Shi'ites and Syrian Ba'athists — were included.

The military organization of the National Movement barely existed since each group insisted on retaining its independence. A few of their militias made an effective contribution to the war, but most of them were small and poorly trained. Only the Mourabitoun, a group of about one thousand militiamen belonging to the Independent Nasserist Movement, was in the same class as the guerrillas of the PLO or the militias of the Lebanese Front. The most surprising military failure was Kamal Jumblatt's. He was prepared to talk about going to war but made few preparations to fight one: indeed it was nearly a year after the Ain el-Roumaneh incident before he organized some of his Druze followers into the 'Fakhreddin Army', but even this was not much of a force. If one looks back at a photograph of Jumblatt with his soldiers in 1976, one is likely to mistake it for a picture of Lawrence's irregulars setting off to fight the Turks in the First World War.

Without at least some of the Palestinian forces, the National Movement would not have been a match for the Maronites. The Palestinians, however, were divided and most of them did not want to fight. Arafat knew that it would be disastrous to become embroiled in Lebanon as he had in Jordan and throughout 1975 he kept his own Fatah group out of the fighting. But, as in Jordan, the radical Palestinian groups refused to listen to him. They argued that the Phalangists and their allies, backed by Israel and the United States, were determined to crush the Resistance and it was therefore the duty of the Palestinians to fight alongside the National Movement. The three groups which were prepared to fight from the beginning were Habash's PFLP, the Iraqi-backed Arab Liberation Front and the PFLP-General Command of Ahmed Jibril. Their involvement did great harm to the Palestinian cause because it provided ammunition for the Maronite thesis that the war was less a civil conflict than a contest between the Lebanese and the Palestinians. Besides, the political damage suffered by the PLO as a result was not offset by any great military advantage to the National Movement. Only Jibril's group won a significant victory when, in alliance with the Mourabitoun, it drove the Phalangists from most of west Beirut in the autumn of 1975.

The fighting had returned to the capital by the middle of September. Three weeks earlier there had been a clash between rival factions in the town of Zahle in the Bekaa valley and the violence had soon spread to the north where gunmen from Frangieh's town of Zghorta confronted Tripoli's Nasserist group, the October 24 Movement. Under pressure, Karami decided to use the army to separate the two sides and police a cease-fire. But this intervention made matters worse since the army allowed the Maronites to violate the cease-fire with impunity while it dealt severely with infractions by the men from Tripoli. In one incident on the coast regular troops engaged the Nasserists in a gun-battle and killed thirteen of them.

On September 17 the Phalangists decided to escalate the crisis. They brought their artillery into the centre of Beirut, positioned their guns on the east side of the central square and started to lob shells into the souqs to the west. After four days of bombardment the one traditional quarter of Beirut was in ruins. Even the Damascus fire brigade was unable to help because the Phalangist gunmen prevented anyone from getting near their targets.

The destruction of the souqs was clearly intended as a warning that the Phalangists were prepared to do almost anything rather than accept Jumblatt's demands. It was a typical show of Maronite defiance and also a bad miscalculation because it brought about the Phalangists' first major defeat. The two most effective militias then supporting the National Movement decided to counter-attack in west Beirut, an area where the Phalangists had always been politically weak. In two phases, at the end of October and again in December, the Nasserists' Mourabitoun and the PFLP-General Command attacked the Phalangists and overran their positions in Kantari and in most of the smart hotel district. Forced back from most of west Beirut, the leading Maronite militia barely succeeded in holding its own headquarters in Sioufi.

By the end of 1975 neither side held a decisive military advantage but it was clear that the Maronites had done much less well than they had expected. Although in theory their military strength exceeded that of the National Movement, their forces were for the most part on the defensive. Moreover, they had been unable to win even though Arafat had stayed out of the war and sent the bulk of his Fatah forces to positions in the south near the Israeli border. Only in their own heartland of Mount Lebanon had the Maronites been able to achieve significant success. Apart from their setbacks in Beirut they had suffered reverses in the Bekaa valley where some of their villages had been captured or were under siege. South of Beirut, Camille Chamoun's Tiger militia were under pressure from forces belonging to the National Movement and the Rejection Front around the town of Damour, while in the north Tony Frangieh's troops from Zghorta had failed to make much impression on the Nasserists in Tripoli.

From December onwards the Lebanese Front decided to concentrate on consolidating its hold on the region stretching north of the Beirut–Damascus road. In this area, which formed a rectangle with Zghorta and the Cedars in the north and east Beirut and Zahle in the south, the Maronites' opponents were to be defeated and then expelled. Accordingly, in early January the Phalangists and their allies went on to the offensive in east Beirut and surrounded the Palestinian refugee camps of Tal Zaatar and Jisr al-Pasha. Although warned by Arafat that he would bring Fatah into the war to save the camps, the Maronites paid no attention and provoked the PLO further by attacking a third camp, Dbayyeh, which they captured on 14 January. The Phalangists followed up this success with an assault on the slum areas of Qarantina, Maslakh and Naba'a. On 18 January they overan Qarantina and Maslakh, shot or deported their inhabitants — a mixture of Kurds, Palestinians and Lebanese Muslims — and brought in bulldozers to flatten the houses and tenement buildings. Qarantina was the worst atrocity of the war so far, more brutal even than the Black Saturday massacre the previous month when the Phalangists murdered 300 Muslim civilians in a single day as a reprisal for the killing of 4 of their own men by unknown assasins.

The blockade of the Palestinian camps in east Beirut finally brought the main PLO forces into the conflict, a development which, as the Maronites should have foreseen, radically altered the balance of power. In order to relieve pressure on the large camp at Tal Zaatar, the Palestinians sent reinforcements to help the National Movement's offensive against the Maronite coastal districts south of Beirut. This was part of Chamoun's 'fief' and its defence was entrusted to the Tigers and directed by the Minister of the Interior himself. Although Chamoun managed to persuade the chief of staff to send in the Lebanese air-force to bomb the PLO supply lines, his militiamen were unable to hold out for long. On 20 January Damour fell and, in retaliation for the massacres at Qarantina and Maslakh, many of its inhabitants were killed — although Chamoun himself was rescued by an army helicopter. Two days later the Tigers surrendered in Chamoun's home village of Saadiyat and the former president's house was blown up by the guerrillas. With the capture of Damour, the Lebanese Front lost its major remaining slice of territory outside the Maronite mountain.

The character of the civil war had changed during the autumn of 1975 and by January of the following year it had assumed a clearer sectarian nature. In the early rounds there had been some bitter fighting but it had not led to an exodus of population. Towards the end of 1975 this changed and Lebanese living in a region under the military control of their opponents were often forced to leave. In the predominantly Sunni region of Akkar north of Tripoli, Christian villagers were leaving their homes and taking refuge in the Mountain, while in the Maronite rectangle the Muslim villages were being cleared and their inhabitants forced out. In the capital, people were beginning to move either side of the battle lines which divided the city into a predominantly Christian sector to the east and a largely Muslim sector to the west. Nevertheless, while very few Lebanese Muslims or Palestinians remained in east Beirut or indeed in any area under the control of the Lebanese Front, a large number of Christians continued living in areas dominated by the PLO or the National Movement. The Maronites' increasing intolerance of other communities living in the areas under their control was a clear warning that they were contemplating partition of the country.

In September 1975, during one of his many visits to Lebanon, the Syrian foreign minister, Abdul Halim Khaddam, had managed to persuade the Maronite Patriarch to announce that he was opposed to partition. But the military defeats over the following months made many Maronites think that partition of the country and the setting-up of a Maronite state perhaps would be the best hope of preserving their identity. By January 1976 the Lebanese Front had reduced its early ambitions and abandoned the aim of suppressing the Palestinian Resistance. But it remained adamant that it would not compromise. If the Maronites were unable to rule over the entire country, at least they would preside over Mount Lebanon. It was this threat of partition which led the Syrians to step up their mediation efforts.

9

The Syrian Intervention

All through 1975 the Syrian government watched the turmoil in Lebanon with growing apprehension. Three times that summer President Assad had sent his foreign minister, Abdul Halim Khaddam, to mediate in Beirut. Each time Khaddam had come away with some success. In May he had persuaded Frangieh to drop the military government and ask Karami to form a civilian one. At the end of June he had managed to reconcile Karami and Camille Chamoun so that they could sit in the same cabinet. And in September he had gone again to Lebanon with the Chief of Staff, General Shihabi, where he had obtained a cease-fire and encouraged the formation of a Committee for National Dialogue. These achievements, however, proved to be ephemeral and they merely managed to delay rather than halt the development of full-scale civil war. By January 1976, Khaddam was back in Lebanon to prevent what Syria regarded as the worst possible outcome — the division of the country — and he warned that any 'move towards partition would mean our immediate intervention'.[1]

After the capture of Damour there seemed only two possible military outcomes to the conflict: a limited defeat for the Maronites which would allow them to set up a separate state in their rectangle, or a victory for the forces of the National Movement and the PLO in the whole of the country. From the Syrian point of view either result would be disastrous. A total victory for Jumblatt and the Palestinians would be unacceptable to Israel and the United States and would certainly lead to an Israel invasion. The partition of Lebanon would mean a tiny Maronite state that would be a natural ally of Israel, with which the Maronites shared pathologically anti-Arab and pro-Western feelings, and a radical Arab nationalist state dominated by the PLO and the National

Movement. Once again such an outcome would be bound to provoke an Israeli invasion and the possible annexation of southern Lebanon.

Both of these results would have also caused major problems for Syria. In the summer of 1975 President Assad had claimed that 'it is difficult to draw a line between Lebanon's security in its broadest sense and Syria's security'[2] and he was right. An Israeli military presence in southern Lebanon would have dislocated Syria's defences on the Golan front and enabled the Israeli army to outflank the Syrians through the Arqoub and the foothills of Mount Hermon. Assad feared that a victory for Jumblatt and the PLO would end in a war between Syria and Israel. After the second Sinai disengagement agreement between Israel and Egypt in September 1975, the Syrian government was feeling particularly vulnerable and insecure. Assad was in no mood to contemplate a contest with Israel and was prepared to go to great lengths to avoid one.

But Syria's opposition to the dismemberment of Lebanon was not merely a matter of pragmatism. It was also a matter of sentiment. Assad exaggerated when he claimed that 'throughout history, Syria and Lebanon have been one country and one people'[3] but there were many people in both who regarded the division between them as unnatural. In spite of different political and economic systems, the two countries had close ties and neither kept an embassy in the other's capital. Moreover, both Syrians and Lebanese could travel freely to each other's countries. There were thousands of Syrian workers taking advantage of Lebanon's more prosperous economy while during the civil war perhaps one-quarter of a million Lebanese went to live in Syria. Reluctantly, the Syrians had come to accept that Lebanon would remain a separate state, but only on condition that it remained the state of the National Pact. Syria was not prepared to allow partition or to see the Israeli army in the south. As Khaddam remarked in January 1976, 'Lebanon was part of Syria before the French mandate. Syria will recover it the moment a serious partitioning attempt gets under way.'[4]

From the beginning of the civil war, Syria's sympathies had been with the National Movement and the Palestinians. Among the Arab countries it regarded itself as the strongest supporter of the Palestinian cause and it had been the only country which had given military help to the PLO in the Jordanian civil war in 1970. It also saw itself as the heart of the Arab nationalist movement with a long tradition of abortive attempts to further the cause of Arab unity. Between the Syrians and the Maronites there existed layers of mistrust that stretched back for centuries and had led the Maronites to look for European protection against a Syrian threat which was often imaginary. So it was logical that Syrian inclinations should have been towards the National Movement, at least when it seemed that Jumblatt and the Palestinians were on the defensive. And in the middle of January 1976 it was the Maronites who were unquestionably the aggressors. From the beginning of the New Year they had launched a series of assaults on the Palestinian and Muslim enclaves in east Beirut with the apparent aim of creating a *de facto* partition of the country. It was as a warning to the Maronites that on 19 January Assad sent into Lebanon troops of the Palestine Liberation Army, a regular force based in Syria with Syrian officers. Two days later the Syrian foreign minister was sent to Beirut to arrange yet another cease-fire.

On this occasion, Khaddam had come to Lebanon not simply to organize a cease-fire or reconcile a couple of old za'ims. He had come to explain a programme of reforms which the Syrians hoped would be acceptable to both sides. Shortly afterwards, President Frangieh visited Damascus, where he was persuaded to agree to the reforms, and on 14 February he announced them in Beirut. This programme, henceforth known as the Constitutional Document, required the Lebanese Front to make a number of minor concessions while it asked the National Movement to content itself with a series of very limited reforms. There were to be three main changes: the Christians would lose their 6:5 advantage in parliamentary representation and the seats would be distributed on a 50:50 basis; the Sunni prime minister would no longer be chosen by the Maronite president but would be elected by parliament; and civil service posts would be awarded on merit and not according to confession, although the confessional principle would still be observed at the higher levels. Apart from these there was not much else the Maronites had to concede. There was a clause which stated that social justice for all should be ensured through financial, economic and social reform, but it looked more like a statement of good intentions than a serious proposal. Considering that many Maronites liked to pretend that they were not Arabs, for them the most galling part of the document was perhaps the opening sentence which declared that 'Lebanon is a sovereign, free, and independent Arab country'.[5]

Kamal Jumblatt complained that the Constitutional Document 'contained only a few timid reforms'[6] but even these were balanced by a reaffirmation of some traditional customs. The distribution of the three main offices of state, for example, was to stay the same and the most important of them, the presidency, would remain a Maronite preserve. The reform of the armed forces, which was demanded not only by Jumblatt but also by the Sunni leaders, was not discussed in the document although the clause affecting the distribution of civil service posts was probably meant to apply to the army as well. The only faction in the civil war to be mentioned was the Palestinians who were gently admonished and told that 'Lebanon . . . is not really the territory of the revolution'. They were also told that 'the situation today requires closer adherence to agreements and greater punctiliousness in their implementation, especially in the case of the Cairo Agreement.'[7]

The Constitutional Document was received with a marked lack of enthusiasm on both sides, particularly by the National Movement which was winning the war and thought it should be rewarded with more serious reforms. Jumblatt, who probably felt that his own ambitions had been thwarted by the stipulation that a Maronite would always be president, seemed unsure of how to react. During the next three weeks, while Khaddam tried to organize a government of national unity to carry out the programme, Jumblatt's behaviour was highly ambiguous. It now seems probable that he was waiting for Muslim officers in the Lebanese army to rebel and bring their garrisons over to his side. Once assured of their support he would then feel strong enough to reject the Syrian initiative and carry on the war.

The first mutiny had taken place at the end of January when a junior Sunni officer, Lieutenant Ahmed Khatib, and a small number of soldiers had revolted and set up their self-styled Arab Army of Lebanon in the Bekaa valley. But it was not until the beginning of March that the Lebanese army really began to disintegrate. Most units expelled their Christian officers and joined Khatib, others joined the Maronite forces and a few remained loyal to the army commander Hanna Said. In three days in the second week of March, 5 garrisons, including 2 of the most important ones in the south, mutinied and joined the Arab Army of Lebanon. The Syrian Chief of Staff was sent to Beirut to prevent a total break-up but he was too late. The one Lebanese institution that had stood in the way of total anarchy and a full-scale civil war had already dissolved.

The army split was caused by the Maronites' attempt to force the government to deploy it on their side. Neither of the two army commanders, or indeed Camille Chamoun who was the most active proponent of army intervention, seem to have realized that the Muslim officers would not participate in attacks on their own communities. General Ghanem was wholly sympathetic to the Lebanese Front and his open partisanship led the prime minister to accuse him of smuggling arms to the Maronite militias.[8] His successor, General Said, proved to be no more impartial and it was his decision to use the air force on the side of Chamoun's militia at Damour which finally provoked Khatib into rebellion.

The disintegration of the army effectively disposed of the Syrians' reform programme. Lieutenant Khatib, now the commander of a serious military force, dismissed the Constitutional Document because 'it does not provide a fundamental solution to the Lebanese crisis and the minor reforms it proposes are not commensurate with the sacrifice that has been made. In any case, the civil war is not over as neither side has achieved what it wanted.'[9] Khatib's first priority was to get rid of the president whom he regarded as one of the chief criminals in the drama. By now this view was widely held and two-thirds of the Lebanese deputies had already signed a petition calling for Frangieh's resignation. When he refused to go, Khatib ordered his troops to attack the presidential palace at Ba'abda. Although the men of the Arab Army of Lebanon found their way blocked by PLA troops loyal to Syria, they were able to train their artillery on the palace and on 25 March Frangieh, though still refusing to resign, left with his family.

The first person to see the possibilities of the new situation was Kamal Jumblatt. The Druze leader's equivocal behaviour at this stage is still somewhat mysterious. In his memoirs he claimed that he tried to prevent the rebellion through negotiations with Khatib's father and his cousin, Zaher Khatib, who was one of Jumblatt's own deputies in the PSP. But the claim is not convincing since he did nothing publicly to discourage the rebellion during February and he was the first to take advantage of it once it had got truly under way in March. In addition, his puzzling attitude towards Khaddam's attempts to put together a cabinet of national unity needs some explanation. If he had come out unequivocally in favour of the Constitutional Document and agreed to co-operate in the formation of the new government, the cease-fire would probably not have collapsed at the beginning of March nor would the army have disintegrated. The fact that his attitude remained so ambiguous during those crucial three weeks does seem to indicate that he had no intention of accepting the Syrians' reforms but was merely waiting for the garrisons to mutiny before going all out for a military victory.

Kamal Jumblatt was the most enigmatic of politicians and it was often difficult to know when he was bluffing and when he was being serious. As the fighting intensified during March he was talking about a 'total and irreversible' military campaign that would lead to 'full military victory' and 'total revolution'.[10] Yet at the same time he was doing little to organize the military campaign and he was perfectly happy to leave the bulk of the fighting to the PLO and the Arab Army of Lebanon. It is reasonably certain, however, that at some moment at the beginning of 1976 Jumblatt decided that it was futile to go on seeking a compromise with the old Lebanon of the National Pact. Once he had realized that the Maronite militias could be defeated, he decided that there was no point in hanging onto the outdated system which had preserved the Maronite ascendancy. It was time for a decisive break. The spring of 1976, he later declared, was the propitious moment for a genuine democratic revolution. It was a 'rendezvous with history' that could not be missed. 'We could not let slip by this historic opportunity finally to transform these confessional and outdated institutions into truly secular and democratic ones'.[11]

When the cease-fire, which had held through February, broke down at the beginning of March, the Syrian government became desperate. Khaddam was sent yet again to try to form a government of national reconciliation but he, like the Syrian Chief of Staff who followed two days later in an attempt to stop the army falling apart, was unsuccessful. So disastrous did the situation seem that President Assad even cancelled an official visit he was on the point of making to France. The Syrians' anxieties were understandable. From the beginning of the conflict they had tried through diplomatic means to bring about a compromise settlement which would satisfy the minimum demands of the National Movement without requiring the Lebanese Front to accept greater concessions than it was prepared to make. They had wished to reform Lebanon but retain the essence of the old system, and they were puzzled and irritated that such a reasonable solution should be unwelcome to both sides. The Syrian position had all along been impartial towards competing Lebanese interests and the Damascus government had not allowed its Arab nationalist leanings to influence its behaviour. In January 1976, when the Maronites launched their offensive in east Beirut, Syria had regarded them as the aggressors and allowed units from the Palestine Liberation Army to enter Lebanon. Two months later, after the failure of the reform programme, Syria blamed Jumblatt for the breakdown and began to increase its pressure on the Druze leader.

Jumblatt, however, had no intention of succumbing to the Syrians. Three times in the second fortnight of March he was invited to Damascus and on each occasion he went out of his way to antagonize the Syrian government. The first time he simply refused to go, declaring bluntly that 'the Syrians should pull out. Their role is finished. The question of government is now purely Lebanese.'[12] The second time he was equally arrogant, informing the Syrians he was unable to travel to Damascus because he was 'too busy directing the battle.'[13] On the third occasion he actually did go to see Assad, but then behaved more offensively than ever. When he learnt that the Syrians had planned a meeting between him and a Phalangist leader, Karim Pakradouni, he left Damascus and hurriedly returned home. On arrival, he issued a statement thanking Assad for lunch and adding that he hoped to invite the

Syrian leaders to a return meal in Bikfaya, the home of the Gemayel family.[14]

As summer approached the Syrians were becoming increasingly impatient with Jumblatt and a show-down between Assad and the Druze leader seemed inevitable. But in the meantime the Damascus government had other problems to deal with. The principal one was the position of the president, Suleiman Frangieh. For many months Frangieh had been behaving more like a Maronite za'im than a president and his resignation was now demanded by most of the non-Maronite population. On 11 March Brigadier Aziz Ahdab mounted a somewhat farcical coup — which soon fizzled out — in an attempt to force Frangieh to resign. A couple of days later the parliamentary deputies signed their petition calling for the president's resignation and shortly afterwards even Frangieh's elder brother suggested he should resign in the interests of the country. The following week the guns of the Arab Army of Lebanon finally forced Frangieh to leave his palace in Ba'abda.

The Syrians had by this time realized that Frangieh's resignation was a prerequisite for a restoration of national unity but they wanted to arrange it in an orderly and constitutional manner. They also wanted to ensure that he was succeeded by someone more amenable and chose as their nominee Elias Sarkis, the man Frangieh had defeated by one vote in the previous election. In early April, Parliament passed a constitutional amendment permitting the deputies to choose the next president six months before the incumbent's term was due to end in September. The election was scheduled to take place on 1 May though it was postponed for a week after Jumblatt accused the Syrians of trying to impose their candidate on the deputies. But it made no difference to the result. Jumblatt's deputies boycotted parliament because they knew there was no chance of electing their choice, the liberal, anti-Syrian leader, Raymond Eddé — one of the few heroes of the war, a Maronite za'im who took no part in the fighting and spent his time working for the release of victims of kidnapping. Sarkis was thus duly chosen though his election did little to improve the situation as Frangieh stubbornly insisted on staying in power until the end of his term. The National Movement, which the day before the elections had called for a general strike, reacted to the result by stepping up hostilities on all fronts.

The fighting had continued since the beginning of March except for a short lull in the middle of April. Most of it had gone against the Maronites. The Mourabitoun and the Palestinians had cleared the Phalangists from their last positions in west Beirut and captured the huge pockmarked block of the Holiday Inn which they had been fighting over for months. In the mountains the PLO, with the help of the National Movement and Khatib's forces, struck north of the Beirut — Damascus highway into the Dhour Shuwair area. As they advanced into the Maronite heartland, they threatened the skiing resort of Faraya and Gemayel's home town Bikfaya. The Maronites became desperate: the Phalangist leader called all able-bodied men and women to join the militias while Chamoun, who had been opposed to the Syrians all his life, now pleaded for their intervention. 'Co-operation with fraternal Syria is necessary at all times' he declared, 'and especially in the present circumstances.'[15]

On the other side, Jumblatt and other National Movement leaders such as Ibrahim Qleilat of the Nasserist Movement saw that victory was in sight and did not stop to think that they might be thwarted by the Syrians. Arafat was more cautious and did what he could to restrain Jumblatt and persuade him to be more conciliatory towards Damascus. But the Palestinian leader failed to divert Jumblatt from his 'rendezvous with history'. Arafat had the strongest military force in Lebanon at that time but his political power was much weaker. A cautious and moderate man by nature, he had allowed himself to be dragged along by Jumblatt and the Palestinian rejectionists so that he had by now lost that independence which he had earlier preserved for his movement. Against his better judgement he followed Jumblatt down the path of confrontation with the Syrians. As Saeb Salam, one of the wisest of the old Sunni za'ims, said later, 'the gravest mistake our Palestinian brothers made was that they allowed Jumblatt to appear as if he were their spokesman . . . while in fact, Jumblatt's objectives were quite different from those of the Palestinian Resistance.'[16]

Arafat understood the Syrian position far better than Jumblatt and knew that Assad was blaming the continuation of the war on the intransigence of the Palestinian-National Movement alliance. Arafat seemed to have some sympathy with the Syrian desire to avoid a new conflict with Israel but Jumblatt merely dismissed Syria's perfectly valid fears as 'quite absurd'.[17] The Druze leader had become obsessed by the idea of a 'military solution' and refused to be deflected from it. When he finally did go to Damascus after his third invitation on 27 March he told an unsympathetic Assad that the Maronites had to be defeated. According to his own account, he told the Syrian president that 'the racist fascism of the Phalangists, of Chamoun and company, first had to be broken militarily if one was later to deal with it politically and, eventually, heal it psychologically.'[18] Assad evidently found Jumblatt's attitude incomprehensible. During a major speech in July the Syrian president gave his version of the meeting:

> [Jumblatt] said: 'Let us discipline [the Maronites]. We must have decisive military action. They have been governing us for 140 years and we want to get rid of them.' At this point, I realized that all the masks had fallen. Therefore, the matter is not as we used to describe it. It is not as we were told. The matter is not between the Right and Left or between progressives and reactionaries. It is not between Muslim and Christian. The matter is one of vengeance. It is a matter of revenge which goes back 140 years.[19]

Allowing for some exaggeration as well as Assad's need to convince a sceptical Syrian people that he had done the right thing, the description sounds plausible. Jumblatt had suddenly become entranced by the prospect of a revolution which he had never actively pursued in the past. The one politician who really understood what was wrong with Lebanon had merely ended up as intransigent and irresponsible as his enemies. His aggressive and myopic attitude towards the Syrians now led to a crippling defeat, political as well as military, for himself and his Palestinian allies.

The Syrian military intervention began on 1 June and within a few days there were 12,000 Syrian troops in the country advancing along two fronts towards Beirut and Sidon. By 7 June they had taken the village of Sofar in the mountains on the Beirut–Damascus road and had reached the suburbs of Sidon in the south. Probably they did not anticipate a tough battle since they expected the support of the Palestine Liberation Army and the pro-Syrian groups inside the PLO. But many of Syria's supporters in Saiqa and the PLA went over to Arafat and the rest were quickly neutralized by Fatah's forces. When the second column reached Sidon it walked into a PLO ambush and lost six of its tanks. A subsequent assault was also unsuccessful.

Assad's reluctance to accept high casualties by pressing on and quickly finishing off the battle was diplomatically disastrous. Within a few days Syria had lost most of its friends and had gained nothing but the dubious award of American approval. The Soviet Union, Syria's protector and arms supplier, was embarrassed and its news agency TASS called for a cease-fire and an end to foreign intervention.[20] Later, Brezhnev was to write to Assad telling him to withdraw his troops.[21] But the reaction in the Arab world was much stronger. The sight of Syria, of all countries, trying to eliminate the PLO, brought almost unanimous criticism from the other states. On 6 June, the day before the Sidon battle, the Arab foreign ministers meeting in Cairo called for the removal of the Syrian troops and their substitution by a mixed Arab force. While Egypt and Saudi Arabia lambasted Damascus through the press, Iraq denounced 'the fascist ruling clique in Damascus for this hideous crime against the Arab people of Palestine' and sent troops to the Syrian border 'to execute their historic duty.'[22] Even in his own country there was much hostility to Assad's sudden alliance with the Maronites. In the eyes of the largely Sunni Syrians, Pierre Gemayel was a villain on a similar level to the CIA and the Israeli prime minister Yitzhak Rabin.

Had Assad pushed on regardless he could no doubt have occupied Beirut and Sidon within a matter of days. But he hesitated and the international outcry increased. Realizing that he had lost his chance of quickly finishing the fighting, he withdrew his troops to positions overlooking the coast and accepted the cease-fire. Soon afterwards, Sudanese and Libyan units of the Arab peace-keeping force

began to arrive and for a while it appeared that the Syrian intervention had ended in humiliation. But the opposing leaders refused
to be diverted by the presence of the Arab forces and the civil war
quickly started up again. The Maronites, profiting from the respite
given them by the battle between the Syrians and the Palestinians,
began an offensive to capture the refugee camps of Tal Zaatar and
Jisr al-Pasha which had been blockaded at the beginning of the
year. On 22 June, a Maronite force, consisting mainly of Chamoun's
Tiger militia backed up by the Phalangists and soldiers who had
defected to the Maronites, attacked the camps and in a few days
overran Jisr al-Pasha. It then began the slow, horrifying, destruction
of Tal Zaatar.

Syria's political role in Lebanon was at this stage highly uncer-
tain but the presence of Syrian troops had a strong influence on
the course of the fighting. It was their pressure on the PLO which
forced the Palestinians to divert their guerrillas away from the
traditional fronts and so enabled the Maronites to capture territory in the north near Tripoli. And it was their blockades, both at
sea and on land, which interrupted the flow of fuel and weapons
to the commando organizations. The most dramatic result of the
Syrian intervention was the fall of Tal Zaatar, the home of 30,000
people, most of them Palestinians, the rest Shi'ite refugees from
southern Lebanon. Living conditions in the camp had always been
terrible: most of the dwellings had no running water, many of
them were without heating or lavatories; six or seven people would
often be found living in the same room. But in the heat and
humidity of that August things were worse than ever. The blockade
had prevented the passage of either food or medical supplies and
now the daily bombardments added to the misery of the refugees.
There was little water in the camp and what there was in the wells
was polluted. By the beginning of August hundreds of people had
died and most of the survivors had dysentery. The Red Cross
managed to get some of the wounded out and others were able to
leave by crossing the lines at night and giving themselves up to the
Phalangists. But most of the camp's inhabitants remained and
waited for the end. It came on 12 August when the Tigers and
Phalangists stormed in after a siege of fifty-three days. Over a
thousand people were killed in the final assault; even more were

lined up and shot immediately afterwards. Chamoun's men killed anyone they could find — doctors, nurses, children and religious leaders. They charged around the camp, kicking in doors and murdering screaming families. While some brought in steam shovels to scoop up the dead, others, assisted by hundreds of Christian civilians, looted the camp, tearing clothes and jewelry from the mutilated bodies. Very few children came out alive of Tal Zaatar.

Syria's military role was not limited to tying down the PLO in order to make the Maronites' task easier. At the end of July, Syrian troops moved against the forces of the PLO–National Movement alliance which were occupying former Maronite territory in the mountains at Dhour Shuwair. In the following month the Phalangists attacked from a different direction but it was not until the end of September that the Syrians stepped up their pressure and finally forced their opponents back towards the Beirut–Damascus road. The Syrian government clearly expected that this setback would force the PLO to concede defeat and they insisted that the Palestinians should break off their alliance with Jumblatt and return to their remaining refugee camps. When they refused, a strong Syrian force from Sofar began to drive over the mountains towards Beirut. On 13 October it engaged the PLO at the village of Bhamdoun which it captured after considerable casualties on both sides. It was at this stage, with the prospect of a long and costly battle between the Syrians and the Palestinians carrying on all the way to Beirut, that Saudi Arabia decided that the war had to end. On 15 October it called for a summit to be held in Riyadh the following day and Assad, believing that Jumblatt and Arafat had been all but defeated, agreed to attend.

By October, Assad was in a much stronger position that he had been in June. The peace-keeping attempt by the Arab ministers had faded away and the countries that mattered — Saudi Arabia, Egypt and Kuwait — were now prepared to accept that a settlement of the Lebanese conflict would be in the hands of Syria. Not that the Syrian role was even mentioned in the resolutions adopted by the Riyadh conference or by the Arab summit meeting in Cairo a week later. But that hardly mattered. There was a tacit understanding among the Arab leaders that the Syrian position had to be accepted and that the 30,000 soldiers of the peace-keeping force called for in the resolutions would in fact be the Syrian army then in Lebanon with a smattering of troops from other countries for cosmetic effect. Of the twenty-one members of the Arab League, only Iraq and Libya failed to join the consensus. The others agreed among themselves that Lebanon would be resurrected under the hand of the new president, Elias Sarkis, and its development guided by Assad. For their part, the Palestinians were made to agree 'to implement the Cairo Agreement . . . in both letter and spirit' and to affirm 'respect for Lebanon's sovereignty and well-being'.[23] Three weeks after the Cairo summit, the Syrian troops, now officially a part of the Arab League force, entered Beirut and the war was declared over.

President Assad had narrowly turned a potential disaster into a triumph. The intervention had been unpopular and costly, and it had been made even more expensive by Saudi Arabia's decision to cut off its US$700 million subsidy. But, in the end, nineteen Arab countries accepted the Syrian role and the Saudi aid was restored. Assad's prestige in the Arab world had increased and the position of his government at home had also improved.

As for Lebanon, Assad was later to claim that Syria's action 'was able to save lives, prevent partition, stop the exodus of Lebanese and Palestinians from Lebanon, and repatriate hundreds of thousands of refugees to Lebanon.'[24] In spite of the human cost, it had been a political success. It had blocked the partition of the country and it had prevented an Israeli invasion of the south. But this was essentially a negative success. Syria had prevented things from getting much worse but it did not appear to have much to offer as to how to make them better. The Syrian leadership had been able to demonstrate what it did *not* want, it was to be less successful in demonstrating what it did.

10

Fragmentation

A year and a half of desperate fighting had left little in the country undamaged. Only the banking system functioned as it had done before, piling up large profits, while the Lebanese pound remained astonishingly stable in a crisis that would have sunk most currencies. Public services — hospitals, roads, schools, the electricity network — had been wrecked throughout the country. Industries and agricultural equipment had been destroyed and damage to the country was estimated at US$2.5 billion. The official casualty figure was given as 30,000 dead[1] but this was probably an understatement and it is possible that 50,000 people were killed and twice that number wounded during the war. More than 600,000 people had abandoned their homes to move to areas where their co-religionists were in control. In Ras Beirut there were thousands of poor Muslims driven from the Maronite areas now squatting in the apartments of middle-class Lebanese who were watching the war from London or Paris.

Elias Sarkis had become president in September 1976 and had promised to maintain 'Lebanon's sovereignty and its territorial and national integrity'.[2] But it was not until the entry of the Syrian army — now forming part of the Arab Deterrent Force (ADF) — into Beirut that he was able to set about rebuilding the country. The problems that faced him were formidable but, during the early months of his presidency, they did not seem incapable of solution. Although he had no army, security was maintained and improved by the ADF. In July 1977, Syria, the government and the PLO signed the Chtaura Agreement designed to regulate the Palestinian armed presence in Lebanon. During the early months of the 'peace', the ADF managed to collect at least some of the heavy weapons belonging to both sides and the militias reduced their presence on the streets.

In January 1977, Sarkis set up the Board of Reconstruction and Development but already by that date there were signs of a revival of economic activity. The airport and the port of Beirut were open once more; so were the gambling rooms of the Casino du Liban and the race course. Banks and businesses began to re-open in the capital and industrial production soon reached a third of its pre-war level. Typically, the most prosperous sector of the post-war economy was real estate. Huge sums were spent on speculation and urban property values doubled during 1977.[3] There was little actual construction, however, to accompany this speculation, and the money, which could have been used to repair factories, was in effect wasted. The new Lebanon seemed intent on repeating the mistakes of the old. In 1978, the Arabian Contracting Company completed 'Summerland' on the southern edge of Beirut at a cost of US$17 million. Summerland was a huge beach complex — apparently the largest and most sumptuous in the Mediterranean — with saunas, night clubs, tennis courts and four swimming pools. It was built next-door to another beach where several thousand destitute refugees were camping miserably in huts.

In spite of the limited economic recovery in 1977, real improvement could not take place without political reconciliation. Salim Hoss, the new prime minister, admitted that vital questions such as the reconstruction of the army and the resettlement of refugees could not be settled without political entente.[4] But there was little sign of the establishment getting down to sort out its differences. After everything which the country had been through it would have been a mockery to try to put together yet another government of elderly za'ims. So the new cabinet consisted of technocrats less interested in political manoeuvring but also lacking the za'ims' strength in the country. Their achievement was bound to be limited without a reconcilation between the quarrelling politicians.

The ADF's success in improving security did not last long. From the spring of 1977 violence began to increase again: kidnappings, bomb explosions, gun-fights between rival militiamen. The worst incident took place in March, when Kamal Jumblatt was assassinated on the way to his home in the Chouf — an event that led to the massacre of a large number of Christian villagers by Jumblatt's Druze followers. The assassins were never found but few people doubted that Jumblatt had been murdered by the Syrians. It was a stupid and pointless crime because Jumblatt's power had already been broken by the Syrian army. He would no doubt have remained a critic of Syrian policy in Lebanon, but his opposition would have been largely vocal. Besides, he still had a useful role to play in politics since he was the only man of authority in the National Movement. Without him that uneasy coalition of Ba'athists, communists and Nasserists became leaderless and disorganized.

Syria had intervened in Lebanon primarily to prevent the partition of the country. But in 1977 partition seemed to be going ahead regardless of the Syrian presence. The ADF did not patrol the Maronite mountains, and control of that rectangle defended by the Christian militias during the war was largely in the hands of the Phalangist Party. Pierre Gemayel was still in favour of the reunification of Lebanon but his younger son Bachir, commander of the Maronite forces and probably by now the most powerful man in the Lebanese Front, seemed determined to set up an autonomous state. A year earlier, L. Dean Brown, an American diplomat sent to Lebanon as the special envoy of President Ford, had spoken to Maronite leaders who were toying with the idea of partition and 'confederation with Israel'.[5] By the spring of 1977 plans seemed well advanced. The Phalangists had organized their own police force and were levying their own taxes. In the north of their rectangle they were building a new airfield to be known as 'Pierre Gemayel International Airport'. The Maronites were careful not provoke Syria by proclaiming independence, but many of them clearly regarded themselves as already belonging to a separate state.

The leaders of the Lebanese Front accompanied these moves by stepping up their criticism of the Palestinian refugees, whom they wished to send to other Arab countries, and of the Syrian army, which, they believed, had outlived its usefulness in Lebanon. Maronite self-confidence, which had been badly bruised by the defeats in the first half of 1976, had been restored by the friendship with Israel, which now emerged as the foremost ally of the

Lebanese Front. The Israelis had been arming the Maronites for some time — according to Dany Chamoun, commander of the NLP forces, 'since early 1976, when we could not get arms from anywhere else'.[6] By the end of the fighting in October 1976, Israeli aid to the Maronites was estimated by Israeli sources to total US$100 million.[7] In the south of the country the Israelis had also been supplying arms and protection to a handful of Maronite villages near the border where they were training a small, largely Maronite, force under the command of a rebel Lebanese officer, Major Saad Haddad. This force, which was intended to fight Palestinian and National Movement units in the south of the country, was reinforced by Maronite militiamen from the north who were taken by boat to Israel and then transferred across the border.

The new militancy of the Maronite politicians, who only a year earlier had been begging the Syrians to rescue them, was encouraged by the Israelis. So was partition, which the Israelis had long seen as an effective means of securing a dependable ally in the region.[8] For their part, the Maronites felt they could afford to criticize Damascus without risk of a Syrian retaliation. The new allies worked hard to cement their friendship and Israeli instructors were regularly sent to Jounieh to show the militiamen how to use their new weapons.

In 1977 there was a general election in Israel and, for the first time in the state's history, the Labour Party was defeated and the right-wing Likud coalition came to power under Menachem Begin. The change-over brought with it a tougher Israeli approach to the Lebanese struggle. Since the establishment of the Zionist state in 1948, its leaders had spent much of their time discussing various ways of intervening in Lebanon. Israel's first prime minister, David Ben Gurion, was even planning to overthrow the Lebanese government in the first year of his country's existence. 'A Christian state ought to be set up there [in Lebanon]', he wrote in his diary, 'with its southern frontier on the Litani.'[9] As he made clear in a later extract from his diary, this development would allow Israel to extend its border as far north as the Litani river and so annex a large area of Lebanese territory inhabited mainly by Shi'ite Muslims.[10] According to Moshe Sharett, who was Israel's foreign minister during the early fifties, Ben Gurion, like his Chief of Staff,

Moshe Dayan, was obsessed by the idea of intervening in Lebanon.[11] Certainly, plans were drawn up for the exploitation of the Litani waters and their diversion to northern Israel.[12]

In spite of the energy spent by Ben Gurion and Dayan discussing plans for an invasion of Lebanon, Israel's military action did not begin until after the 1967 war. It started on a relatively small scale. There were the dramatic expeditions to Beirut, to blow up civilian aeroplanes at the international airport (1968) or to murder Palestinian leaders (1973). There were the bombing raids on Lebanese villages and Palestinian refugee camps; there were the land and sea expeditions to harass the local population, abduct its leaders and destroy the infrastructure. Roads and bridges were dynamited, houses blown up and crops wrecked. As we have already seen, tens of thousands of Shi'ite villagers fled their homes as a result and went to settle in the 'belt of misery' around Beirut.

The policies of Israel's Labour governments after 1967 were not difficult to understand. The destruction of Lebanese property and the humiliation of the country's security forces were obvious attempts to persuade the Lebanese to deal with the PLO in the same way as King Hussein was to do in Jordan in 1970. Israel was bluntly telling the Lebanese that the cost of harbouring the guerrillas would become increasingly high. However, whereas Hussein could count on the loyalty of his well-organized army in a confrontation with the Palestinians, the Lebanese government, even had it wished to, knew that it could not use its weak and divided army in an attempt to suppress the PLO. The Israelis therefore failed to provoke a war between the Lebanese and the guerrillas, but they did manage to make the Palestinian question the chief issue of Lebanese politics. They were thus largely responsible for dividing the country between those who supported the Palestinian presence in Lebanon and those who opposed it.

Having failed to 'Jordanize' the Lebanese situation, it was only logical that Israel should encourage the Maronite militias to attack the PLO by themselves. As we have seen, Israel had become their chief arms supplier by at least the beginning of 1976 and may well have been shipping them weapons even before then. The Maronites, however, proved incapable of the task allotted them and were only saved from a resounding defeat by the intervention of the Syrian army. Shortly after the ADF had driven into Beirut, Menachem Begin became prime minister in Israel.

Begin had made his name in Palestine in the 1940s as the leader of the Zionist terrorist group, the Irgun Zvai Leumi. The most spectacular act of terrorism against the British mandate — the blowing up of the King David Hotel with the loss of 91 lives — and the most spectacular butchery of Arab civilians — the massacre of 254 people at the village of Deir Yassin — were carried out on his orders. Over the next 35 years his attitude towards the Palestinians did not change. He did not accept the UN Partition Plan in 1947 and as prime minister he still insisted that the West Bank, the area intended by the United Nations to be the heart of the Palestinian Arab state, should become a part of Israel. The central aim of his government was to absorb the West Bank — which he insisted on calling Judaea and Samaria — by settling thousands of Jews on expropriated Arab land. This policy and the brutality which characterized Israel's occupation helped to radicalize the West Bank so that almost its entire population became supporters of the PLO. It was largely in order to destroy Palestinian nationalism in the West Bank and thus facilitate the eventual annexation of the area that Begin set out to destroy the PLO in its headquarters in Lebanon. He made his first attempt in 1978 and the second in 1982.

The pretext for Israel's first invasion was supplied by a group of Fatah guerrillas who on 11 March 1978 managed to land on the coast south of Haifa and seize an Israeli bus. They then drove south along the Tel Aviv highway firing from the windows and in the subsequent shoot-out with Israeli security forces most of the occupants of the bus were killed. By the time the fighting ended, 37 Israelis had died as well as 9 guerrillas. The following day, Begin held a press conference and promised retribution against an organization he claimed was similar to the Nazis[13] — a comparison he was fond of making on the eve of ordering an operation in which thousands of Arab civilians were likely to be killed. On 15 March, four days after the Palestinian raid, an Israeli force of 25,000 men crossed the Lebanese frontier. Accompanied by air strikes against the refugee camps and naval bombardments along the coastline, the Israeli army easily pushed backed the lightly-armed guerrillas of the PLO — estimated by the Israeli chief of staff at 2,000[14] — and seized a 'security-belt' about 6 miles deep along the border. Although at the beginning of the campaign they claimed that this 'corridor' was their objective, the Israeli columns continued to move northwards and within a few days they had captured all of Lebanon south of the Litani river, an area of some 425 square miles.

If the aim of the invasion was to inflict a heavy defeat on the PLO, it was a failure. The Palestinians lost a relatively small number of their fighters and were able to withdraw the rest with their equipment north of the Litani river. Those who suffered most — as always — from the Israeli incursion, were the Arab civilians, both Lebanese and Palestinian. According to estimates by Western correspondents, 2,000 civilians were killed during the various bombardments,[15] many of them by lethal American-made cluster bombs which Israel was using in contravention of an agreement with the United States restricting their use to defence purposes. There was also a huge number of new refugees, the United Nations calculating that the invasion had made one-quarter of a million people homeless.[16] Many of these were Shi'ites who had been made homeless twice already — once by Israeli raids in the early seventies which had forced them to move to Beirut, and again when the civil war in the capital had persuaded them that it was safer to return to their original homes.

The invasion probably had several objectives, not all of them well thought-out. Apart from avenging the victims of the bus-raid — though even by Israeli standards the killing of 2,000 Arabs for the loss of 37 Israeli lives, a ratio of 54:1, was excessive — Israel appears to have had two military aims: to defeat the guerrillas and to prevent them from launching further raids against Israel. Neither aim was achieved. The PLO was not defeated and Israel preferred to bomb the refugee camps rather than engage the bulk of the Palestinian forces around Tyre. Nor did the Israelis achieve much by setting up their 'security belt'. The guerrillas no longer made cross-border raids and in any case their Katyusha rockets could still reach Israeli settlements from emplacements north of the Litani. Moreover, they could still attack Israel by sea as the bus-raiders had done.

Perhaps a more important, though undeclared, aim was the

wrecking of attempts at reconciliation between Palestinians, Lebanese and Syrians. The destruction of so much Lebanese property and the looting of Shi'ite homes was clearly intentional. According to the United Nations, about a hundred Lebanese villages were attacked and this resulted in the complete demolition of 2,500 houses and the partial destruction of a further 5,200.[17] This wreckage, and the new wave of refugees it created, naturally undermined such post-war stability that Lebanon had achieved and eroded the prestige of the Syrian and Lebanese governments. It also destroyed much of the credibility of the 1977 Chtaura Agreement upon which the new Syrian–Lebanese–Palestinian consensus was supposed to be built.

The concessions this agreement had required from the PLO were substantial. The Palestinians agreed to give up their heavy weapons in Beirut, allowed ADF-Lebanese-PLO check points to be set up at the entrances to their refugee camps in the capital, and promised not to launch operations into Israel or even to station troops within 6 miles of the border. Once the PLO had pulled back, units from the reconstituted Lebanese army were supposed to take up position along the border and restore the government's authority. Such a plan, had it worked, would surely have led to the pacification of the south, which was the government's biggest single problem. That it did not work was due to Israel and its protégé Major Haddad. In September 1977, days before the Lebanese army units were scheduled to move into their new positions, Haddad's men, backed by Israeli artillery, attacked PLO forces nearby. The fighting that followed, in which Israeli soldiers had to enter Lebanon in order to rescue Haddad from defeat, prevented the Lebanese army from entering the battle zone and postponed the implementation of the Chtaura Agreement. The full-scale Israeli invasion a few months later effectively sabotaged the agreement altogether.

On 19 March 1978, the UN Security Council passed two resolutions on Lebanon. The first, resolution 425, called 'upon Israel immediately to cease its military action against Lebanese territorial integrity and withdraw forthwith its forces from all Lebanese territory'.[18] The second dealt with the setting up of a special UN force in southern Lebanon 'for the purpose of confirming the withdrawal of Israeli forces, restoring international peace and security and assisting the government of Lebanon in ensuring the return of its effective authority in the area'.[19] Within two weeks of the resolution, the UN secretary-general Dr Waldheim had gathered together a mixed force — contributed by Canada, France, Iran, Norway and Sweden — to be called the United Nations Interim Force in Lebanon (UNIFIL). By the end of April UNIFIL had been reinforced by contingents from Nepal, Nigeria and Senegal, and now totalled 4,000 men. In response to Israel's demands that the force should be increased still further, the UN Security Council agreed in May to raise another 2,000 men.

Israel, which seems to have been surprised by the UN's unambiguous demands for its evacuation, began to pull its troops back on 7 April and by the end of the month it had withdrawn from everywhere except the so-called 'security belt', which included the villages controlled by Haddad's Israeli-trained Maronites. There was then a six-week delay while Begin decided what to do with this area. The Security Council was unequivocal that 'all Lebanese territory' had to be evacuated and equally insistent that the authority of the Lebanese government should be restored, with the help of UNIFIL, throughout southern Lebanon. The Israelis realized, however, that if they complied with the UN's wishes they would lose Haddad who was proving to be a useful puppet for them. In the event, Begin preferred to antagonize the international community rather than give up Haddad and on 12 June, the day before Israel's final withdrawal, he handed over the final stretch of territory to Haddad's rebel troops. From then on this force, which with the influx of northern Maronites now totalled some 3,000 men, controlled the border country. It remained, as always, paid, armed and supplied by the Israelis.

Begin's decision naturally prevented UNIFIL from carrying out a major part of its mandate. The UN force had managed to bring about a full if delayed Israeli withdrawal and it was able to control an area between Haddad's men and the PLO guerrillas which prevented serious clashes between the two forces. But it was unable to achieve more than this and assist the Lebanese government to extend its authority to the south, because Haddad's Israeli protectors refused to allow the Lebanese army to come within several miles of the border. A year after the Israeli invasion the Lebanese government tried again to send a unit to the south to co-operate with UNIFIL. Haddad responded to the challenge by shelling the UN forces and thus preventing the army unit from taking up its intended positions. He followed this up by grandly announcing that the area under his control should henceforth be known as 'Free Lebanon'.

Whatever chance of success Sarkis and the Syrians might have had in patching up Lebanon were dashed by Israel's invasion and its behaviour afterwards. The nation became a mosaic of warring factions that controlled most of the country and gave only token recognition to the government in Beirut. In the east of the capital and in the Maronite mountain, no attention was paid to the government, whose authority was further weakened when Camille Chamoun came out in support of Haddad's mutineers and recognized 'Free Lebanon'. Further north, in the Tripoli and Akkar regions, the Christian and Muslim politicians were on closer terms with the Syrians and inclined to be more co-operative with the government. But the difficulty of communicating with Beirut made them virtually independent. If Walid Jumblatt, who inherited his father's political jobs as president of the Progressive Socialist Party and spokesman for the National Movement, wished to meet his allies in Tripoli, he had to travel five sides of a hexagon, a day's journey, via Damascus and Homs. Before the war the trip took an hour and a half along the coast. South and east of Beirut the position was more complicated. In most of the area the Syrian army was in overall control, although it was interspersed with detachments of Palestinians and the National Movement militias. South of the Syrians, the PLO controlled a stretch of territory east of Zahrani and Tyre, and beyond were UNIFIL and the thwarted unit of the Lebanese army. Finally, just north of the Israeli border, lay the 120 square miles of 'Free Lebanon'.

The government had little control over any of these groups and, being unable to govern, it was reduced to a mere mediating role between the factions. Salim Hoss, the prime minister, had no illusions about the extent of his authority. He knew there were a dozen leaders in the country who had more power than he did. On one occasion he was attending a private lunch party in a village near Beirut when the telephone rang and he was summoned to an adjoining room. When he came back ten minutes later, one of the guests asked him whether anything was wrong. 'No, no', replied the prime minister. 'It was just some fellow who's had his car stolen and wants me to get it back.' The anecdote illustrates the nature of Hoss's problems. There was nothing more useful he was able to do, so he might as well help someone to look for his car.

In the spring of 1979 Lebanon was limping along in a manner described by an American embassy official as 'functional anarchy'. The banks were, as usual, doing business and the Lebanese pound remained stable. In the fashionable areas, smart restaurants were open and full, but public services were terrible. As was to be expected in Lebanon, private enterprise managed to survive successive disasters while the public sector collapsed completely. Garbage was not being collected, water and electricity services were not repaired and the law courts had practically ceased to function. In the region dominated by the Lebanese Front, administration and public services were usually in the hands of the Phalangist Party and were relatively efficient. In other areas, where the PLO or the National Movement were in control, the system of administration was much less effective. This was partly because of the incessant squabbling among different factions of the coalition and partly because they had long feared that the establishment of separate civil administrations would create a climate favourable to eventual partition.

The only positive development was the building of a national consensus in parliament. Under the leadership of the Shi'ite speaker, Kamal Asaad, more than half the deputies (who were still those elected to the 1972 parliament since it had not been possible to hold elections during the civil war) had joined the consensus. It was not a powerful group, largely because nobody with a militia, least of all the important Maronite za'ims, belonged to it. But in the conditions of 1978–79 it was remarkable that it should have existed at all. Its major achievement – a reform long overdue – was the passing of a Defence Law and the establishment of an Army Council in which all the communities were represented. The main provision of this law was to limit the powers of the Maronite commander to actual operations and allow matters of policy and promotion to be decided by the Army Council — an important move if the newly reconstituted army was to be impartial.

The refusal of the Maronite leaders to join the consensus was largely a consequence of Israeli aid and the Israeli invasion. Assured of Zionist help, the Phalangist Party and the National Liberals had stepped up their demands for the departure of 'foreign forces' (i.e. the Syrians and the Palestinians) from Lebanon. They had also become increasingly intolerant of those Christians who refused to share their stand. Camille Chamoun declared that there were now two categories of Christians in the Middle East: free Christians, like himself, and those who had 'submitted to the Muslim caliphs and who pay ransom in order to survive'.[20] Two Christian leaders who, according to Chamoun, were members of the second category and no longer 'belonged to the Lebanese race' were the Patriarchs of the Greek Catholic and Greek Orthodox churches. Another Christian who refused to go along with Chamoun and Gemayel and their pro-Israeli stance was the former president, Suleiman Frangieh, who had links with Syria that stretched back to the days of his exile there twenty years earlier. He now left the Lebanese Front, made up his long-standing quarrel with Rashid Karami in Tripoli, and aligned himself firmly with the Syrian position. The Phalangists' reaction to this 'apostasy' reflected their confidence in the Israeli alliance. Their military commander, Bachir Gemayel, ordered a strong detachment of Phalangist militia to attack Frangieh's mountain stronghold at Ehden where they killed his son, Tony Frangieh, together with his wife and baby daughter, as well as thirty-two of the clan's followers.

It would perhaps have been better for Lebanon if the Syrians had used the murder of the Frangiehs as a pretext to occupy the Maronite areas in the same way that they had occupied most of the rest of the country. Such a move would at least have curbed the Maronite arrogance that was doing so much to hinder the reconciliation of the Lebanese. Unfortunately the Syrians reacted in the worst possible way. Instead of taking over east Beirut they trained their artillery against it and over the following three months they succeeded in killing a large number of Christians in Ashrafiyeh. This move was presumably intended to discipline the

Maronites and bring them to heel. If so, it showed an astonishing ignorance of Maronite psychology. The bombardment merely strengthened their defiance and Camille Chamoun clearly relished his new role directing the resistance. He was much photographed striding through the rubble of Ashrafiyeh in his shirt sleeves promising to fight on 'until the last Syrian soldier leaves Lebanon'. The elderly, white-haired former president, who only two years earlier had asked 'fraternal Syria' to come to Lebanon's aid, now insisted that there would be peace between the Lebanese only after the departure of the Syrians: 'For God's sake, let them leave the country, for this will be the only means of keeping some feeling of friendship between the Lebanese and Syrian peoples. There will be peace in Lebanon if they withdraw, because all the troubles we have seen have been created by Syrian policy.'[21] Against all the evidence accumulated over more than three years of violence, Chamoun claimed that the ADF was not needed. He appealed to the government not to renew the force's mandate for a further six months and told the ministers they would be 'traitors to the nation' if they did.[22]

Chamoun might be regarded as the symbol of Maronite resistance to the Syrians but as he approached his eightieth birthday he was plainly losing influence. In Maronite Lebanon, power was being concentrated more and more in the hands of Bachir Gemayel, the short, strutting son of the founder of the *Phalanges*. Bachir's elder brother Amin represented the moderate wing of the party, which was prepared to open a dialogue not only with the more conservative Sunni politicians but with Walid Jumblatt as well. Bachir opposed his brother's attempts at reconciliation and, since he commanded the militia, he was able to carry the party with him. His aim was to make the Phalangist Party the strongest power in the country and to get himself elected president when Sarkis's term of office came to an end in 1982. National unity, he believed, would not be obtained by persuading all the different factions to start talking to each other. It could only be achieved if it was imposed by force — in other words by the Phalangist Party.

But before he could impose unity on the other Lebanese communities, Bachir had to establish the Phalangists' total domination over the Maronites. In 1978 he had moved against one old ally, former president Frangieh; in July 1980 he turned against the other, former president Chamoun. The second was a far bloodier operation designed to bring about the virtual extinction of the National Liberal Party. In Amin Gemayel's 'fief' in north Metn the Phalangists' subjugation of their one-time allies was carried out without bloodshed. But in other parts of the mountain and in east Beirut there was considerable slaughter. No member of Chamoun's family was killed, though his grand-daughter was wounded, but some 500 people, many of them civilians with few connections with the NLP, were shot by Bachir's rampaging militiamen. Chamoun, who had long lost his traditional base in the Chouf and knew he could not compete with the Phalangists in the Maronite Mountain, tried to persuade Gemayel to accept some compromise, but the Phalangist commander refused. Bachir knew what he wanted and he insisted on having it. Chamoun and his family could remain as objects of veneration for the Maronite faithful but from then on political power would be with Bachir Gemayel.

The Israeli invasion and the renewed militancy of the Phalangists made it impossible for Sarkis and his government to proceed effectively with their plans for national reconciliation. These developments also did irreparable harm to the entire Syrian venture in Lebanon. The credibility of the Damascus government was weakened by its refusal to oppose the Israeli invasion; it was further damaged by Assad's inability to persuade the Maronites to take part in Sarkis's efforts to rebuild the state. The Syrian president was indeed in an impossible situation. He was unable to extricate his country from the Lebanese conflict but he was also being prevented from dealing effectively with the crisis by the Israeli–Maronite alliance. Syria's main error may have been its failure to occupy the Maronite areas in 1976 when Chamoun and Gemayel were still grateful for their rescue. It could still probably have achieved something had it dealt roughly with the Maronites after the Ehden massacre in 1978. No doubt Assad feared the Israelis would retaliate if Syrian troops entered the Maronite enclave – as indeed they did later in the year when their navy attacked Syrian and Palestinian positions along the coast to put pressure on the Syrians to stop their bombardment of Ashrafiyeh. But the timing for a Syrian move in June 1978 had been right. The

Frangiehs had been murdered on the very day when the Israelis withdrew their last troops from Lebanon and it is unlikely that even Begin would have risked the international uproar that a fresh piece of Israeli aggression would have provoked.

Syria's position between the two Israeli invasions was an almost hopeless one. It could encourage Sarkis's efforts and help to rebuild the Lebanese army but it could not begin to tackle the real problems. Syrian policy had arguably never done anything to resolve the Lebanese crisis but had merely prolonged the agony of civil war. In 1975 and the early part of 1976, Syria had tried to end the war with a compromise acceptable to both sides. In June 1976 it had sent its army into Lebanon to prevent partition and a victory for one side. All along it had tried to produce a solution which would preserve the main features of the pre-war Lebanese system. It was a thankless task, resented by both sides, and Syria ended up having to fight each of them. Anyone was prepared to accept Syrian help when under pressure but neither of the opposing sides wanted a Syrian role in Lebanon. Both the Maronites and the National Movement shared a common aim: each wanted to destroy the other and set up a regime it could dominate. Outright military victory, the division of a people into victors and vanquished, is the usual way in which civil wars end. Perhaps the Syrians' basic mistake was that they were not ruthless enough − they tried to end the civil war in Lebanon without allowing either side to destroy the other.

11

Israel's Second Invasion of Lebanon

During the four years that followed Israel's invasion of 1978 there was little improvement in Lebanon's position. The country remained tense and fragmented. The government was unable to make progress towards the political and economic reconstruction of the country because of the recurrence of sporadic fighting in different regions. The occasional attempts it made to assert its authority were usually blocked by the Phalangists in east Beirut and the Maronite mountain, by Palestinians and radical groups in west Beirut, and by Saad Haddad's militiamen in the south. None of these forces would allow the Lebanese army to patrol areas under their control.

The situation in southern Lebanon remained the government's most intractable problem. At the beginning of March 1981 President Sarkis of Lebanon and President Assad of Syria met in Damascus and agreed once again to send a detachment of the Lebanese army to join up with UNIFIL. Saad Haddad's reaction to this attempt to extend government control to his area was typical. He bombarded UN positions and killed three Nigerian soldiers serving with UNIFIL. This action had the required effect because the Lebanese made no further attempt to move into the border area. Meanwhile, in an effort to carry out his particular mandate, the UNIFIL commander, General William Callaghan, asked the Israelis to leave Lebanon altogether, to stop supporting Haddad and to allow UNIFIL to police the whole area occupied by Israel in 1978. The Israelis refused.

The following month, heavy fighting broke out between Phalangists and the Syrian army in the Bekaa town of Zahle. The Syrians had occupied Zahle in 1976 but had later withdrawn when the government announced its intention of installing a detachment of Lebanese gendarmerie there. Instead of the gendarmes, however, Phalangist militiamen arrived in large numbers with heavy artillery and started to build a road to connect Zahle with the Maronite mountain. This development angered the Syrians who realized that in the event of a war between their army and the Maronite–Israeli alliance, Zahle would be a position of vital strategic importance. Determined to prevent the Phalangists from digging themselves in around the town, Syrian troops therefore moved against the militiamen and defeated them. For reasons that are not altogether clear, the Israelis only intervened after their allies had been beaten and then only to shoot down two Syrian helicopters. However, when the Syrians installed Sam-6 anti-aircraft missiles in the Bekaa valley to protect their own air-force, the Israelis became more bellicose. Although the missiles were by definition defensive and were stationed deep inside Lebanon far from the Israeli border, Mr Begin demanded their immediate withdrawal and was only prevented from launching an air-strike against them by American diplomatic pressure.

In the spring of 1981, Begin's Likud Party was preparing for a general election it looked certain to lose. Corruption and incompetence in internal policies, in addition to one of the highest inflation rates in the world, were responsible for giving the opposition Labour Party a massive lead in the opinion polls. Begin and his ministers realized that an election fought on domestic issues would lead to an overwhelming defeat. They therefore decided to appeal to the voters through an aggressively anti-Arab foreign policy. The Syrian missile crisis was one part of this policy and the bombing of the Baghdad nuclear reactor on 7 June was another. A third part of this strategy – it was so successful that in spite of his government's appalling record Begin did win the election – was a revival of the war against the Palestinians. Israel began a new round of air raids and commando attacks on Palestinian positions in April, which was complemented on Easter Sunday by a bombardment of Sidon by Haddad's men in which 16 civilians were killed. In late May, the raids started up again and on 10 July Begin decided to wage 'unremitting war' on the Palestinians. The PLO retaliated by training its rockets on the settlements of northern Galilee and 6 Israelis were killed. But as usual the casualty lists were heavily one-sided. On 17 July, Israeli aeroplanes bombed Beirut destroying tall apartment blocks in the Fakhani quarter and killing 350 people. A week later the American special envoy, Philp Habib, succeeded in arranging a cease-fire.

The cease-fire was successful, to the evident annoyance of the Israelis. The Begin government had wanted to destroy the PLO in 1978 and it had failed. In 1981 it wanted to have another go but was prevented from so doing by the United States. The Israeli Chief of Staff, General Eitan, has even admitted that 'the Israeli invasion of Lebanon [of 1982] had been planned to take place in July 1981 and had been postponed after a cease-fire had been arranged by Philip Habib.'[1] Neither Eitan nor General Sharon, the new defence minister, were prepared to see a third chance wasted. In the middle of the 1982 invasion Sharon confessed that he had been planning the operation since taking office in July 1981[2] and also admitted that he had gone secretly to Beirut in January 1982 to make his plans on the ground.[3] His only problem was that the PLO refused to break the cease-fire and thus give him a pretext to put his plans into operation. He sent troops into Lebanon on three occasions in the early months of 1982 but each time failed to provoke a response from the PLO. In April, an Israeli vehicle illegally patrolling southern Lebanon hit a mine and a soldier was killed, an event which led to a retaliatory air strike in which 35 people died. Once again the Palestinians refused to respond. On 9 May, the Israeli air-force went into action once more and PLO gunners replied by shelling northern Israel — at the same time, however, deliberately avoiding causing casualties that might have given Sharon a pretext to invade. Following an assassination attempt on the Israeli ambassador in London by anti-PLO Arab gunmen on 4 June, Israeli aircraft bombed Palestinian positions in southern Lebanon and west Beirut. This time the PLO did reply and its bombardment — which incidentally did not kill a single Israeli — was sufficient excuse for Sharon to launch his absurdly-named 'Operation Peace for Galilee'.

On 6 June, the Israeli army invaded Lebanon with instructions from the cabinet 'to place all the civilian population of the Galilee beyond the range of the terrorists' fire from Lebanon'.[4] While the Israeli air-force and navy pounded Palestinian positions along the coast, the army attacked on three fronts: in the Bekaa valley, against the PLO forces around Beaufort Castle near the Litani river, and along the coast road to Tyre. UNIFIL's peace-keeping force was pushed aside as Israeli columns — outnumbering their Palestinian opponents by about ten to one — swept north towards Sidon and Jezzine. Beaufort Castle fell after savage hand-to-hand fighting and shortly afterwards Nabatiya was captured. By 10 June, four days after the start of the invasion, Israeli troops had reached Beirut. According to their spokesmen. Tyre, Sidon and Damour had all been taken but in fact Palestinian resistance held out against long odds in all these places for at least a week after the 'official' capture. There was comparatively little fighting on the Bekaa front although the Syrian Mig fighters suffered heavy losses to Israel's superior air-force. Syria was plainly anxious to avoid a full-scale war and its forces retreated northwards up the Bekaa valley before agreeing to a cease-fire on 11 June.

At the beginning of the invasion, Israeli spokesmen announced that their aim was to drive the PLO beyond a line 25 miles from the border so that, according to the Israeli Chief of Staff, 'Israel would no longer be within PLO artillery range'.[5] Within a couple of days, however, the Israeli army had gone well beyond the 25-mile zone and when commando units tried (and failed) to land on the beaches near Beirut, which is about 60 miles from the border at Rosh Haniqra, it became clear that the professed aim was simply a ruse to deceive international opinion. Later, Israel's deputy prime minister admitted as much when he said on television that Beirut was from the outset one of Israel's goals.[6] The Israelis knew that if they were going to gain any international sympathy for the invasion they would have to lie about their real aims and pretend they had been forced into a war against implacable and powerful 'terrorists'. It was for this reason that they deliberately exaggerated the military strength of the PLO in south Lebanon. Israeli spokesmen claimed that 500 modern tanks had been captured and the government declared that it had been faced by a 'vast terrorist arsenal of thousands of tons of weapons, ammunition, missiles and heavy artillery equipment, all of which constituted a direct, immediate and actual threat to Israel's security'.[7] Some time later, after Israeli propaganda had begun to have an effect in the United

States and elsewhere, Israeli journalists discovered that instead of the 500 modern tanks which the government claimed to have seized, less than 90 old-fashioned models, many of which may have belonged to the Syrians rather than the PLO, had been captured.[8]

For anyone who knew anything about the Israeli army, the idea that it could be vulnerable to any guerrilla force was of course laughable. Israelis have claimed that theirs is the third or fourth military power in the world and General Eitan has gone even further, declaring that 'if the Russians start a war against Israel, the Israeli Defence Forces will win'.[9] How the same man can also claim that the PLO represented a serious military threat to Israel is a mystery. An equally unconvincing argument was put forward by Israel's ambassador to the United Nations: Israel's military actions were a consequence of 'constant terrorist provocations since July 1981'.[10] As we have seen, the PLO was notably restrained in its behaviour after the July cease-fire and indeed, when the ambassador gave details of casualties which these 'provocations' had caused, he produced a figure of 8 Israelis, 7 of whom had in fact been killed long *before* the 1981 agreement.[11] He added a further 9 Jews who had allegedly been killed abroad by the PLO but he did not say that they were Israelis, nor did he provide any proof that the PLO was responsible.

Once the huge death toll from the invasion of Lebanon had become known to the outside world, Sharon tried to counter this by announcing that since the 1960s 'terrorists' had killed 1,002 Israelis.[12] A fortnight afterwards he amended this figure upwards, alleging that 1,392 Israelis had been killed since the 1967 war.[13] This announcement prompted the Israeli newspaper *Ha'aretz* to investigate the claims and it discovered that a majority of the people in Sharon's figure were not Israelis at all: most of these were Arabs and the rest were nationals of other countries who had been killed by terrorists of one sort or another who — and we have only Israel's word for this — were affiliated to the PLO. Even when *Ha'aretz* looked at the figure for Israeli casualties it found out that most of them were soldiers killed in Lebanon or the Occupied Territories where their presence was in any case illegal. For an accurate figure of Israeli civilians killed by the PLO in fifteen years of fighting Israel, the newspaper came up with 282,[14] or rather less than the number of Arab civilians killed in Israel's 10-minute blitz on Beirut in July 1981.

According to Professor Yehoshua Porath, one of Israel's finest historians, the decision to invade

> resulted from the fact that the cease-fire had held . . . Yasser Arafat had succeeded in doing the impossible. He managed an indirect agreement, through American mediation, with Israel and even managed to keep it for a whole year . . . this was a disaster for Israel. If the PLO agreed upon and maintained a cease-fire they may in the future agree to a more far-reaching political settlement and maintain that too.[15]

In other words the PLO was attacked not because it was assaulting Israelis but because it was not assaulting them. It had become respectable and had made large diplomatic gains in Europe and elsewhere. The moderation and responsibility which Arafat had been showing were an obvious threat to the expansionist aims of Israel's leaders and for that reason the PLO had to be destroyed.

During Israel's siege of Beirut in July 1982 Begin claimed that 'nothing happened in this war that was not planned'[16] and we can, therefore, assume that the professed aim of creating a 25-mile cordon sanitaire was a lie even at the time it was stated. Even when the world was being told about the campaign's ostensible objective, Israeli officers were being briefed that the real aims were to advance as far north as the Beirut–Damascus road and to set up a new regime in Lebanon.[17] The Begin-Sharon plan gradually became apparent: to clear the Syrians out of Beirut and central Lebanon and to install a client regime based on the Phalangist Party which would sign a peace treaty with Israel. As for the PLO, there was to be no question of merely pushing it back 25 miles; it was to be expelled from Lebanon and, if possible, destroyed altogether. On 30 June Sharon told the Israeli parliament that the government had decided that 'the PLO must cease to exist'.[18]

Israel's further aims for Lebanon, which may or may not include the annexation of a part or all of the south, are not yet sufficiently clear. But nobody can be in any doubt about the real aim of the invasion as far as the Palestinians were concerned. It was quite simply the destruction of Palestinian nationalism. If the PLO was annihilated in Beirut, argued Sharon, then the Palestinians of the West Bank and Gaza, who regarded Arafat as their leader, would become more amenable to his type of coercion. As the defence minister himself explained, 'the bigger the blow and the more we damage the PLO infrastructure, the more the Arabs in Judaea and Samaria [sic] and Gaza will be ready to negotiate with us and establish co-existence'[19] – in other words, the easier Israel would find it to colonize and annex these remaining areas of Arab Palestine. Professor Yuval Ne'eman, Israel's minister of science and technology, put the argument more succinctly: 'the war is in two parts. One is what is happening up there in Lebanon, and the other is to create a situation in which there will be practically nowhere, no place left, to create a Palestinian state . . . . It is now a matter of working every day and every month to accelerate the Jewish colonization of Judaea and Samaria and Gaza.'[20]

Israel has invaded Arab countries in 1956, 1967, 1978 and, on a smaller scale, on numerous other occasions as well, but never has the destruction or the civilian casualties been comparable to those inflicted in the 1982 aggression. According to *The Times* Beirut correspondent, who carefully examined the figures given by the Red Cross and the Lebanese police for every town and village, 14,000 people were killed and 20,000 wounded during the first fortnight of the war.[21] A couple of months later, after the bombardment of Beirut had ended, two Lebanese papers using government sources gave figures of 18,000 dead and 30,000 wounded.[22] Nearly 90 per cent of the casualties were civilians.

The staggeringly high proportion of civilian casualties was a direct consequence of the tactics used by the Israelis. The government decided that the invasion had to be swift and successful and that no time could, therefore, be wasted laying siege to towns that blocked the route to Beirut. Nor was it prepared to lose men in costly infantry assaults. As the only means of quickly capturing a town without suffering heavy casualties is to bombard it into submission, this was the tactic employed. Parts of Tyre and Sidon, and many other towns and villages as well, were obliterated for this reason. According to the United Nations High Commission for Refugees (UNHCR), 1,000 buildings in Sidon were completely destroyed and another 1,500 damaged.[23] One Israeli writer travelling in southern Lebanon admitted that he could not remember having seen a single undamaged house since crossing the border.[24] Among the destroyed or damaged buildings in Tyre and Sidon were 27 schools and 13 hospitals.[25] At the time Israel and its apologists in the West made every effort to minimize the damage caused by the invasion and the Israeli embassy in London made the astonishing claim that throughout the whole operation 'the Israel defence forces took maximum precautions to ensure that the civilian population would not be harmed'.[26] It is true, as the Israelis claimed, that their air-force sometimes dropped leaflets on their targets encouraging the inhabitants to leave the area but it is also true that these leaflets were sometimes dropped after the bombardment had taken place. This was certainly the case in Sidon which suffered 36 hours of continuous bombing before the leaflets were dropped.[27] The town's municipality later revealed that 1,278 people were killed during the bombing while another 600 were missing presumed dead[28] — and this figure includes only Lebanese civilians and not the even larger number of Palestinian victims from the refugee camps on the town's outskirts.

As was to be expected, the Palestinian refugee camps were even more savagely dealt with than the Lebanese towns. Some of these were partially destroyed during the bombardment and were later to be completely flattened by Israeli bulldozers. According to UNRWA, half of the refugees' homes in the southern camps were destroyed during the invasion. Again, Israel claimed to have warned the occupants beforehand and again it later transpired that the warnings came too late. At the huge camp of Ain el-Hilweh outside Sidon the Israeli air-force dropped leaflets warning the refugees to 'flee for your lives' because there was to be a bombardment in two hours' time. That was on 9 June. Ain el-Hilweh had first been bombed — from land, sea and air — on 6 June. It was to be bombed again, repeatedly, on the 7th, 8th and 9th. As one British journal reported, 'the bombing continued without cease as the leaflets flooded down amidst the rubble. All roads out of the camp were under intense attack throughout the ten days. If the leaflets were of help to Israeli embassies abroad, they were useless to the victim populace.'[29]

Horrifying though the destruction of Tyre and Sidon were, television viewers throughout the world were soon presented with an even more appalling spectacle: the bombardment of west Beirut. The siege of Lebanon's capital began a week after the invasion and lasted for two months. The Israeli position was clear from the start: the PLO forces in Beirut, estimated at about 9,000, must surrender or leave the country, along with any Syrian forces still in the city, or the Israeli army would go in and expel them. Meanwhile, as American diplomats tried frantically to arrange an agreement leading to the evacuation of the guerrillas, the Israelis kept up the pressure with a sustained and ferocious bombardment of the city. Beirut was bombed almost constantly from 13 June to 12 August with two short intervals of about a week each at the end of June and the middle of July. During that period it was subjected to air raids, naval bombardment, heavy artillery barrages (155 mm guns and 121 mm howitzers) and fire from tanks, mortars and rocket launchers.

The Israeli government claimed all along that its forces were aiming only at military targets but to anybody living in Beirut it was clear that the bombardment was almost indiscriminate. The Canadian ambassador and his staff surveyed 55 separate areas of Beirut that had been hit and declared that none of them were Palestinian military targets.[30] The American ambassador, reporting on one night's bombing, cabled to Washington: 'Simply put, tonight's saturation shelling was as intense as anything we have seen. There was no "pinpoint accuracy" against targets in "open space". It was not a response to Palestinian fire. This was a blitz against west Beirut.'[31] According to the *Sunday Times*, among the targets hit by the Israelis in the two months following their arrival in Beirut were 'five UN buildings, 134 embassies or diplomatic residences, six hospitals or clinics, one mental institute, the Central Bank, five hotels, the Red Cross, Lebanese and foreign media outlets and innumerable private homes.'[32] But in spite of the evidence of shattered schools and burning hospitals, the Israelis continued to deny that they were hitting civilian targets. The deputy director of the Israeli foreign ministry said smugly, 'It is accepted, I think, that our Air Force is very accurate',[33] but the pilots themselves did not seem to agree. One air-force officer, ordered to destroy apartment blocks in Beirut, described his mission as follows:

> The first couple [of aeroplanes] hit them directly. I was in the second couple and it was our mission to bomb again and make sure the hit was perfect. When we got closer we saw the hits: the large housing blocks collapsed in an enormous cloud of fire, smoke and dust. We released the bombs not seeing the target clearly. From the 'after' picture, it seems we missed a bit, we hit the next block of houses, and it collapsed. It is hard to believe that anyone got out alive.[34]

All the evidence suggests not only that the air-force was often inaccurate but also that that it was specifically ordered to bomb a large number of non-military targets. How else can one explain the bombing in a single day of the prime minister's office, the Central Bank, the ministries of information and tourism, the offices of *Newsweek* and UPI — none of which were anywhere near Palestinian or other military targets? How else can one explain the destruction of hospitals, even though they were flying Red Cross flags, or the damaged French schools housing dozens of refugee families, or the embassies which, with the interesting exception of the American one, were nearly all hit. One of the most terrible examples of Israeli brutality was the destruction of the DOHA (Development Organization for Human Abilities) Centre at Aramoun south of Beirut. This had been built only the year before during the International Year of the Handicapped and it housed 650 handicapped children in various institutions for the blind, deaf, physically handicapped and mentally retarded. In spite of the fact that the DOHA Centre was very far from PLO or other military positions, and although it was clearly marked as a medical institution, it was the target of nine air raids on 10 and 11 June. The Centre was completely destroyed and months later, when an International Commission visited the ruins, there were still unexploded bombs on the premises.[35]

In Beirut, as in Tyre and Sidon, the civilians were the chief victims of the bombardment. A Red Cross representative in the capital reported that at least 80 per cent of the casualties were civilians but a Norwegian surgeon working in one of the hospitals put the figure at more than 90 per cent.[36] It was obvious to any neutral observer that the Israeli government was simply refusing to make a distinction between military and civilian targets and Begin even justified the casualties in the Knesset by insisting that the 'civilian population deserves punishment'.[37] On another occasion he declared, 'there is no room for humanitarianism. To make an omelette you have to crack eggs.'[38]

The instruments used by Begin and Sharon to crack Beirut included some of the most lethal and barbaric weapons ever invented, bombs and shells deliberately designed to cause maximum casualties in the target area. One of the worst was the suction bomb which implodes rather than explodes and causes entire buildings to collapse inwards; on 12 August one such bomb hit the Maksour building in Borj al-Barajneh and killed 120 people. Still nastier weapons are phosphorous shells, which cause so much internal burning that people wounded by one need a quick amputation of the injured limb if they are to stay alive. One doctor described to *The Times* correspondent how she had found two 5-day-old twins who had been killed by one of these shells. 'I had to take the babies and put them in buckets of water to put out the flames,' she said. 'When I took them out half an hour later, they were still burning. Even in the mortuary they smouldered for hours.'[39] Among the several targets of phosphorous shells — several hundred of which were fired into Beirut in the first three weeks of the siege — were one Red Cross office, two hospitals and the Hamra boulevard.[40]

The most destructive of all these weapons, however, was the cluster bomb, a canister which contains — depending on the type — up to 650 small bombs that can wipe out anything and anybody in an area of 5,000 square yards. Israel had used American-supplied cluster bombs in its 1978 invasion and in a subsequent agreement the United States insisted that Israel should not use them except in combat with 'two or more Arab states' and then 'only for defensive purposes'.[41] It was Sharon himself who decided to use the cluster bombs[42] and he tried to justify his decision by pointing out that Syria was also involved in the fighting — although attacking a retreating Syrian army in the Bekaa valley could hardly be described as a 'defensive purpose', and in any case Syria was no longer fighting when the cluster bombs were used against Beirut. According to an American expert who visited Beirut during the siege, cluster bombs were dropped in at least sixteen different areas of the city.[43]

At the beginning of the siege there were more than half a million people in west Beirut, of whom less than 3 per cent were combatants. During the following weeks perhaps one-third of the civilians left the city because of the appalling conditions inside. From the beginning of the invasion, Israel had prevented relief organizations from getting much-needed supplies to the civilian population. A UNICEF relief aeroplane was turned away from Lydda airport and a Red Cross boat carrying 550 tons of supplies was denied permission to disembark at Sidon. On 20 June, the *Sunday Times* said in an editorial: 'Hundreds of thousands of ordinary people are on the move, needing urgent help and Israel is putting politics before their plight. It is refusing to allow UN agencies to use the food, medicines and disaster experts that have rushed to the borders of Lebanon'. In Beirut, as the siege dragged on, the situation became desperate. While the Israeli navy blockaded the north and west of the city, the army controlled the southern approaches and along the line that divided west Beirut from the Christian sectors of the city it sealed off the exits with the help of the Phalangist militia. At various stages during the siege the Israelis prevented the delivery of food, fuel and other necessities to west Beirut and they also turned off the electricity and water supplies.

The civil war confrontation between the Maronites and the alliance of radical Arab nationalists and Palestinians survived the Israeli invasion. The PLO and the several militias of the National Movement fought together against the invaders in the south and in Beirut. The Palestinians, who had managed to alienate Lebanese Muslims by their insensitive behaviour in areas under their control were nevertheless supported by leaders such as Walid Jumblatt and Ibrahim Qleilat and also by the Shi'ite militia Amal, which carried out some of the most determined operations against the Israeli army around Beirut airport. Although Amal had quarrelled bitterly with the PLO in the south and blamed the Palestinians for many of their troubles with Israel, the Shi'ite militiamen were sufficiently patriotic to forget their differences during the invasion.

The Phalangists and their allies, however, who regarded themselves as the only true Lebanese patriots, did not find the sight of a foreign army smashing up Lebanese towns as a sufficiently good reason to oppose it. Although they did not actually fight alongside the Israeli army, the Phalangists welcomed the invasion and saw the opportunities it would give them to achieve their ambitions. For them the invasion would be the last, decisive act in the civil war which, by disposing of the Syrians and the PLO, would leave them in control of post-war Lebanon. During the siege of Beirut, therefore, they echoed the demand of their Israeli allies that the PLO should be expelled from Lebanon and coupled this with a call for the removal of the Palestinian refugees as well and their dispersal around the Arab world. At the same time, the militias of both the Phalangist Party and Saad Haddad began to step up their activities in areas that had previously been under the control of the Syrians or the Palestinian-National Movement alliance. Phalangist militiamen infiltrated the Chouf at the end of June and later began a series of attacks against the Druze villages which supported Walid Jumblatt. In the south, the militias harried the now destitute Palestinians and at the Mieh Mieh refugee camp they burned and looted many of the remaining houses. In the town of Nabatiya, Haddad's men evicted Palestinian families and told the local lawyers not to accept Palestinian clients.

In late August the Maronites could claim that they — or rather their Israeli allies — had finally won the Lebanese civil war. The victory was symbolized by two major events: the departure of the PLO and the election of Bachir Gemayel as president of Lebanon. On 21 August, after weeks of negotiations, the PLO finally began its evacuation of Beirut. The Palestinians left in order to save what remained of the city and to end the slaughter of civilians, both Palestinians and Lebanese. The morale of their 9,000 fighters was high and they had shown on several occasions — in Sidon, Tyre, Damour and Beirut itself — that they were a match for the Israelis in urban hand-to-hand fighting. Through weight of numbers —

Israel was estimated to have 90,000 men in Lebanon[44] — and superior weapons, the Israelis would no doubt have captured west Beirut. But they would have taken a lot of casualties as they discovered in August when they were forced to abandon two offensives across Beirut's central dividing line. That is why they preferred to bombard the city in the hope that the damage caused would persuade the Palestinians to withdraw. The tactic worked and by the end of August the PLO had left the city that had been its headquarters for twelve years. Its newsagency *Wafa* was dismantled and moved to Nicosia, its radio station *Voice of Palestine* was closed down and some of the PLO offices in the ruins of the Fakhani district were turned over to refugees from the Beirut camps. Yasser Arafat himself took a boat to Athens, a destination which perhaps symbolized the Palestinians' disgust at the failure of the Arab states to come to their help.

Two days after the withdrawal of the Palestinians began, Bachir Gemayel was chosen as president by 62 deputies. This event was just as much a consequence of the Israeli invasion as the evacuation of the PLO, because in normal times Gemayel would not have received more than the 20 or so votes belonging to the Phalangists and Chamoun's National Liberal Party. In other circumstances, Raymond Eddé, the politician supported by the National Movement, might have won easily. But the National Movement had been beaten and its power had gone. Many deputies, particularly the Shi'ites and Druzes, who would have been inclined to vote for Eddé in peacetime, went for Gemayel because in the aftermath of the invasion they understood that there was no real alternative. Israel and the Phalangists had won the war and it would have been pointless to resist the imposition of their candidate. Besides, many of them realized that, however much they might detest Gemayel and his violent, neo-fascist politics, the country needed at that moment a strong and ruthless leader, not a decent liberal like Eddé.

Bachir Gemayel was the Israelis' candidate and he had collaborated freely with them for years. But it was by no means certain that he would continue to do so. He had used the Israelis to get himself elected but he was an ambitious man, as well as a tough one, and it is probable that he saw his future as the leader of a resurrected, independent Lebanon and not as a stooge of the Israelis. During his three weeks as president-elect he began to distance himself from his Israeli allies. At the beginning of September he met Begin and Sharon in northern Israel where the Israeli leaders tried to force him to agree to a peace treaty. Gemayel refused and later complained that he 'had been treated like a bell-boy'.[45] A few days before his assassination he began a dialogue with his Lebanese opponents and at a meeting with Saeb Salam he announced that the Lebanese parliament rather than the president would decide whether to sign a treaty with Israel.

According to an agreement, negotiated once again by the American envoy, Philp Habib, between Israel, Lebanon and the PLO, a multinational force was to arrive in Beirut to supervize the Palestinian withdrawal *and* to protect the inhabitants of west Beirut from the Israelis and the Maronite militias. On 25 August, French and Italian soldiers, as well as a detachment of American marines, disembarked at Beirut. On 10 September, after the PLO's evacuation had been completed, they began to leave again, although the Habib plan had envisaged that they would remain for at least another fortnight. Their hurried departure was much criticized by the now unprotected population of west Beirut which accused the multinational forces of fulfilling only the first part of their mission. As the Lebanese prime minister, Shafiq Wazzan, afterwards complained, their quick withdrawal made it seem 'as if the purpose of their arrival was just to evacuate the Palestinian fighters. There was another purpose — the protection of both the civilians and the Palestinian [refugees].'[46] Wazzan was right to oppose the hasty retreat of the multinational forces. Had they remained until their planned date of withdrawal, the worst massacre of the Lebanese war would have been avoided.

No one will ever know whether Bachir Gemayel would have emerged as the strong leader his country then needed because on 14 September, before he had even assumed the presidency, he was killed by a large bomb explosion at the Phalangist Party headquarters. Nobody knew who had planted the bomb but it is significant that Phalangists blamed neither the Palestinians nor the National Movement for the assassination. Nor was Suleiman Frangieh, who had vowed to revenge the murder of his son Tony by Phalangists four years earlier, one of the main suspects. Some Maronites accused the Syrians but most blamed the Israelis or the pro-Israeli, 'Sharonist' faction of the Phalangist Party for having killed Bachir because he was showing signs of too much independence. However that may be, the only people to gain any immediate advantage from the crime were the Israelis and the most extreme anti-Palestinian Phalangists. On Tuesday 14 September Bachir Gemayel was killed. On 15 September the Israeli army moved into west Beirut in contravention of the Habib agreement. The following day Phalangist militiamen launched the massacres of Sabra and Chatila.

Begin and Sharon justified their decision to occupy west Beirut by claiming they were going 'to maintain law and order', although the city had in fact been quiet ever since the end of the bombardment. The Israeli cabinet subsequently issued a statement on 17 September claiming that the occupation had been carried out 'in order to prevent the danger of violence, bloodshed and anarchy, while about 2,000 terrorists, equipped with modern and heavy weapons, remained in west Beirut, thus blatantly violating the departure agreement'.[47] Whether Sharon really believed that there were 2,000 Palestinian guerrillas still in the city, or whether he simply invented the figure as an excuse to send in the tanks, is not certain. What is certain is that there was no sign of the 2,000 men — or indeed of any Palestinian force at all — when the Israelis took over. If there had been any guerrillas in Beirut they would presumably have resisted the Israelis just as they would have defended their refugee camps against the Phalangist killers. The fact that the Israeli army was unopposed except by a small number of Muslim Lebanese, together with the fact that the Phalangists were able to carry out their ghastly massacre unhindered, surely indicate that Sharon's accusation was baseless.

On Wednesday 15 September at 3.30 a.m., only hours after Bachir Gemayel's assassination, the Israeli chief of staff, General Eitan, and the northern commander, General Drori, held a meeting with Phalangist officers in Beirut.[48] They agreed that Phalangist militiamen would hunt out 'terrorists' in the refugee camps of Sabra and Chatila — a part of Beirut's 'belt of misery' south-east of the city centre inhabited by a large number of poor Lebanese as well as Palestinian refugees. At noon the following day there was another meeting to finalize details. Two Phalangists present were Fady Frem, recently appointed as commander of the Lebanese Forces,* and Elias Hobeika, the Phalangist intelligence chief and one of the men responsible for the massacre of Palestinians in the Tal Zaatar refugee camp in 1976. It was agreed that Hobeika would be in charge of the operation and at 5.00 p.m. his force assembled at Beirut airport. Israeli paratroop units were ordered to assist the Phalangists' entry into the camps and shortly afterwards the militiamen reached Chatila. At 11.00 p.m. that evening Hobeika told the Israeli commander in Beirut that 'until now 300 civilians and terrorists have been killed', a message that was sent immediately to Tel Aviv where about twenty senior Israeli officers saw it.

The following morning, at 11.30 a.m. on Friday 17 September, General Drori ordered the militiamen to stop their operation, but after a further meeting with Phalangist officers the Israelis agreed to let them remain in the camps until the following day. Hobeika was also given permission to use two battalions of fresh troops and in the afternoon another force of militiamen entered the camps where they began a new round of killing. The Israeli commander in Beirut, General Yaron, has since admitted that, in spite of the fact that Israeli officers had known for several hours that the massacres were taking place, the Phalangists were allowed to call up reinforcements and remain in the camps for a further thirty-six hours.[49] The militiamen rampaged round Sabra and Chatila until Saturday morning killing indiscriminately: nurses were raped by the killer gangs and then shot, children were scalped, patients from two hospitals were dragged from their beds and knifed to death. The Phalangists left most of their victims where they had killed them, in their homes or in the streets, but some of them borrowed Israeli bulldozers and tried to cover up their deeds by shovelling corpses into mass graves. Because some of the victims were taken away and never seen again, and because it was decided

---

*Bachir Gemayel had incorporated the Phalangists and other Maronite militias such as the Guardians of the Cedars into the 'Lebanese Forces'. Phalangist militiamen comprised 80 per cent of their strength.

not to open up some of the graves, it will never be known how many people were butchered. But perhaps as many as 2,000 people were killed and not even Sharon can pretend that these were the 'terrorists' he was allegedly looking for.

The chief villains of the atrocity were obviously those responsible for carrying it out. The majority of them were undoubtedly Phalangists and they have made little attempt to deny their role in the killings. Some of them may have come from Damour or Saadiyat which were sacked by their opponents in the civil war — a fact which may make the atrocity more explicable as an act of vengeance but which makes it all the more incredible that they should have been allowed anywhere near the refugee camps by the Israelis. Saad Haddad has consistently denied that his militia was involved in the massacre but the evidence suggests that some of his troops played at least a subsidiary role. Too many witnesses recognized the southern accents and militia insignia of their attackers for his denial to be convincing.

But if the murderers themselves were the Maronite militiamen, ultimate responsibility for the murders must lie with the Israelis, and in particular, as the Israeli Commission of Enquiry later reported, with the defence minister and chief of staff. They were the people who planned the operation and they were the ones who allowed the militias into the camps and then assisted them once they were there. On the morning of 18 September, Morris Draper, another of President Reagan's envoys despatched to Beirut, sent a message to Sharon alleging Israeli responsibility: 'You must stop the massacres. They are obscene. I have an officer in the camp counting the bodies. You ought to be ashamed. The situation is rotten and terrible. They are killing children. You are in absolute control of the area, and therefore responsible for that area.'[50] But the responsibility was greater than Draper suggested. On 15 September Israeli troops had surrounded Sabra and Chatila. They were never more than 300 yards away from the camps and sometimes as close as 50 yards. Moreover, Israeli soldiers were on the roof of the Kuwait embassy nearby and could see what was happening in both camps. There is a mass of evidence to show that the Israelis knew that a massacre was in progress by Thursday evening but did nothing to stop it until the Saturday morning.

Apart from Hobeika's admission that his men had killed 300 people by 11.00 p.m. on Thursday, it is known that the Israelis and the Phalangists were in constant radio contact with each other and that there was an Israeli liaison officer with the Phalangists. Furthermore, although it was known what was happening on the Thursday evening, General Drori's order to stop the operation the next morning was not implemented and Israeli generals gave permission to the Phalangists to stay in the camps until Saturday.

There is further evidence which indicates the extent of Israel's complicity in the massacre. The discovery in one of the camps of an Israeli sergeant's identity tag does not prove that he actually took part in the killing but it is significant that the Israeli army did not allow him to appear before the Israeli Commission of Enquiry. More importantly, the Israelis were prepared to assist their Phalangist allies in a number of different ways: they lent bulldozers so that the killers could bury some of the dead; they fired flares throughout the night of 16 September – at a rate of two a minute according to one Israeli soldier[51] – so that the killers could see what they were doing; worst of all, they prevented civilians from fleeing and forced those who tried to escape back into the camps.

When questioned by the Israeli Commission of Enquiry, both Begin and Sharon claimed that it had not occurred to them, when they planned the operation, that there might be a massacre. Sharon declared that 'no-one foresaw – nor could have foreseen – the atrocities committed in the neighbourhood of Sabra and Chatila'.[52] At best this was an admission of almost unbelievable ignorance. As Israel's opposition leader, Shimon Peres, remarked, 'even a village policeman' would have anticipated the danger. Had the Israeli defence minister heard nothing of the career of Elias Hobeika? Did neither Begin nor Sharon know what had happened at Qarantina or Tal Zaatar or the Black Saturday bloodbath?

After the massacres, the multinational forces came back again to protect the survivors and Lebanon continued to be a country divided into three parts. Following Bachir Gemayel's assassination, his more moderate elder brother Amin was elected president but the area under his control consisted only of Beirut and the middle section of Mount Lebanon. In the north the Syrians still dominated Tripoli, Akkar and the northern Bekaa. In the southern half of the country the Israelis had reluctantly pulled back from west Beirut but they only withdrew to positions a couple of miles south of the city and then set about consolidating their hold on the areas under their control. The only thing the three zones had in common was continuing violence. In Tripoli there was constant fighting between pro- and anti-Syrian groups and in Beirut Walid Jumblatt was wounded in an assassination attempt that killed his bodyguard and several other people. In the south, there were clashes between Druze and Maronite villagers, while from behind the Israeli lines PLO guerrillas who had avoided Israel's 'mopping up' operations in the south carried out a series of successful raids. On 11 November the Israeli headquarters in Tyre were blown up and 75 soldiers and intelligence officers, as well as 15 Arab prisoners, were killed. Israel blamed the explosion on a gas leak but as Lebanon has no mains gas supply it was an unconvincing theory.

The Israeli occupation of southern Lebanon was characterized by widespread looting and destruction. Israeli soldiers broke into Beirut shops to steal cameras, watches and other goods. They forced their way into the homes of Palestinians and Lebanese Muslims taking what they wanted and then wrecking apartments by smashing furniture and defecating on the carpets. There was a good deal of 'official' looting as well. This took the form of removing equipment from research centres and science laboratories, stealing tractors, lorries and other vehicles, and ransacking Beirut airport and the offices of Middle East Airlines. The Ghandour biscuit factory, one of the largest in the Middle East, was pillaged and then destroyed. A number of modern hotels were deliberately wrecked and many orange groves in the south were cut down, allegedly because 'terrorists' might hide in them.[53]

Life in Israeli-occupied Lebanon was unpleasant for everyone — except for the Maronite militiamen who were allowed to roam around the countryside doing pretty much what they liked — but it was particularly hard for the Palestinians. On 20 July 1982 OXFAM reported that there were 175,000 Palestinians 'in dire need' in southern Lebanon while another 60,000 homeless refugees were in Beirut. Thousands of Palestinians had been either killed or arrested. In June, Israelis took 14,000 men prisoner and herded them into detention centres in the south. Half of them were confined within the barbed wire and watchtowers of the Ansar prison camp on the road between Tyre and Nabatiya. One Canadian doctor, Christopher Giannou, who was arrested along with the Palestinians, has described how the entire male population of Sidon was paraded before three hooded collaborators who advised the Israelis which ones should be detained.[54] The process was repeated in Tyre and in this way 14,000 men, who knew neither their accusers nor the accusations, were locked away.

Conditions inside the over-crowded camps were appalling: the stifling heat, the lack of food and water, the disgusting sanitary conditions. According to Giannou and other witnesses, prisoners were regularly interrogated and beaten up by the Israeli guards.[55] *The Times* correspondent went to Sidon and found convincing evidence that at least four men had died after being beaten up by the Israelis,[56] while a Red Cross worker, who was among the prisoners, reported: 'They held us for four days, almost all the time out in the open. They gave us water but no food and ten men died near me. I saw one man — I think he was a Palestinian — and he asked for food. A soldier hit him in the stomach with his rifle and the man collapsed and died.'[57] Two months later conditions were much the same. On 19 August *New Society* reported that 'about 10,000 civilians remain in detention camps. They are without rights. They are subjected to torture and beatings. Their families are denied all knowledge of their whereabouts. Neither legal representatives nor international agencies are permitted access to them.'[58] One of the Israeli guards at Ansar prison camp has described the pitiful sight of Palestinian women coming to the edge of the prison day after day begging the guards to tell them whether their husbands, sons and brothers were inside.[59]

The plight of the Palestinian refugees in south Lebanon who had not been arrested was also desperate. Many of them had lost their menfolk and half of them had lost their homes. Some of the refugee camps, such as Ain el-Hilweh and Rashidiyeh, had been systematically destroyed by the Israelis long after the fighting was over. One senior Israeli officer declared that Rashidiyeh was being demolished two weeks after all its inhabitants had fled 'so that it shall never again give shelter to them'.[60] But who or what *would* give shelter to them was a question which neither the Israelis nor the Lebanese government seemed prepared to answer. When Israel's energy minister, Ya'acov Meridor, visited Sidon and was asked to explain his government's policy towards the Palestinian refugees, he replied: ' "They should be driven eastward" — waving his arms in the direction of Syria — "Let them go there and don't let them return".'[61] The Lebanese government refused to issue a statement on the status of the refugees but *L'Orient-Le Jour* reported an apparently official plan to reduce the number of Palestinians in Lebanon through the application of stricter controls on residence and work permits.[62] Other newspapers demanded more extreme solutions such as the destruction of the refugee camps and the removal of all Palestinians.[63]

Apart from the brutality of the Israelis and the indifference and hostility of the Lebanese government, the refugees also suffered from the depredations of marauding Maronite militiamen. The Phalangists, who had never had much support in the south, now entered the region in large numbers and based themselves in a few Christian villages east of Sidon. They began a campaign of harassing the local population, setting up check points and making arbitrary arrests. Large numbers of Palestinians and Druzes were seized and beaten up during the autumn of 1982, and several people were kidnapped and then killed. The Israeli occupying forces knew of these events and could presumably have stopped them had they wished. Instead they went out of their way to encourage the Phalangists at the expense of the Lebanese army. When the Israelis entered Sidon in June they disarmed the regular army at the same time that they began a programme of equipping the local Phalangists. In the Chouf they helped to establish a Phalangist output at Beiteddine.

Apart from these, the Israelis were helping several other militias as well. There was Haddad, of course, who was now more than ever a tool of his protectors — in September he told *The Times* that his forces 'do nothing without the co-ordination of the Israeli army'[64] — and a number of new ones also. The Israelis helped to set up local Shi'ite militias in Tyre and Jouaiya. In the village of Nasrat Chaban they armed yet another group while in Hasbaya they were giving weapons to the local Druzes. To those who belonged to these and other 'approved' militias, the Israelis gave yellow identity cards printed in Hebrew which entitled them to carry weapons in areas under Israeli control.

At first sight, Israel's policy of arming and training all these militias was incomprehensible. What, for example, was the point of giving weapons to both the Phalangists and the Druzes so that they could use them to fight each other in the Chouf? One former Druze minister declared that Israeli officials had offered to create Druze militias to be used as a counter-balance to the Phalangists, which would indicate that Israeli policy was simply a variation of 'divide and rule'. But there is another explanation, as one senior Israeli officer revealed to Agence France Presse. When asked why they were setting up all these militias, the officer replied: 'these units will one day be part of the Israeli forces if Israel is to stay in south Lebanon.'[65]

Whether Israel does or does not stay in Lebanon — or whether, like last time, it goes and then comes back again — is a question beyond the scope of this book. The answer probably depends on the degree of pressure which the international community, especially the United States, is prepared to put on Israel to bring about a complete withdrawal. We know that many Israelis would like to stay in south Lebanon and colonize the area as they have done in the West Bank and Gaza. There are certainly enough zealots around to claim that the region once belonged to the Tribe of Asher and is therefore 'an integral part of the Jewish patrimony'. Zionists from Chaim Weizmann to Ben Gurion, from Dayan to Ne'eman, have argued that Israel should extend its borders as far north as the Litani river and maybe it will, perhaps now, perhaps sometime in the future. Whatever happens, it will be a long time before Lebanese, Palestinians and other Arabs can feel that they are safe from the threat of Israeli expansionism. The ambitions of Begin and Sharon are little different — though even more ruthless — from those of the late Moshe Dayan, who once proudly proclaimed:

Our fathers had reached the frontiers which were recognized in the Partition Plan. Our generation reached the frontiers of 1949. Now the six-day generation has managed to reach Suez, Jordan and the Golan Heights. This is not the end. After the present cease-fire lines, there will be new ones. They will extend beyond Jordan — perhaps to Lebanon and perhaps to central Syria as well.[66]

12

The Revolt of '83

Between 1975 and the end of 1983 there were about 180 cease-fires in Lebanon. Almost all of them were greeted with the usual Lebanese optimism, but on only two occasions did it seem that the fighting had really come to an end: in November 1976, when Syrian troops entered Beirut, and in the summer of 1982, when the Israeli army invaded Lebanon, defeated the Syrians, over-whelmed the radical Lebanese militias and forced the PLO to evacuate.

President Assad had sent his army into Lebanon in 1976 to prevent the defeat of the Maronite forces and to preserve a balance between the opposing sides. Syria was invited into the country by the Lebanese government and remained there, with the sanction of the Lebanese and the Arab League, to prevent a renewal of civil war. The aim of its intervention was to prevent an outright victory for either side, and it remained faithful to that objective during the subsequent years. As the Syrian foreign minister stressed in May 1983, 'we came in [to Lebanon] at the request of the Christians in 1976 to avoid Muslim domination. We will not allow Christian domination of the Muslims now.'[1]

The Israelis' objective was very different. They invaded Lebanon not in order to preserve a balance but to ally themselves with one party so as to destroy the other. Civil wars generally end only when one side has crushed the other, and the Israelis believed that the Lebanese conflict would be no exception. Their principal aim, therefore, was to defeat or expel the enemies of the Maronites and to set up a new regime, dominated by the Phalangist Party and closely allied to Israel. In the aftermath of the invasion it seemed as if the Israelis had been successful. Opposition to the Maronites collapsed, a Gemayel occupied the presidential palace, and Phalangist militiamen swarmed over central and southern Lebanon convinced that the war had been won.

But the war was not over. An artificial situation had been created, sustained by American support and Israel's military might. With Syria defeated, the Palestinians dispersed and the radicals demoralized, the new government could hold Beirut and its hinterland. But it could not do so indefinitely without making an honest and determined effort to unite the country. The Gemayel brothers were elected presidents because Israel had won their war for them; there was no other reason. Although they were both elected, more or less constitutionally, by the Lebanese parliament, every Lebanese knew that Bachir was the choice of the Israelis and Amin his natural successor. In spite of this disadvantage, however, the new regime might have survived, without Israeli help, had it tried to reconcile the Lebanese. But the Phalangists were in no mood for reconciliation. Aggressive, over-confident and insensitive to the resentments of the Muslim communities, they were determined to take advantage of 'their' victory and to 'Phalangize' the institutions of the country. The arrogance of their behaviour during the year following the Israeli invasion finally drove their Lebanese opponents into revolt.

If he had lived, Bachir Gemayel might have been able to control the extremists inside his party. He was a hardline Phalangist himself and the man who had made the party militia — now known, misleadingly, as the 'Lebanese Forces' — the largest and best-armed fighting group in the country. But his elder brother Amin, elected shortly after Bachir's assassination, was a moderate, perhaps the most reasonable and conciliatory of all the Maronite leaders involved in the fighting. Lacking the 'macho' glamour and brutal record of his brother, Amin was probably the best candidate — in the conditions that existed after the invasion — for the task of uniting his countrymen. Perhaps his principal problem was that he was not trusted by his party's militia leaders, the savage, uncompromising fanatics who had planned and directed the massacres at Sabra and Chatila.

Amin Gemayel was prepared to go some way towards national reconciliation, further than most of his traditional supporters, and for this reason his election was welcomed more by the Muslims than by the Phalangists. In the months after he became president, Amin's posters were plastered all over west Beirut but in the Christian areas of the east Bachir's photograph still predominated.

The Muslims voted for Amin because they hoped he would obstruct the efforts of the extremist Phalangists to carry out their programme. Saeb Salam, still the pre-eminent Sunni politician of Beirut, convinced many Muslims and Druzes that the election of Gemayel could lead to peace and national unity. The elderly former prime minister was prepared to go to almost any lengths to build bridges between the Lebanese, even to the extent of absolving the Phalangists of responsibility for the murders at Sabra and Chatila and placing the blame entirely on the Israelis. By the autumn of 1982 a clear majority of the Muslim and Druze population supported the new president. Amin Gemayel thus found himself with two very different sets of supporters and he tried to position his government somewhere midway between them. If he inclined towards the Phalangists, notably in his lists of new appointments, he was sufficiently conciliatory towards the Muslims to be dubbed 'Muhammad Amin' by the more intolerant Maronites. Furthermore, he resisted their calls for a full peace treaty with the Israelis, which he realized would lead to subservience to the Zionist state and fresh conflict among the Lebanese. But he needed an alternative ally and thus he turned to the United States.

America was not a happy choice. Apart from the inability of the Reagan administration to understand the complexities of the Lebanese conflict, there was the problem of American credibility in the Arab world. The United States was already playing several different and contradictory roles in Lebanon. It saw itself variously as the preserver of order, the builder of a new Lebanon, the ally of Israel, the enemy of the Soviet Union and the architect of a general Middle East peace — and it wanted to be all these things in Lebanon. But the Lebanese Muslims and most of the Arab world refused to trust the Americans. They knew that the then secretary of state, Alexander Haig, had encouraged the Israelis to invade Lebanon in 1982. And they could not see how a state, which had been an accomplice to the devastation and massive casualties caused by that invasion, could pose as a credible peace-maker a month or so later.

During the first twelve months of Amin Gemayel's presidency, the ambiguities of America's role became steadily more pronounced. US marines were stationed in Beirut to protect the civilian popula-tion from further massacres but other American soldiers were in Lebanon to advise and train the Lebanese army. The Americans made themselves the guarantors of a regime which gradually alien-ated a growing number of the Lebanese population. And they were prepared, as events proved, to use force to back that regime at a time when it was manifestly unpopular and unrepresenta-tive. Not surprisingly, many Arabs came to believe that the United States was not in Lebanon to promote a just peace, but to turn the country into an ally of the West and to achieve a settlement accept-able to Israel.

On 1st September 1982, shortly after the PLO's evacuation from Beirut, President Reagan announced a new plan to settle the Arab–Israeli conflict. His chief proposal, which every country in the world except Israel had long since accepted, was that the ter-ritories occupied by Israel since 1967 should be returned to the Arabs, although the Americans remained opposed to the creation of a Palestinian state in the West Bank and Gaza and called for 'self-government' there in 'association with Jordan'. The plan was immediately rejected by Israel while the Arab states countered a week later with their own proposals, which were similar to Reagan's and implicitly recognized Israel's right to exist. Once their plan had been broadcast, however, the Americans decided not to do anything actively to promote it and they concentrated instead on more minor matters. When the new secretary of state, George Shultz, embarked on his first round of Middle East diplomacy, he made no attempt to achieve an overall settlement of the Arab–Israeli conflict but simply to solve the problem that seemed to Washington to be the most urgent: the withdrawal of foreign forces — Syrians, Israelis as well as those Palestinian units still in the north of the country — from Lebanese soil. Curiously enough, he thought it superfluous to talk to the Syrians or Pales-

tinians about this project. He evidently thought it sufficient to
negotiate the withdrawal of the Israelis, after which the others
would voluntarily leave.

Throughout the autumn of 1982 American diplomats shuffled
between Lebanon and Israel and held a series of fruitless discussions with both sides. Not until January of the following year
did the two countries even agree on an agenda for the negotiations.
Each of them had very different priorities. The Lebanese wanted
to discuss the withdrawal of the Israeli army and were prepared,
as a concession, to make some security arrangements along their
mutual border. Withdrawal, however, was not the Israelis' chief
concern. They were prepared to go if they got what they asked
for, but they were quite happy to stay if the Lebanese proved to
be unco-operative. The first thing they wanted was 'normalization
of relations' between the two countries, if possible a formal peace
treaty but if not, something that closely resembled one. Their
next concern was to erect a powerful 'security' barrier over southern
Lebanon. The defence minister Sharon demanded that Israel
should retain military bases in the area. He also insisted that the
Lebanese should put Saad Haddad, the rebel Lebanese officer, in
charge of the south. Understandably, the Beirut government
rejected both of these suggestions, arguing that Israel had only one
legitimate demand, and that was that Lebanon should never again
be used as a base for operations against it.

Negotiations between the two countries remained barren until
the end of April when Shultz, eight months after the announcement of the Reagan Plan, finally decided to visit the Middle East.
After a series of consultations with Arab and Israeli leaders, the
secretary of state was able to persuade the two governments to
sign on 17 May an agreement providing for the withdrawal of
Israeli troops from Lebanon. While Israel did not manage to
achieve some of the more ambitious security demands which
Sharon had been making — there were to be no military bases in
the south and Haddad was not given command of the area — the
agreement did provide for the establishment of joint Israeli–
Lebanese patrols working inside the Lebanese border. Although
the terms were somewhat disappointing to Israel's most hawkish
leaders, one senior politician argued that the agreement achieved

'the major goal of neutralizing Lebanon and putting it in the American sphere of influence'.[2]

Shultz's handling of the negotiations was a personal achievement but it was soon nullified by his clumsy treatment of the Syrians. The Israeli government had made it clear that any agreement to pull back its troops was conditional on a commitment from the Syrians to withdraw their army simultaneously from the Bekaa valley. It should have been obvious, therefore, that the Americans would have to exercise some diplomacy with the Damascus regime. Astonishingly, Shultz decided initially to ignore Assad altogether and later to try to bully him into accepting the agreement. At no time did he offer the Syrians an incentive to co-operate. As Philip Habib, Reagan's special envoy to the Middle East, told a British journalist at the time, 'we know Syria won't willingly accept the terms of this accord. It must now accept them unwillingly.'[3]

The Syrian government quickly denounced the agreement, complaining that it infringed Lebanese sovereignty and turned the country into an Israeli protectorate. The first claim was only technically true and the second was entirely untrue. Had the agreement been carried out, Lebanon might possibly have become a sort of American protectorate but it would not have become an Israeli one. Most Lebanese were surprised that the agreement had not given more to the Israelis and a large majority would have welcomed its implementation. Had the United States accomplished the agreement in the autumn of 1982, it might have persuaded the Syrian government, demoralized by its brisk military defeat in June, to accept it. But by May of the following year, when Syria was enjoying closer ties with the Soviet Union and receiving quantities of Soviet weapons, Assad's position had hardened. Humiliated by American diplomacy, which entirely ignored his own country's interests, he was disinclined to accept an agreement that seemed to benefit only the United States, Israel and the pro-Western government of Amin Gemayel. 1982 had been a disastrous year for the Syrians and they were determined to recover their losses. The Israelis, who had recently annexed the Syrian Golan Heights and whose guns could bombard Damascus without difficulty, were now in occupation of the southern half of Lebanon, while an anti-Syrian government was installed in

Beirut. The Syrians' influence in a country which many of them still regarded as an extension of their own, was thus reduced to the northern regions.

That the United States believed that Assad would willingly accept an agreement which confirmed Syria's loss of influence in Lebanon is an indication of the quality of American foreign policy. Only one thing could have induced the Syrians to leave Lebanon at that time — a commitment from the Americans to persuade the Israelis to withdraw from the West Bank and the Golan Heights. But if the Americans were not prepared to co-operate with Syria over its legitimate grievances, then Syria was not prepared to co-operate with the Americans over Lebanon.

Shortly after the announcement of the Shultz agreement, a Lebanese opposition group calling itself the National Salvation Front was formed. Its three leaders were Suleiman Frangieh, the former president, Rashid Karami, the former prime minister, and Walid Jumblatt, the Druze leader and president of the Progressive Socialist Party. The front was clearly inspired by Syria and was prepared to co-operate with Assad, but its leaders were not simply Syrian stooges. They represented a growing number of Lebanese who were becoming disenchanted with Amin Gemayel's regime, and in particular with the president's failure to curb the Phalangists. It was not only the Druzes or the Sunnis of the north who had turned against Gemayel. The Shi'ites and the Sunni community of Beirut had also lost faith in his ability to reunite the country. Even Saeb Salam, Gemayel's most respected Muslim ally, began to criticize the Maronites for their overbearing behaviour.

From the beginning of Amin Gemayel's presidency it was clear that the Phalangists were not going to abide by the traditional Lebanese formula, 'no victor, no vanquished'. They considered themselves as victors — although in fact their 'victory' had been won not by them but by their Israeli allies — and they were determined to behave as such. They were prepared to co-operate with the new president on condition that he recognized their predominance in the new regime and, to 'encourage' him to do so, they made it clear they they would not disband their powerful militia of 25,000 men. Gemayel was thus hampered from the outset by the existence of a military force — larger, better-armed and more highly motivated than the Lebanese army — which appointed itself overseer of his government's actions. Inhibited by this threatening posture, he decided, probably with reluctance, that the Phalangists would have to be treated with the deference they were demanding. Considering that he himself was one of the party's deputies, that his father was the party's founder and that his late brother had been the party's militia leader, this was perhaps not surprising. It was, nonetheless, a disastrous decision. Within weeks of his election, Lebanon's Muslims had been warned that they were to be treated very differently from the country's Christians. Following Israel's withdrawal from west Beirut after the Sabra/Chatila massacres, the Lebanese army moved swiftly into the city and hauled off hundreds of Muslims for interrogation. Its 'cleaning-up' operation was carried out harshly and with uncharacteristic vigour in the western half of the capital. But there was no corresponding move into the eastern districts. Amin Gemayel did not dare to send the army into areas controlled by the Phalangists and backed away from a possible confrontation. Eventually some army units did cross into east Beirut but they formed only a token force and they did not go anywhere where their presence might have been resented.

While the Phalangists kept their militia in readiness to thwart the president should he prove too conciliatory, they also demanded a large share of appointments in the army and government service. Once again Gemayel acquiesced. In the foreign service, for example, career diplomats were shunted aside to make way for political appointments. In Washington, where the embassy was traditionally given to a Muslim, the new ambassador was a pro-Phalangist Maronite; in London his counterpart was a pro-Gemayel Muslim. In the universities it was a similar story. The president of the American University of Beirut (AUB) was told by Gemayel himself to 'Lebanize' the university.[4] The AUB, which had long been a centre of Arab nationalism, suddenly found itself besieged by Phalangists wanting places and teaching positions. In the past the Maronites had ignored the AUB, preferring to send their children to the French-speaking St Joseph University instead. But now they were determined to penetrate the American University and purge the Arab nationalists. Phalangists tried to gain control of the student union but later forced the cancellation of elections when it was obvious that they were going to lose them. The strength of the Phalangist assault on the university became clear in May 1983 when the government refused to renew the residence permits of three faculty members of Palestinian origin.

Gemayel's worst mistake was his failure to control the behaviour of the Phalangist militiamen. For seven years they had been cooped up in east Beirut and the Maronite regions to the north and, now that the Israelis had disposed of their enemies, they felt like expanding their presence to the south. With full Israeli co-operation they entered west Beirut, where they carried out the massacres of Sabra and Chatila; the Chouf, where they began fighting the Druzes; and the south, where they harassed the Muslim population and the surviving Palestinian refugees. In none of these areas had they had a significant presence before and their behaviour, which consisted largely of looting and kidnapping, was bound to provoke retaliation. The Phalangist commanders were determined to make national reconciliation impossible and to frustrate any concessions the president might wish to make to the Muslims or to the Arab world. They were prepared to embarrass Gemayel and, if possible, force him to take a stronger pro-Israeli line. In the summer of 1983 they opened ostentatious new barracks in east Beirut, although technically the Lebanese army was meant to be the only military force in the capital, and they even entertained the new Israeli defence minister, Moshe Arens. As in 1975 they were provocative, over-confident and longing for a fight: 'Let the war take place and let the strongest win', declared Pierre Gemayel in early August.[5] As in 1975 they got their war, and as in 1975 they lost it.

The underlying cause of the 'September War' of 1983 was the behaviour of the Phalangist Party during the previous twelve months. The immediate cause was the behaviour of its militiamen in the Chouf. From the beginning of the civil war in 1975 the mountainous region to the south of the Beirut—Damascus road had been one of the few comparatively peaceful areas of the country. There had been a bad outbreak of sectarian killing in March 1977, when Kamal Jumblatt was assassinated, but this had been brought to an end by his son Walid. During the seven years of almost continuous warfare in Lebanon, there had been no other fighting in the region. The Chouf was inhabited by people from different sects, including a considerable number of Maronites, but it was generally accepted that it was the homeland of the Druze community. The traditional za'ims were Jumblatt and Camille Chamoun and, although they disliked each other intensely, they agreed not to settle their differences in the Chouf. The loyalty of the local Maronites to Chamoun and his party meant that there was no room for the Phalangists in the region and this contributed to its tranquility. But the situation changed in the summer of 1982 when the Israelis brought the Phalangists into the Chouf and encouraged them to set up outposts. The militiamen decided to assert their superiority by harassing the local population, and the Druzes retaliated. Within a short time the Chouf had become the scene of a savage little war of kidnapping and killings.

The leader of the Druzes was Walid Jumblatt, a young man in his mid-thirties who had, in true Lebanese style, 'inherited' his father's positions both as the pre-eminent Druze sheikh and spokesman of the Lebanese left. Owing to his casual appearance, his flippant manner with journalists and his rather wild rhetoric, Walid Jumblatt was treated somewhat contemptuously by the foreign media; the Middle East correspondent of *The Times*, an otherwise excellent reporter, abandoned all normal conventions of journalism when discussing him. Yet behind the frivolity and the sardonic humour, Jumblatt was an intelligent man with a strong sense of obligation towards the Druze community. In the summer of 1983 both the Phalangists and the Israelis occupied the Chouf. The fact that neither of them were still there after the September fighting is a tribute both to his political skills and to the fighting qualities of his followers.

Amin Gemayel's government badly miscalculated over Walid Jumblatt. Like the foreign media, it underestimated the Druze leader, believing that without Palestinian or radical Lebanese support, he had become powerless. With the Chouf under Israeli–Phalangist control, and Jumblatt choosing to live in Amman or Damascus rather than in his occupied homeland, it was con-

fidently assumed that he could be ignored. When Jumblatt tried
to see Amin Gemayel in the autumn of 1983 he was told to come
back several weeks later. When he asked the president to remove
the Phalangist militiamen from the Chouf in order to avoid further
bloodshed, his request was turned down. Through its own blindness
the Lebanese government thus turned the Druze leader into its
most formidable opponent.

Walid Jumblatt's objectives were two-fold. He wanted to get
the Phalangist militia out of the Chouf and he wanted to reverse
the process of 'Phalangization' by forcing Amin Gemayel to
choose a government more representative of the country's Muslim
majority. But he knew that he needed the support of the Syrians
or the Israelis before he could achieve either aim. As his plans
coincided with those of the Syrians, he naturally enlisted their
support, but he also managed to acquire some help from the
Israelis. A year after the invasion, many Israelis were disillusioned
by their government's policy in Lebanon. Apart from all the
destruction and the massive Arab casualties, 500 Israeli soldiers
had been killed and people from all sides were clamouring for an
end to the occupation. A powerful voice was added to Begin's
critics when Shlomo Argov, the former Israeli ambassador whose
near-fatal shooting in London had triggered off the invasion,
denounced the war altogether. 'Only the charlatans can say that
the war was worthwhile,' he declared. 'Those who initiated the
war and led the nation towards it should have thought twice
about the cost, especially the cost in human life . . . Israel must
keep away from useless military adventures.'[6] In response to so
much criticism, the Israeli government began to discuss proposals
for a limited withdrawal of its troops to the Awali river north of
Sidon.

One of the Israelis' principal complaints was that they were
regularly losing men in ambushes and bomb attacks without
making any political advances. The year before everything had
seemed so simple: Sharon would charge into Lebanon, bash the
Syrians, expel the PLO, install a puppet government, leave Haddad
in charge of the south, and then the Israelis would go home and
enjoy the fruits of neo-imperialism. But it turned out to be more
complicated than that. In spite of their military and political

weakness, the Lebanese were not prepared to submit to the Begin–Sharon diktat because they knew submission would split the country irredeemably. The Israelis became impatient, both with the Beirut government and with their main ally, the Phalangist Party. They had had high hopes of the Phalangists and had chosen them as partners in their Lebanese venture. But the Phalangists had not co-operated. Instead of helping the Israelis during the invasion they had stood aside and had only become involved when the PLO had left and they were able to butcher unarmed refugees without fear of retaliation. The Israelis helped the Phalangists establish themselves around Sidon and in the Chouf but later they seem to have regretted it. At the beginning of August 1983 they ordered the Phalangists to move out of their main base in southern Lebanon. Several months earlier they had begun helping the Druzes stand up to the militiamen in the Chouf.

Although the Israelis had introduced the Phalangists to the Chouf, they were reluctant to let them maltreat the Druze population, because Israel had its own Druze citizens who had strong feelings of kinship with their Lebanese co-religionists. Moreover, the Israeli Druzes were well represented in the army and many of them were then serving in Lebanon. Walid Jumblatt was not, of course, an ideal ally for the Israelis and they at first tried to set up and arm rival Druze groups. But when these failed they offered to help him, on condition that he did not allow PLO units back into the Chouf. For Jumblatt it was a question of survival and he was prepared to accept assistance from anyone willing to help him get rid of the Phalangists. In the spring and summer of 1983 the Israeli-occupied Chouf thus became a battlefield between Israeli-armed Druzes and Israeli-armed Phalangists who were only there in the first place because the Israelis had put them there. The fighting, which usually went in favour of the Druzes, was savage enough even when the Israelis were occupying the region. But everyone knew it would be far worse if the Israelis made a precipitate withdrawal to the Awali river.

By the beginning of August 1983 the most vital question in Lebanon had become: what would happen in the Chouf after the Israelis had withdrawn? The government was insistent that the area should be occupied by the Lebanese army, and in normal conditions this would have seemed a reasonable answer. But the conditions were far from normal. The army was not the neutral force whose impartiality a quarter of a century earlier had prevented a previous civil war from escalating. It was armed and trained by the United States, and commanded by a Phalangist president. From the point of view of the Druzes, the difference between the reconstituted army and the Phalangist militia was insignificant. If the army was allowed into the Chouf after the Israeli withdrawal, it was bound to favour the Phalangists in their battles with the Druzes. Jumblatt thus informed Gemayel that his men would not allow the army into their area without a prior political agreement leading to the creation of a more representative government. When the president once again ignored him, Jumblatt took the initiative and on 10 August his artillery shelled Beirut airport and some positions of the Lebanese army.

While the government was preparing its troops for an assault on the Chouf once the Israelis had left, it also decided to reassert its authority in west Beirut. At the end of August an army force confronted armed Shi'ites in the capital and, although it was unable to break through to Amal's headquarters in Borj al-Barajneh, it performed effectively against the Muslim militiamen. Shortly afterwards, in order to make matters as difficult as possible for Gemayel, the Israelis pulled back without warning from the Chouf. As the government's most reliable battalions were in west Beirut and as the Israelis took only six hours to evacuate, it was obviously impossible for the army to reach the region before full-scale fighting broke out. The Druzes and Phalangists attacked each other immediately and, after some ferocious battles, Jumblatt's forces were victorious, driving their opponents from almost the entire region in a matter of days. Having earlier lost the town of Aley, the Phalangists now lost their stronghold at Bhamdoun while at Deir el-Qamar they retreated into the town and sent out frantic requests for help. The foremost Maronite militia, which considered itself the most powerful indigenous force in Lebanon, thus found itself, after more than eight years of fighting, still unable to claim a single military victory against an *armed* opponent. Even when the army joined in the fighting, collaborating closely with the Phalangists, they were unable to regain the lost ground.

The army thus sided with one faction of the Lebanese against another and the country was once again at war with itself. As in the nineteenth century, Druzes and Maronites were fighting each other with peculiar savagery in the Lebanese mountains. But the government and its American backers refused to recognize that this was a civil conflict. The Americans, still incensed by the Syrian sabotage of the Shultz agreement, claimed that the fighting was a plot originating in Moscow and orchestrated in Damascus. Gemayel agreed, announcing that his army was not fighting other Lebanese but Syrians and Palestinians.

Certainly the Syrians provided the Druzes with weapons and some artillery support, but they did not do any of the fighting. Nor, it appears, did the Palestinians, at least in any significant numbers. There may have been PLO guerrillas with Jumblatt's men but there was little evidence of them. When a senior journalist on *The Times* went to the Chouf looking for Palestinians, he had to report that he had been unable to find any.[7] The truth, which neither the Lebanese nor the American governments were prepared to face, was the Lebanon's civil war had started up again. The Druzes, who were fighting in the mountains, and their Shi'ite allies, who were attacking the army as well as US marine positions around Beirut, were opposing a government that had come to represent little more than the Maronite interest.

Nevertheless, the United States argued that it was supporting a legitimate government in danger of being overthrown by 'foreigners' and thus decided to intervene militarily in Gemayel's favour. By the fourth week in September government troops were under siege in Souk al-Garb, a resort town in the Chouf foothills overlooking Beirut. If they had been left to fight it out with the Druzes by themselves, there is no doubt that the town would have fallen. But suddenly Souk al-Garb was transformed, by the Americans, into a Lebanese Verdun. No matter what had happened elsewhere, through Souk al-Garb the Druzes would not be allowed to pass. American officers were thus sent up to the town to direct its defence while ships from the US navy bombarded Druze and Syrian positions nearby. For a few days the Americans placed the credibility of their Lebanese policy on the retention of a small town which few people outside Lebanon had ever heard of.

The American action could well have been the beginning of a further escalation and the involvement of other powers. But for once common sense prevailed. On 25 September a cease-fire was agreed, brought about by concessions made by both sides. Jumblatt and his allies no longer insisted on an immediate change of government, while Gemayel abandoned his attempt to deploy the army in the Chouf. Meanwhile all Lebanese factions were to be represented by a National Reconciliation Committee which would meet to sort out the country's problems.

The composition of this committee, announced the following day, was not, however, encouraging. The familiar names were all there — Chamoun, Gemayel, Frangieh, Karami, Salam, Eddé, Osseiran* — the gang of septuagenarian za'ims who had presided over, and been in large part responsible for, Lebanon's tragic history. Any list of politicians since the 1930s would have included them, or their fathers or brothers; only the Shi'ite leader Nabih Berri did not belong to the za'ims' club. As usual after a crisis, they were being asked to congregate and settle their differences. If the historical precedents were anything to go by, the chances of success were poor. In the autumn of 1975 a similar committee, composed of much the same people, was set up to end the fighting of that year. Not only did they fail to co-operate then, most of them could not even be bothered to attend the committee meetings. Besides, it was difficult to be optimistic of the chances of reconciliation between the Lebanese communities when many of their leaders were not even on speaking terms, or when two of them, Frangieh and Pierre Gemayel, had had a blood feud since Frangieh's son and grandchild were murdered by Phalangists in 1978.

After a long squabble over where it was to meet, the National Reconciliation Committee finally gathered in Geneva on the last

---

* The three younger members of the committee were Walid Jumblatt, Nabih Berri and Amin Gemayel, who was chairman. The only member who refused to participate was Raymond Eddé, who had been living in voluntary exile in Paris for the previous few years.

day of October. There were then more squabbles, firstly over the shape of the negotiating table, and then over the indignity of having to walk through metal detectors — even when Frangieh had reluctantly left his gun behind, the machine was still set off by his gold cigarette case. The youngest of the delegates, Walid Jumblatt, livened up the proceedings by trying to take a camera into the conference room so that he could photograph 'these antiques', as he referred to his fellow delegates. But beyond the farcical, prima donna aspect of the conference, the old za'ims were at last beginning to sit down and patch up their quarrels. The well-publicized embrace between Frangieh and Amin Gemayel was widely believed to have cancelled the blood feud between the two families. Frangieh also made it up with Camille Chamoun who, over the previous thirty years, had several times been both a close ally and a bitter opponent. Having not spoken for five years, the 83-year-old Chamoun dropped into Frangieh's hotel suite and re-established cordial relations by talking about the handsome French shotgun he had just bought at a Geneva gunsmith's.

The conference was, thus, a modest success. It produced a new formula for Lebanon which described it as 'an Arab country, a founder member of the Arab League [which] is bound by all the obligations of that membership'. The delegates also agreed that while the Shultz agreement of 17 May would not be ratified, neither would it be abrogated. President Gemayel was then urged by the whole committee to work out a replacement document which would lead to the withdrawal of Israeli troops.

A week before the delegates arrived in Geneva, two 'kamikaze' lorries packed with explosive were driven into the compounds of the French and American peace-keeping units in Beirut. In the explosions nearly 300 marines and French paratroopers were killed. During the conference itself another suicide lorry destroyed most of the Israeli army headquarters in Tyre and left a further 60 people dead. Although Lebanon was still supposedly governed by the 25 September cease-fire, there was continous sniping going on in the outskirts of Beirut while, in the north, rebel Palestinian groups backed by Syria besieged Yasser Arafat and his loyalist Fatah guerrillas in two refugee camps outside Tripoli. The prospect of peace for the shattered country looked as distant as ever. Yet neither the cease-fire nor the subsequent conference in Geneva should be considered a waste of effort. They did bring about a basic, grudging unity among the Lebanese leaders, who were at last able to agree on some fundamental points. They did reflect certain truths about Lebanon, historical, political and geographical truths which have long been ignored, by France during the mandate, by the Maronite Christians for most of this century, by the United States and Israel in recent years. The first and most obvious of these is that Lebanon, whatever else it may be besides, is an Arab country and a part of the Arab world. Israeli attempts to set up a client state headed by the Phalangist Party, or American attempts to rebuild the country in a Western mould, will only lead to instability and violence. The second important truth is that Syria, for a variety of historical and other reasons, will always be the most important foreign country for Lebanon. This may or may not be regrettable but it is a fact of Lebanese life and, as President Reagan belatedly discovered, it is dangerous to ignore it.

The inability of Lebanon's leaders to stop the violence even when they were for once in agreement reflected yet another truth: that their country's problems probably cannot be solved con-clusively except in the context of an overall peace settlement in the Fertile Crescent. The Lebanese war, in origin and in essence, is a civil war between Lebanese factions. But it has become far more than that. It is a part of the Arab—Israeli conflict and should be treated as such. Reconciliation between the Lebanese would be a fine thing but its success will depend as much on others as on the Lebanese themselves. Lebanon is too complicated to be solved by the simplistic approach of the Americans and the Israelis. Superimposed upon its original conflict between Francophiles and Arab nationalists are a mass of other overlapping conflicts — social, religious and political: Chamounists against Nasserists, Phalangists against Palestinians, Israelis against Palestinians, Syrians against Israelis, Druzes against Maronites and so on — there are many others.

It is impossible to try to solve one of these conflicts by itself. There can only be peace if there is a regional settlement, where all parties get something tangible in addition to peace. 'There is room for everybody in the Middle East,' Kamal Jumblatt once rightly said, 'but not for every ambition.'[8] There can be peace in the Middle East but not if certain peoples and certain communities insist on fulfilling their own ambitions at the expense of all the others. Both Lebanon and Israel/Palestine must be shared by the peoples of those countries. The Maronites tried to 'Maronize' Lebanon and thus reduced their country to a rubble. The Israelis have tried to 'Zionize' Palestine — without leaving the Palestinians a square inch of their own — and they have turned the Middle East into the world's powder keg. Only when justice has been done to the region's dispossessed peoples will there be a chance for real peace. Without it, the future holds only a further succession of wars and occupations and atrocities. At the heart of the conflict, the sufferings of the Lebanese and Palestinian people will continue into yet another generation.

References

Chapter 1   Modern Lebanon

1. Survey by Associated Business Consultants, George Murray, *Lebanon: the New Future* (1974) p. 206.
2. See Michael C. Hudson, *The Precarious Republic* (1968) p. 63.
3. Quoted in David R. Smock and Audrey C. Smock, *The Politics of Pluralism* (1975) p. 154.
4. See David C. Gordon, *Lebanon: the Fragmented Nation* (1980) p. 127.
5. Halim Said Abu-Izzedin (ed), *Lebanon and its Provinces: a study by the governors of five provinces*, (1963) p. 105.
6. See the article by Johnny Rizq and Harry Turnbull, 'Hostility to proposed rent law stalls action on housing', *MEED*, 17 February 1978.
7. Figures given by IRFED, *Besoins et Possibilités de Développement du Liban*, Ministry of General Planning, Beirut 1960–61.
8. See the article by Charles Issawi, 'Economic Development and Political Liberalism in Lebanon' in Leonard Binder (ed), *Politics in Lebanon* (1966) p. 79.
9. Kamal Jumblatt, *I Speak for Lebanon* (1982) p. 49.
10. Eric Rouleau, *Le Monde*, 23 September 1975.
11. Abu-Izzedin, *op. cit.* p. 114.
12. See Michael Wall, 'The tightrope country: a survey of Lebanon', *The Economist*, 26 January 1974.
13. For a discussion of the importance of the family in Lebanese life see Samih K. Farsoun, 'Family Structure and Society in Modern Lebanon' in Louise E. Sweet (ed), *Peoples and Cultures of the Middle East*, (1970) pp 257–307.
14. Y. Sayigh, *Entrepreneurs of Lebanon* (1962) p. 54.
15. Elie Adib Salem, *Modernization without Revolution: Lebanon's Experience* (1973) p. 50.
16. Abu-Izzedin, *op. cit.* p. 63.

17. *Ibid*. pp. 58—61.
18. See Murray, *op. cit*. p. 65.
19. Ministry of Health figures quoted in Murray, *op. cit*. p. 61.
20. Gordon, *op. cit*. p. 137.
21. Rashid Karami. Quoted in Salem, *op. cit*. p. 121.
22. This was the IRFED study, *op. cit*.
23. Salem, *op. cit*. p. 169.

Chapter 2   The Religious Factor

1. Michael C. Hudson, *The Precarious Republic* (1968) p. 34.
2. Quoted in Walid Khalidi, *Conflict and Violence in Lebanon*, (1979) p. 162.
3. Quoted in Elie Adib Salem, *Modernization without Revolution: Lebanon's Experience* (1973) p. 165.
4. Quoted in David R. Smock and Audrey C. Smock, *The Politics of Pluralism* (1975) p. 85.
5. Clovis Maksoud in 'Lebanon and Arab Nationalism' in Leonard Binder (ed), *Politics in Lebanon* (1966) p. 251.
6. Smock and Smock, *op. cit*. p. 169.
7. Quoted in Desmond Stewart, *Turmoil in Beirut* (1958) p. 88.
8. The text of the Eisenhower Doctrine is reprinted in Leila M. T. Meo, *Lebanon: Improbable Nation* (1965) pp. 219—21.
9. Quoted in Odd Bull, *War and Peace in the Middle East* (1976) p. 20.
10. In conversation with Desmond Stewart, *op. cit*. p. 75.

Chapter 3   Democracy: the Lebanese Version

1. Georges Naccache, who was then (1952) editor of *L'Orient*. Quoted in David R. Smock and Audrey C. Smock, *The Politics of Pluralism* (1975) p. 144.
2. See Arnold Hottinger, 'Zu'ama' in Historical Perspective' in Leonard Binder (ed), *Politics in Lebanon* (1966) p. 97.
3. Jumblatt, *op. cit*. p. 32.
4. See Hottinger, *op. cit*. pp. 88—93.
5. Edward Shils, 'The Prospect for Lebanese Civility' in Binder, *op. cit*. p. 4.
6. John P. Entelis, *Pluralism and Party Transformation in Lebanon*, (1974) p. 140.
7. Michael C. Hudson, *The Precarious Republic* (1968) p. 255.
8. See Jamal Toubi, 'Social Dynamics in War-Torn Lebanon' in *The Jerusalem Quarterly*, Autumn 1980, pp. 96—98.

9. Ralph E. Crow, 'Parliament in the Lebanese Political System' in Allan Kornberg and Lloyd D. Musolf (eds), *Legislatures in Developmental Perspective* (1970) p. 294.
10. See John Bulloch, *Death of a Country* (1977) p. 63.
11. Smock and Smock, *op. cit.* p. 115.
12. See article by Malcolm H. Kerr, 'Political Decision Making in a Confessional Democracy' in Binder, *op. cit.* pp. 196–200.
13. Roger Owen, 'The political economy of the Grand Liban, 1920–1970', in Roger Owen (ed), *Essays on the Crisis in Lebanon* (1976) p. 31.
14. See Kamal Salibi, *Crossroads to Civil War: Lebanon 1958–1976* (1976) p. 56.
15. Elie Adib Salem, *Modernization without Revolution: Lebanon's Experience* (1973) p. 101.
16. Quoted in Salem, *op. cit.* p. 90.
17. Desmond Stewart, *Orphan with a hoop: the Life of Emile Bustani*, (1967) p. 130.
18. Elie Adib Salem, 'Lebanon's Political Maze: the Search for Peace in a Turbulent Land' in *The Middle East Journal*, Autumn 1979, p. 450.
19. Jumblatt, *op. cit.* p. 48.
20. Quoted in David C. Gordon, *Lebanon: the Fragmented Nation* (1980) p. 101.

Chapter 4   The Arab Nationalists

1. Quoted in A. L. Tibawi, *A Modern History of Syria* (1969) p. 159.
2. See George Antonius, *The Arab Awakening* (1938) Chapters 3 and 5. Tibawi, *op. cit.* finds Antonius's account exaggerated, see pp. 163–7.
3. Quoted in E. S. Stevens, *Cedars, Saints and Sinners in Syria*, (no date) p. 251.
4. Cited in S. H. Longrigg, *Syria and Lebanon under French Mandate*, Oxford University Press, Oxford, 1958, p. 45.
5. From Sharif Hussein's fourth note to Sir Henry McMahon, 1 January 1916. The text is published in Antonius, *op. cit.* pp. 424–6.
6. The text of the declaration is published in Antonius, *op. cit.* pp. 435–6.
7. Cited in Zeine N. Zeine, *The Struggle for Arab Independence* (1960) p. 122.
8. Edward Spears, *Fulfilment of a Mission: Syria and Lebanon 1941–1944*, (1977) p. 82.
9. Those parts of the King-Crane commission dealing with Syria-Palestine and Iraq are reproduced in Antonius, *op. cit.* pp. 443–58.

10. See Walid Khalidi, *Conflict and Violence in Lebanon* (1979) p. 159.
11. Harry N. Howard, *The King-Crane Commission* (1963) pp. 143–5.
12. See Antonius, *op. cit.* pp. 443–58.
13. See Labib Zuwiyya Yamak, *The Syrian Social Nationalist Party* (1966) p. 39.
14. Spears, *op. cit.* p. 14.
15. Quoted in Spears, *Ibid.* p. 249.
16. *Ibid.*
17. Kamal Jumblatt, *I Speak for Lebanon* (1982) p. 33.
18. *Ibid.* p. 32.
19. Quoted in David C. Gordon, *Lebanon: the Fragmented Nation* (1980) p. 158.

Chapter 5   Libanisme and the Maronites

1. Quoted in Fernand Braudel, *The Mediterranean* Vol. I (1970) p. 40.
2. Quoted in Tewfik Khalaf, 'The Phalange and the Maronite Community', Roger Owen (ed) *Essays on the Crisis in Lebanon*, (1976) p. 43.
3. Jumblatt, *op. cit.* p. 39.
4. Quoted in E. S. Stevens, *Cedars, Saints and Sinners in Syria*, (no date) p. 257.
5. See Ilya Harik, 'The Maronite Church and Political Change in Lebanon' in Leonard Binder (ed), *Politics in Lebanon* (1966) pp. 49–50.
6. Kamal Salibi, *The Modern History of Lebanon* (1965) p. 163.
7. R. Hrair Dekmejian, *Patterns of Political Leadership* (1975) p. 74.
8. George Murray, *Lebanon: the New Future* (1974) p. 116.
9. Labib Zuwiyya Yamak, *The Syrian Social Nationalist Party*, (1966) p. 36.
10. *Ibid.* p. 51.
11. John P. Entelis, *Pluralism and Party Transformation in Lebanon* (1974) p. 77.
12. Zuwiyya Yamak, *op. cit.* p. 48.
13. Quoted in Tewfik Khalaf, 'The Phalange and the Maronite Community' in Roger Owen (ed), *Essays on the Crisis in Lebanon* (1976) p. 46.
14. Quoted in Labib Zuwiyya Yamak, 'Party Politics in the Lebanese Political System' in Binder, *op. cit.* p. 151.
15. Salibi, *op. cit.* p. 87.
16. *The Times*, 10 February 1976.
17. Entelis, *op. cit.* p. 46.
18. *Ibid.* p. 52.

19. Eric Rouleau, quoted in Michael C. Hudson, 'The Lebanese Crisis: the Limits of Consociational Democracy', *The Journal of Palestine Studies*, Spring—Summer 1976, p. 120.
20. See David C. Gordon, *Lebanon: the Fragmented Nation* (1980) p. 150.

Chapter 6   The Palestinian Presence

1. *Ha Sepher Ha Palmach*, Vol. 2, p. 286; cited in David Hirst, *The Gun and the Olive Branch* (1977) p. 41.
2. For an excellent description of the campaign in Galilee see Nafez Nazzal, *The Palestinian Exodus from Galilee* (1978).
3. UNRWA newsletter, April—May 1964.
4. Quoted in Rosemary Sayigh, *Palestinians: From Peasants to Revolutionaries* (1979) p. 115.
5. Fawaz Turki, *The Disinherited: Journal of a Palestinian Exile* (2nd ed.) (1974) p. 41.
6. Bassem Sirhan, 'Palestinian Refugee Camp Life in Lebanon', *Journal of Palestine Studies*, 14 (Winter 1975), p. 101.
7. *Ibid.*
8. Quoted in Sabri Jiryis, 'The Nature of the Palestine Liberation Movement', a paper delivered at a seminar organized by the Committee on the Exercise of the Inalienable Rights of the Palestinian People in Vienna, August 1980. UAR, Ministry of National Guidance, *Documents and Papers on the Palestine Question*, Cairo 1969, Vol. 2, p. 1373.
9. From a speech at the fifteenth annual conference of the Phalangist Party at Chtaura, 22 September 1972.
10. Quoted in David C. Gordon, *Lebanon: the Fragmented Nation* (1980) p. 68.
11. Cable from the National Assembly of Egypt to the Chamber of Deputies of Lebanon, 10 December 1972.
12. The Cairo Agreement is reproduced in Walid Khalidi, *Conflict and Violence in Lebanon* (1979) pp. 185—7.

Chapter 7   The Maronite Reaction

1. Quoted in Frank Stoakes, 'The Supervigilantes: the Lebanese Ketaeb Party as a Builder, Surrogate and Defender of the State', *Middle Eastern Studies*, October 1975, p. 222.
2. From a statement by President Frangieh on 2 June 1972.

3. Jean-Pierre Haddad, *Le Combat du Liban* (1977) p. 26.
4. Kamal Jumblatt, *I Speak for Lebanon* (1982) p. 94.
5. Quoted in David C. Gordon, *Lebanon: the Fragmented Nation*, (1980) p. 86.
6. Quoted in Haddad, *op. cit.* p. 45.
7. *Ibid.* p. 37.
8. See for example the article by Yvonne Sursock Cochrane, a passionate supporter of the Phalangist Party, in *The Times*, 5 May 1976.
9. Cited in *Al-Bayrak*, 31 May 1976.
10. Quoted in Haddad, *op. cit.* p. 136.

Chapter 8   Civil War

1. See Walid Khalidi, *Conflict and Violence in Lebanon*, (1979) p. 67.
2. *The Times*, 19 April 1975.
3. *Daily Star*, 18 June 1975. Quoted in David C. Gordon, *Lebanon: the Fragmented Nation* (1980) p. 240.
4. See John Bulloch, *Death of a Country* (1977) p. 94.
5. See Kamal Salibi, *Crossroads to Civil War: Lebanon 1958—1976*, (1976) p. 135.
6. *Events*, 11 August 1978.
7. See Anthony Sampson, *The Arms Bazaar* (1977) pp. 15—24.
8. See Salibi, *op. cit.* p. 145.
9. Kamal Jumblatt, *I Speak for Lebanon* (1982) p. 91.
10. *Ibid.* pp. 92—3.

Chapter 9   The Syrian Intervention

1. In an interview with the Kuwaiti newspaper, *Al-Rai al-'Amm* 7 January 1976.
2. British Broadcasting Corporation, *Summary of World Broadcasts* (hereafter *SWB*), ME/494/A2, 31 May 1975. Quoted in Adeed I. Dawisha, *Syria and the Lebanese Crisis* (1980) p. 89.
3. *SWB*, ME/5266/A/2, 22 July 1976. Quoted in Dawisha, *op. cit.* p. 37.
4. *Facts on File*, 10 January 1976, p. 1. Quoted in Peter B. Heller, 'The Syrian Factor in the Lebanese Civil War', in *Journal of South Asian and Middle Eastern Studies*, Autumn 1980, p. 57.
5. *An-Nahar*, 15 February 1976. Translated by the Institute for Palestine Studies, Beirut.

6. Jumblatt, *op. cit.* p. 16.

7. *An-Nahar, op. cit.*

8. Cited in Walid Khalidid, *Conflict and Violence in Lebanon*, (1979) p. 167.

9. Quoted in John Bulloch, *Death of a Country* (1977) p. 118.

10. Khalidi, *op. cit.* pp. 54—5.

11. Jumblatt, *op. cit.* pp. 15, 18.

12. *International Herald Tribune*, 17 March 1976.

13. Quoted in Bulloch, *op. cit.* p. 126.

14. *Ibid.* p. 128.

15. *SWB*, ME/5186/A/6, 15 April 1976. Quoted in Dawisha, *op. cit.* p. 131.

16. *SWB*, ME/5330/A/5, 6 October 1976. Quoted in Dawisha, *op. cit.* p. 161.

17. Jumblatt, *op. cit.* p. 17.

18. *Ibid.* p. 74.

19. *SWB*, ME/5266/A/10. Quoted in Sam Younger, 'The Syrian Stake in Lebanon', *The World Today*, November 1976.

20. Ilana Kass, 'Moscow and the Lebanese Triangle' in *The Middle East Journal*, Spring 1979, pp. 172—3.

21. Dawisha, *op. cit.* pp. 136—7.

22. *Al-Thawra*, 2 June 1976 and 9 June 1976. Quoted in Dawisha, *op. cit.* p. 136.

Chapter 10   Fragmentation

1. See Walid Khalidi, *Conflict and Violence in Lebanon*, (1979) pp. 104, 174.

2. *Ibid.* pp. 193—4.

3. See Harry Turnbull, 'Real estate market thrives at expense of producers' in *MEED*, 10 February 1978.

4. See article by Johnny Rizq, 'Government hoping for political entente and a national outlook' in *MEED*, 29 July 1977.

5. See David Binder, 'US Troubleshooter in Beirut', in *Middle East International*, July 1976.

6. Quoted in *Events*, 11 August 1978.

7. See *Time*, 22 August 1977.

8. See Livia Rokach, *Israel's Sacred Terrorism*, Association of Arab-American University Graduates, 1980, pp. 28—9.

9. See Michael Bar-Zohar, *The Armed Prophet* (1967) p. 139.

10. *Ibid.* (Hebrew edition), Am Oved, Tel Aviv 1977, Vol. 3, pp. 1234—5.

11. See Rokach *op. cit.* pp. 28—9.

12. See the article by Thomas Staufer, 'The Lure of the Litani', in *Middle East International*, 30 July 1982.
13. Seth P. Tillman, *The United States in the Middle East*, (1982) p. 180.
14. *Time*, 27 March 1978.
15. *Time*, 3 April 1978.
16. Figures given by UN Press Section, New York, 23 March 1978.
17. Figures given by United Nations High Commissioner for Refugees, Beirut, 19 May 1978.
18. UN Security Council Resolution 425, 19 March 1978.
19. *Ibid.*
20. *Témoignage Chrétien*, 10 August 1978.
21. Quoted in Adeed I. Dawisha, *Syria and the Lebanese Crisis*, (1980) p. 189.
22. *The Times*, 12 September 1978.

Chapter 11   Israel's Second Invasion of Lebanon

1. *Financial Times*, 3 July 1982.
2. *Jerusalem Post*, 9 July 1982. Quoted in Michael Jansen, *The Battle of Beirut* (1982) p. 124.
3. See Jansen, *op. cit.* p. 124.
4. See the speech of the Israeli representative to the United Nations at the meeting of the UN Security Council, 5 June 1982.
5. This was the reason given by the Israeli chief of staff to the commander of UNIFIL. See the report of the UN Secretary General, 11 June 1982.
6. See *Israel in Lebanon*, the Report of the International Commission, (1983) p. 143.
7. Israeli Government Briefing, 18 July 1982.
8. See Jansen, *op. cit.* pp. 5–6 and Jacobo Timerman, *The Longest War* (1982) p. 87.
9. General Eytan's claim was reported in *Ha'aretz*, 28 December 1979.
10. See the speech of the Israeli representative to the United Nations at the meeting of the UN Security Council, 5 June 1982.
11. *Ibid.*
12. *Ha'aretz*, 30 June 1982. Quoted in Jansen, *op. cit.* p. 130.
13. *Ha'aretz*, 16 July 1982. Quoted in Jansen, *op. cit.* p. 130.
14. Quoted in Jansen, *op. cit.* p. 130.
15. *Ha'aretz*, 25 June 1982.
16. *Jerusalem Post*, 27 July 1982.
17. *Guardian*, 20 October 1982.
18. Quoted in Jansen, *op. cit.* p. 11.

19. *The Times*, 5 August 1982.
20. Quoted in Christopher Hitchens, 'Mr Begin's Grand Design', *Spectator*, 28 August 1982.
21. *The Times*, 21 June 1982.
22. *An-Nahar* and *L'Orient-Le Jour*, 2 September 1982.
23. Report dated 12 July 1982. Cited in *Israel in Lebanon*, *op. cit.* p. 43.
24. Timerman, *op. cit.* p. 29.
25. Report dated 12 July 1982. Cited in *Israel in Lebanon*, *op. cit.* pp. 32, 41–2.
26. Letter to *The Times*, 19 June 1982.
27. *Financial Times*, 17 June 1982.
28. As told to an Oxfam worker, Mr David MacDowell. Cited in *Israel in Lebanon*, *op. cit.* p. 52.
29. *New Society*, 19 August 1982.
30. Quoted in *Israel in Lebanon*, *op. cit.* p. 45.
31. Quoted in the *Sunday Times*, 8 August 1982.
32. *Ibid.*
33. *Daily Telegraph*, 10 August 1982.
34. *Israel in Lebanon*, p. 82.
35. *Ibid.* p. 40.
36. *Ibid.* p. 64.
37. *Ibid.* p. 57.
38. Quoted in the *Guardian*, 14 December 1982.
39. *The Times*, 2 August 1982.
40. See *The Times*, 2 July 1982, and the *Washington Post*, 21 August 1982.
41. *New York Times*, 1 July 1982.
42. *Jerusalem Post*, 15 August 1982.
43. Testimony of Franklin Lamb, consultant to several US congressmen. Quoted in *Israel in Lebanon*, pp. 226–37.
44. Associated Press depatch, 23 June 1982.
45. Jansen, *op. cit*, p. 93.
46. Beirut Home Service, 19 September 1982. Quoted in *Israel in Lebanon*, *op. cit.* p. 165.
47. Quoted in *Israel in Lebanon*, *op. cit.* p. 167.
48. The account of the massacre is based primarily on the evidence and findings of the Israeli Commission of Enquiry which published its report on 8 February 1983, and on the evidence reproduced in *Israel in Lebanon*, *op. cit.*
49. Testimony of General Yaron to the Israeli Commission of Enquiry.
50. Quoted to the Israeli Commission of Enquiry, 21 November 1982.
51. *Jerusalem Post*, 21 September 1982.

52. Testimony of General Sharon to Israel Commission of Enquiry, 25 October 1982.
53. See interview with Marwan Hamade, Lebanese Minister of Tourism, in Beirut, 3 September 1982. Quoted in *Israel in Lebanon, op. cit.* pp. 220–1.
54. Testimony before House Foreign Affairs Committee in Washington.
55. *Ibid.*
56. *The Scotsman*, 19 June 1982.
57. *Ibid.*
58. *New Society*, 19 August 1982.
59. *Ha'aretz*, 5 September 1982.
60. Quoted in Jansen *op. cit.* pp. 29–30.
61. *Ibid.*
62. See *Middle East International*, 15 October 1982.
63. *Ibid.*
64. Interview with Robert Fisk, *The Times*, 23 September 1982.
65. Middle East Reporter, 30 November 1982.
66. Cited in *The Times*, 25 June 1969.

Chapter 12   The Revolt of '83

1. Quoted in the *Daily Telegraph*, 17 May 1983.
2. Cited in *Davar*, 17 May 1983.
3. Reported by Patrick Seale in *The Observer*, 30 October 1983.
4. See the article in *Middle East International*, 8 July 1983, pp. 13–14.
5. Quoted in *The Guardian*, 12 August 1983.
6. See the *Jewish Chronicle*, 15 July 1983.
7. Edward Mortimer in *The Times*, 29 September 1983.
8. Kamal Jumblatt, *I Speak for Lebanon* (1982), p. 11.

Bibliography

Abou, S. *Liban déraciné*, Plon, Paris 1978.

Abu-Izzedin, H. S. (ed), *Lebanon and its Provinces*, Khayats, Beirut 1963.

Antonius, G. *The Arab Awakening: the story of the Arab national movement*, Khayats, Beirut 1938.

Awwad, T. Y. *Death in Beirut*, Heinemann, London 1976.

Baron, X. *Les Palestiniens: Un Peuple*, Le Sycomore, Paris 1977.

Betts, R. B. *Christians in the Arab East*, SPCK, London 1979.

Binder L. (ed), *Politics in Lebanon*, John Wiley and Sons, New York 1966.

Braudel, F. *The Mediterranean* (2 vols.), Collins, London 1970.

Bull, O. *War and Peace in the Middle East*, Leo Cooper, London 1976.

Bulloch, J. *Death of a Country: the Civil War in Lebanon*, Weidenfeld and Nicolson, London 1977.

Bulloch, J. *The Making of a War: the Middle East from 1967 to 1973*, Longman, London 1974.

Chaliand, G. *The Palestinian Resistance*, Penguin, London 1972.

Chamoun, C. *Crise au Liban*, Beirut 1977.

Churchill, C. H. *Mount Lebanon: A Ten Years' Residence from 1842 to 1852.*

Cooley, J. *Green March, Black September: the story of the Palestinian Arabs*, Frank Cass, London 1973.

Dawisha, A. *Syria and the Lebanese Crisis*, Macmillan, London 1980.

Dekmejian, R. H. *Patterns of Political Leadership: Egypt, Israel, Lebanon*, State University of New York Press, Albany 1975.

Dimbleby, J. *The Palestinians*, Quartet, London 1979.

Entelis, J. P. *Pluralism and Party Transformation in Lebanon: Al-Kata'ib 1936–1970*, E. J. Brill, Leiden 1974.

Epp, F. H. *The Palestinians: Portrait of a People in Conflict*, McClelland and Stewart, Toronto 1975.

Fedden, R. *Syria and Lebanon* (3rd ed), John Murray, London 1965.

Furlonge, G. *Palestine is My Country: the story of Musa Alami*, John Murray, London 1969.

Gibran, K. *The Garden of the Prophet*, Heinemann, London 1934.

Gordon, D. C. *Lebanon: the Fragmented Nation*, Croom Helm, London 1980.

Haddad, J.-P. *Le Combat du Liban*, Henri Conchon, Paris 1977.

Heikal, M. *The Road to Ramadan*, Collins, London 1975.

Hirst, D. *The Gun and the Olive Branch: the roots of violence in the Middle East*, Faber and Faber, London 1977.

Hitti, P. *A Short History of Lebanon*, Macmillan, London 1965.

Hourani, A. *Minorities in the Arab World*, Oxford University Press, Oxford 1946.

Hourani, A. *Syria and Lebanon*, Oxford University Press, Oxford 1946.

Howard, H. *The King-Crane Commission*, Khayats, Beirut 1963.

Hudson M. *The Electoral Process and Political Development in Lebanon*, New York 1962.

Hudson, M. *The Precarious Republic: Modernization in Lebanon*, Random House, New York 1968.

IRFED, *Besoins et Possibilités de Developpement du Liban*, Ministry of General Planning, Beirut 1960–61.

Ismael, T. Y. *The Arab Left*, Syracuse University Press, New York 1976.

Jansen, M. *The Battle of Beirut*, Zed Press, London 1982.

Jumblatt, K. *I Speak for Lebanon*, Zed Press, London 1982.

Jureidini, P. A. and Hazen, W. E. *The Palestinian Movement in Politics*, D. G. Heath and Co., Lexington 1976.

Khaled, L. *My People Shall Live; the autobiography of a revolutionary*, Hodder and Stoughton, London 1973.

Khalidi, W. *Conflict and Violence in Lebanon*, Harvard Center for International Affairs, Cambridge Mass. 1979.

Khayat M. K. and Keatinge, M. C. *Lebanon: Land of the Cedars*, Khayats, Beirut, 1960.

Kornberg, A. and Musolf, L. D. (eds) *Legislatures in Developmental Perspective*, Duke University Press, Durham 1970.

Longrigg, S. H. *Syria and Lebanon under French Mandate*, Oxford University Press, Oxford 1958.

Meo, L. M. T. *Lebanon: Improbable Nation*, Indiana University Press, Bloomington 1965.

Mikdadi Tabbara, L. *Survival in Beirut*, Onyx Press, London 1979.

Murray, G. T. *Lebanon: the New Future*, Thomson Rizk, Beirut 1974.

Nazzal, N. *The Palestinian Exodus from Galilee 1948*, Institute for Palestine Studies, Beirut 1978.

Nielsen, J. (ed.) *International Documents on Palestine 1972*, Institute for Palestine Studies, Beirut 1975.

Owen, R. (ed) *Essays on the Crisis in Lebanon*, Ithaca Press, London 1976.

Quandt, W., Jabber, F., Lesch, A. M. *The Politics of Palestinian Nationalism*, University of California Press, Berkeley 1973.

Qubain, F. I. *Crisis in Lebanon*, The Middle East Institute, Washington 1961.

El-Rayyes, R. and Dunia Nahas, *Guerrillas for Palestine*, Croom Helm, London 1976.

Riad, M. *The Struggle for Peace in the Middle East*, Quartet, London 1981.

Rodinson, M. *Marxisme et Monde Musulman*, Editions du Seuil, Paris 1972.

Rokach, L. *Israel's Sacred Terrorism*, Association of Arab-American Graduates, 1980.

Said, E. *The Question of Palestine*, Routledge and Kegan Paul, London 1979.

Salem, E. A. *Modernisation without Revolution: Lebanon's Experience*, Indiana University Press, Bloomington 1973.

Salibi, K. S. *Crossroads to Civil War: Lebanon 1958–1976*, Ithaca Press, London 1976.

Salibi, K. S. *The Modern History of Lebanon*, Weidenfeld and Nicolson, London 1965.

Sampson, A. *The Arms Bazaar*, Hodder and Stoughton, London 1977.

Sayigh, R. *Palestinians: from Peasants to Revolutionaries*, Zed Press, London 1979.

Sayigh, Y. *Entrepreneurs of Lebanon*, Harvard University Press, Cambridge Mass. 1962.

Seale, P. *The Struggle for Syria*, Oxford University Press, Oxford 1965.

Spears, Sir Edward. *Fulfilment of a Mission: Syria and Lebanon 1941–1944*, Leo Cooper, London, 1977.

Stewart, D. *Orphan with a Hoop: the Life of Emile Bustani*, Chapman and Hall, London 1967.

Stewart, D. *The Palestinians: Victims of Expediency*, Quartet, London, 1982.

Stewart, D. *Turmoil in Beirut*, Allan Wingate, London 1958.

Smock, D. R. and Smock, A. C. *The Politics of Pluralism: a Comparative Study of Lebanon and Ghana*, Elsevier, New York 1975.

Stevens, E. S. *Cedars, Saints and Sinners in Syria*, Hurst and Blackett, London (no date).

Suleiman, M. W. *Political Parties in Lebanon*, Cornell University Press, Ithaca 1967.

Sweet, L. E. (ed), *Peoples and Cultures of the Middle East* (2 vols.), Natural History Press, New York 1970.

Tibawi, A. L. *A Modern History of Syria, including Lebanon and Palestine*, Macmillan, London 1969.

Tillman, S. P. *The United States in the Middle East*, Indiana University Press, Bloomington 1982.

Timerman, J. *The Longest War*, Chatto and Windus, London 1982.

Turki, F. *The Disinherited: Journal of a Palestinian Exile*, Monthly Review Press, New York 1972.

Waddy C. *Baalbek Caravans*, Librairie du Liban, Beirut 1967.

Ward, P. *Touring Lebanon*, Faber and Faber, London 1971.

Willets, P. (ed) *Pressure Groups in the Global System*, Frances Pinter, London 1982.

Zeine, Z. N. *The Struggle for Arab Independence*, Khayats, Beirut 1960.

Ziadeh, N. A. *Syria and Lebanon*, Ernest Benn, London 1957.

Zuwiyya Yamak, L. *The Syrian Social Nationalist Party*, Harvard Middle Eastern Monograph Studies, Cambridge Mass. 1966.

Index